Interdependent Development

Harold Brookfield

Methuen & Co Ltd

First published 1975
by Methuen & Co Ltd
11 New Fetter Lane, London EC4P 4EE

© 1975 by Harold Brookfield

Typeset in IBM by
William Clowes & Sons Limited
London, Colchester and Beccles
and printed by
Cambridge University Press

(c

ISBN (hardbound) 0416 78070 9
ISBN (paperback) 0416 78090 6

TO THE UNTROUBLED ONES:
Vicki, Ché and Jumbuck *

* Cats, in whose house this book was written

Contents

Preface

This is not a book about development. It is a book about ideas about development, designed principally for those drawn by a combination of concern over social injustice, and a world view, into the development studies field. Its principal, but not exclusive target is geographers within that larger class, since the contribution of geographers in the development area has thus far been minimal, while their potential contribution is vast. What I attempt to do is to offer a highly selective review of the streams of thought about world development, leading towards a particular view of development within which I suggest it may be possible to synthesize the various strands. This is hardly a textbook, nor is it a research essay: its object is to lead the reader forward through an interdisciplinary literature, stimulate him to disagree or to remark on the purblindness of the author, and form his own ideas from which productive work might follow.

The book therefore assumes some understanding of the dimensions and nature of the world inequality which we call the problem of development. Empirical material is introduced only indirectly, where it is necessary to understand the empirical base of ideas. With Edmund Wilson (1940/1960R: 488) I assume also a concern that 'the superior development of some' be not 'paid for by the exploitation, that is, by the deliberate degradation of others'. This belief underlies the theme of the book, implicit in the earlier chapters and made explicit toward the end, that development is a 'totality' which cannot be properly understood by separation into parts. That is to say, the development of North America or Western Europe or Japan toward a high-production/high-consumption society is also part of the development of Africa or Asia or Latin America or the Pacific islands towards a dependent, skewed economy which we describe as 'underdeveloped'. For this reason, the terms 'developed' and 'underdeveloped' occur within quotation marks wherever they appear, for the fundamental argument is that there is only development, but development of different qualitative orders.

The method adopted is essentially epistemological. I am concerned with the evolution of ideas about development. This leads me into a serious difficulty which is bound to cause me trouble with reviewers and readers. I am by training a geographer. However, very few geographers, and not many more geographical ideas and concepts, are treated in this book. My justification is three-fold. First, I am convinced that one reason for the poor performance of geographers and some others in the development field is their want of understanding of the present 'state of play' in this interdisciplinary area, coupled with a conviction that a vast and complex literature has already anticipated their potential efforts. Second, if a job of interpretation needs to be done, it should begin at the beginning, with the simplicities of the present state of knowledge: there is moreover a good principle in translation that one should only translate into one's own mother tongue. Third, there is every reason to believe that a 'scientific revolution' is beginning to take place in the development field, as the existing conventional wisdom is found wanting by the hard test of empiricism. In this change, which will probably occupy much of the next decade before a new paradigm is achieved, there is abundant scope of new ideas and new entrants.

The third justification is the most important. It is why I have come to write a book so alien to my accustomed style, transgressing so far beyond the limits of naiveté as to be unusual even in these days of collapsing disciplinary boundaries. My experience in this area began at the empirical level, with some twenty years of work in what we call 'developing' countries. Though much of this work was in fields such as population geography and cultural ecology, I became more and more involved with the interpretation of change: my early efforts included some disastrous failures. These led me into an extensive programme of reading and thinking. At first, as a geographer of strongly empirical bent, it is difficult to say whether I was more frustrated by the futility of my own discipline or by the spatial and ecological blindness of others. Later I became much more frustrated by the 'scientism' of much of the development literature — its detachment from reality, its widespread tendency to reason from first principles not soundly based in fact. The core of the problem is clearly the anti-historicism which has prevailed among a whole generation of social scientists, and which also afflicts part of geography. The assumption that an essentially deductive calculus would supersede anything which history might teach extended into a disdain for other forms of empirical relevance. But as I read on, I found I was not alone in my view. A tide is now running strongly in the direction of greater empirical relevance in the development field, and this is perhaps a good moment for weak swimmers, such as anti-positivist geographers, to plunge in.

My methodological position, which I develop in the course of writing, is thus nailed to the mast. Since I adopt an essentially epistemological method of exposition, there is much more reference to anti-historicism in the text than to neglect of the spatial view, for anti-historicism has become the central bone of contention. But my belief is that the empirical relevance of assumptions and theories is involved in a more general sense, and that a review such as this can bring out the possibilities of the spatial dimension as well as that of time. Geographers are therefore invited to think about the relevance of the theoretical streams here imperfectly traced out: I offer comparatively little direct exhortation. For my own part, I have now found the approaches I was seeking, and am beginning to explore these in an empirical context. This has narrowed my reading, and for the writing of a book of this nature, then, it was now or never.

The reader will, however, expect me to offer some definition of development, and he will be disappointed. I can say that my reason is that the whole book constitutes an approach toward a definition of development, since 'development' is what it has come to mean in the hands of numerous writers of very different persuasion, and hence there is no more agreement on this topic than there is over a definition of geography. In parenthesis, this may be a further excellent reason for geographers to enter this field. But I can at least say that development is most certainly not economic growth: very few writers in the 1970s fail to make this distinction. The popular trend is to define development in terms of progress toward a complex of welfare goals, such as reduction of poverty and unemployment, and diminution of inequality. But the view I take here is very different. It seems to me impossible to separate the positive from the negative consequences of change, yet evident that change is accelerating and that its impact has become universal. I prefer to adopt a goal-free definition that, in one sense, is so broad as to be meaningless: development is the whole process of change brought about by the creation and expansion of an interdependent world system. Development is therefore positive and negative, according to one's goals; it is good and bad; it is capable of being defined by progress toward 'one world' or by the satisfactory adaptation of older structures into a new frame. Development is the modern dynamic. Development of the poorer countries of the world may even make their people poorer, but it is still development. To justify this position requires, in fact, the whole space of this book. Were I writing a book about the alleviation of social and economic injustice, I would adopt a much stricter definition, but this is a far more restricted problem than the one with which I am here concerned. At an initial stage, especially in a book concerned to review ideas, nothing but a comprehensive definition of this order can prove helpful. My values, I think, are obvious enough, but my chosen method demands that I do not restrict my discussion to progress toward their achievement.

A few further comments are necessary. I have tried to assume as little comprehension of economics as possible, and have confined my discussion of economic concepts to the level that can be explained verbally: since the basic ideas are very simple, this is less difficult than it might seem. I have, however, assumed of my readers some basic comprehension of the few geographical concepts which are introduced. Because of these assumptions, and the assumption of knowledge of the nature, scale and distribution of the 'development' problem, this is not an introductory book. However, most elementary geographical texts would provide all the necessary background. P. Haggett (1972) omits little that is truly relevant.

Because of my irritation with the anti-historicism of many of the writers I discuss, and also because of my epistemological approach, I have tried so far as possible to give references by their date of original publication, rather than to the latest edition as is most usual: I may have made some errors, easy in a field where so much of the literature has been reprinted or translated by editors and publishers often careless of bibliographic detail. The rather unusual conventions employed are explained at the head of the list of references. Referencing is, however, only partial: to provide a complete bibliographic companion to a book of this order would be a task well beyond my present intention.

Finally, this is the place for some acknowledgements. This book has been written entirely since the spring of 1973; no one has read more than small pieces of it, so I have no possibility of distributing the responsibility for error. I am grateful to Anne Taper for typing most of the manuscript and refraining from suitable comment; I am grateful to Jim Gilmour for a continuing, if intermittent, discussion since early 1971, which has had more to do with the shaping of ideas than he will recognize. A few late revisions, made since the main manuscript was completed, owe much to ideas gleaned in the Institute of Development Studies at Sussex, where I have been a Visiting Fellow since January 1974. However, most of the book was written in Montréal in the house of the three helpmates to whom it is dedicated. The first few months of a Fellowship awarded by the John Simon Guggenheim Foundation provided the necessary and invaluable freedom. The writing of the book followed a graduate seminar at McGill University in 1972-3, and my thanks also go to the sufferers of that seminar, which at least taught me how the book should not be written. I have now left McGill and will, for a space, be an 'international civil servant' with UNESCO, but I should at least thank McGill University for maintaining its Centre for Developing Area Studies after the desertion of international support: it was in that meeting ground for students of and from the 'world periphery' that many of the ideas presented here were generated.

My work with UNESCO will involve me, in Fiji, with the elaboration and testing of ideas sketched out in chapter 7. A late revision of part of this chapter owes much to an exchange of thoughts on the man/environment paradigm with Anne Kirkby. The whole book has benefited from some critical comments made by Janice Price, who combined tact with editorial firmness. But the greatest number of such comments were made — as always — by Muriel Brookfield, who in addition provided the necessary support of meals, cups of tea and glasses of whisky at suitable moments within her own busy working schedule. To all these people and institutions, my thanks, but I need hardly add that the many faults remaining are all my own.

Brighton, March and July 1974   Harold Brookfield

1: From the beginning

Almost five hundred years ago, in the closing decade of the fifteenth century, two bold voyages from Iberia resulted in a chain of events that made the world one, but have not yet ceased to widen the disparities between different areal groupings of mankind. Two types of European dominance, two types of dependence, were initiated by these voyages. The western voyage of Columbus opened the way for exploitative colonization and the direct control of one society by another; the eastern voyage of da Gama began the more enduring commercial dominance/dependence relationship supported by sea-borne power.

What began in so small a way in 1492 and 1498 was the process of 'interdependent development'. The sort of long distance relationship that was created was new in world history. The whole contemporary world problem that we call variously that of 'under-development', 'modernization' or the 'economic development of the Third World' is concerned at base with a dominance/dependence relationship that is expressed in a great many ways. Most obviously, it is expressed in the contrast between the rich and the poor countries, the former group enjoying average *per capita* incomes ten to twelve times larger than those of the latter group. But there are rich people in poor countries and poor people in rich countries, and neither wealth nor poverty can be measured adequately in money terms alone. No less important, but less easily quantified, is the more insidious contrast in the span of the power of nations and their élites. Some have little control over their own destinies, while others may determine the fate of people far beyond their own borders. All people touched by the integrated system of world power relation-ships have experienced 'development', but of very different kinds. Notwithstanding conventional wisdom, the state of development is not time-dependent, nor is progress simply diffused. Northern Haiti is one of the world's poorest regions, yet Columbus made his landfall there. By contrast, Australia was untouched until the late eighteenth century, yet now houses a rich and fortunate people, influential out of all proportion to their numbers.

Modern thinking on development has been slow to come to grips with historical reality, even though before World War II 'economic development' was conceived of as being part of the domain of economic history. In our day, many have come to believe that 'we' have found the key to unlock the world's treasure house, and all that 'they' need is some help in acquiring our domestic arrangements and virtues in order to find their own road to plenty. No Melanesian cargo-cult prophet has been more emphatic in his assertions of revealed truth than have some of our development economists, more insistent in their prescription for finding the 'road bilong cargo'. Yet even the Melanesian cargo cultist recognized something that many of our modern prophets have declined to see; in most cargo cults, the 'cargo' is seen as having been intercepted and appropriated by the alien colonizers and exploiters.

The argument that some call 'dependent development', but which I prefer to designate as 'interdependent development', is elaborated further in the final chapters. In between, however, there is an immense amount of ground to be covered. In a few chapters I set out to delineate elements of certain main lines of development theory; I give weight to those that have a spatial dimension, but it is not possible to consider these exclusively. I do not pretend to be 'value free': I have my biases just as others have who have written on this topic. I intend to trace out streams of thought, all of which, even though I seek to discredit some of them, have something to contribute toward greater understanding. Most of what I recount is the product of a strictly modern period, since 1945, but it will help to begin with a brief overview of what was said and done before our time.

Development thinking before 'development' began

Exploitation, protection and mercantilism

Some of the ideas assembled under the jargon-word 'development' have a long antiquity. The realization of unacceptably low living standards among national populations as a whole is certainly the youngest, yet it can be traced back into the eighteenth century. The view of development as the realization of economic potential is far more ancient, and the germ of the concept of economic and social progress goes back to classical times. Tacitus, for example, remarked on the economic progress of the Britons, and noted sadly that their acculturation to Roman ways was really a 'feature of enslavement' which they regarded as civilization. The initial impact of Spanish exploitation on the Caribbean region was so wholly disastrous for the indigenous inhabitants that it could hardly fail to arouse a response. Fray Bartolomé de las Casas, and the Dominican order which he joined, were strident voices for the rights of the fast-vanishing Indian inhabitants of the Antilles, and paved the way for regulatory policies which muted the later impact on Mexico and Peru just sufficiently to ensure some measure of survival for the conquered people (las Casas 1971T).

The debate in the early Spanish empire was over the means by which people were enforced to labour for the exploiters and colonists, whether by *corvée*, by slavery, or by reduction to serfdom through deprivation of land. The objectives of empire gave rise to fewer questions: the enrichment of the metropole, its citizens and especially its rulers was only lightly dressed in the clothing of a civilizing and proselytizing mission. But the early Spanish empire failed in its aims, partly because of destruction of the labour on which exploitation depended, partly because the enrichment at home did not generate any significant multiplier effect. Much later, in the eighteenth century, Spain and Portugal attempted anew to generate growth and to diversify the export production of their empires, but they failed a second time. The Iberian market for colonial produce was limited; a mass of protectionist barriers blocked the path to wider sales; most fundamentally, perhaps, Spain and Portugal were unable to supply exports of manufactured goods to stimulate colonial demand (C. Furtado 1969/1970T).

The empires which the countries of northwest Europe began to build in the seventeenth century had a wider base. After the initial period, agricultural produce rather than precious metals and scarce goods such as spices became the established export staples. Wealth was generated for the metropole, but for the benefit of a much larger merchant class which was able to utilize the gains for substantial reinvestment; in Britain, a high proportion of the reinvestment went into expansion of the merchant marine, its protecting navy, the ports and industries which served both, and into a series of wars which were fought largely for the defence and expansion of empire. Something like an integrated development policy was evolved around the mercantilist principle of the enlargement of national wealth, regulated by the concentration of trade in national vessels through national ports. In the British case, even the Irish ports were excluded from direct commerce with the colonies. The labour problem in the colonies was overcome in the Asian regions of dense population by an adequate system of forced deliveries, combined with stimulation of demand through exports of manufactured goods. Elsewhere it was solved by a massive expansion of the slave trade, which became West Africa's outstanding contribution to the system. Eric Williams (1964) has forcefully argued that the surplus appropriated from the slave-plantation colonies provided the critical stimulus to investment, which supported the 'improvements' that were the dynamic of growth in eighteenth century Western Europe. On a wider basis, Eric Hobsbawm (1968) demonstrates that while the home market in Britain promoted economic growth, it was the more volatile but unlimited overseas market captured by British commerce through empire and naval control that made possible the first industrial revolution in this one country. But if a lead in the competition for successful empire[1] made possible the industrialization of Britain, there is also an obverse. In 1700 British textile manufacturers won protection from imports of Indian cloth; in 1813 the East India Company lost its monopoly and India was opened to British textile exports. Deindustrialization of India thus flowed from British industrialization.

The rise of economic liberalism

The aggressiveness displayed by the metropolitan manufacturers and exporters lent power to a rising set of voices arguing against the web of mercantilist restrictions, which were seen as stifling the continued expansion of international trade. Although there were precursors of his ideas, the real beginning of the new movement was with the publication of Adam Smith's *Wealth of Nations* in 1776. But this book, often regarded as the first major writing on economic development, forms only a part of the general climate of liberalism.

---

[1] Tracing the chain a little further back, Hobsbawm attributes this success to the crucial willingness of Britain to subordinate foreign policy to economic ends. In explaining this phenomenon he contrasts the continuity of aristocratic control in continental Europe with the incorporation of commercial interests in the power system that followed the seventeenth century revolutions in Britain. The Cromwellian expedition to Hispaniola and Jamaica in 1655 was the first British war of colonial expansion. It is worth recording that in this same valued region a large British army was unsuccessfully employed in trying to wrest western Hispaniola (Haiti) from the French and the black

This also included the influence of Newtonian science making possible a breakaway from the old static concept of a designed earth and the introduction of belief in unlimited technical progress (Glacken 1967): similarly, Adam Smith's belief in the aggregate good yielded by the unbridled effects of individual economic self-interest meshed at several points with Jean-Jacques Rousseau's more idealistic insistence on the rights of all men to freedom of action. To more and more thinking men, the doctrine of *laissez-faire* appealed not only to a will to liberate individual enterprise, but also to a belief that such liberation would lead inevitably to the long-run betterment of all.

A new and wider sense of natural order thus replaced the old, and all that seemed necessary was liberation from the dead hand of regulation. Even the very arrangement of the world into differing ecological zones existed in order that:

> the exchange of commodities may be accomplished by the . . . diffusion of knowledge — by the interchange of mutual benefits engendering mutual kind feelings . . . It is, that commerce may go freely forth, leading civilization with one hand, and peace with the other, to render mankind happier, wiser, better. (Lord Palmerston, *Hansard* 16, February 1842, cited in Robinson, Gallagher and Denny 1961: 2)

Unfettered commerce should thus go hand in hand with philanthropy, and trade was the key to betterment. Ricardo provided theoretical justification with his doctrine of comparative costs, under which:

> if trade is left free each country in the long run tends to specialize in the production of and to export those commodities in which production it enjoys a comparative advantage in terms

---

revolutionaries during the years 1793–8. The losses suffered in this operation were greater than those of the whole Peninsular War, and it was in this forgotten war, not in the Russo-Japanese war of 1905 as is so often stated, that a major European power met its first crucial defeat at the hands of a non-European nation. The Haitian resistance to a colonial campaign, deemed 'the first point to make certain' by the British Prime Minister, greatly weakened British ability to fight a new sort of war in Europe against revolutionary France.

of real costs, and to obtain by importation those commodities which could be produced at home only at a comparative disadvantage in terms of real costs, and such specialization is to the mutual advantage of the countries participating in it. (J. Viner 1937: 438)

But it was the most aggressive industrial and trading nations that benefited most, and especially Britain. Britain could afford to let drop the protective barriers around her own international system in order to gain access to others. The absolute control over the high seas gained by Britain during the French wars made possible strong pressure on other countries to open their trade, and effective support was given to independence movements in countries which, freed of colonial control, would become commercially satellite to the world's only modern industrial economy. This is especially true of Latin America where:

Spain's policy totally obstructed and thwarted the economic development of its colonies by not permitting them to trade with any other nation and by reserving to itself the privileges of the mother country to monopolize all commerce and business carried on in its dominions.

The producing forces of the colonies naturally sought to shake off these fetters ... From the standpoint of world history, South America's independence was determined by the needs of the development of Western or, more precisely, capitalist civilization. The rise of capitalism has a much more decisive and profound, if less apparent and recognizable, influence on the evolution of independence than the philosophy and literature of the Encyclopedists ... England — with the clear sense of destiny and historic mission that was to gain it hegemony in capitalist civilization — played a leading role in South America's independence ...

Spain could supply its colonies only with priests, lawyers and nobles. Its colonies craved more practical and modern instruments, and, consequently, turned to England's industrialists and bankers. Acting as agents of an empire created by a manufacturing and free trade economy, the new-style colonizers wanted, in turn, to dominate these markets.

The economic interests of the Spanish colonies and of the capitalist West coincided exactly, although, as often happens in history, neither of the parties concerned was aware of this fact. (J. C. Mariátegui 1928/1971T: 7–8)

More effective resistance to British pressure was offered by the Dutch, who on returning to Java in 1815 found that the reforms introduced during the short period of British rule had included not only a substantial liberalization of Javanese enterprise but also considerable redirection of trade toward Britain. An essentially mercantilist system was by degrees re-established coupled with a system of forced deliveries of produce in lieu of taxes to a State buying organization which also handled exports. This 'culture and consignment system' was highly profitable for several years, and was capped by the infamous *batig slot* — the surplus balance in the colonial budget which was contributed to the revenues of the Netherlands. Not until much later in the nineteenth century did liberalism, in the form of freedom for entrepreneurs and planters, finally displace this elaboration of ancient practices from Indonesia.

Theory about growth, irrelevant to dependent economies

The theoretical justification of economic liberalism was also the foundation of economics, and most economic writing of this early period was concerned with growth. Hence it forms also the basis for the modern theory of growth and development, as applied to dependent developing countries. But early growth theory was conceived in the very different context of a unique industrial revolution in an otherwise unindustrialized world. To Adam Smith and most of his successors colonial economies were simply an extension of metropolitan economies; international trade was the trade between independent countries. Smith regarded dependencies as a burden, though recognizing the wealth that flowed from the West Indies. The enlightenment treated political control as a necessary evil; the objective was freedom for trade and enterprise throughout the world and great was the chagrin when newly independent countries raised tariff barriers for their own protection. One set of principles, one theory, should suffice for all, and very many years passed before the need for autonomous theory to explain persistent underdevelopment was even suggested.

Adam Smith sought the factors on which depended the evident augmentation of the productive power of human labour. He emphasized the division of labour, discovered the principle of economies of scale, and remarked that the division of labour is limited by the size of the market. His more basic argument, however, concerned the role of capital formation and accumulation, the means by which 'improvements' facilitated output. In common with succeeding 'classical' economists he viewed production as a function of inputs, classified into labour, land and capital, with technology and entrepreneurship as additional and more shadowy variables. Some later writers, such as Marx, incorporated technical change within the concept of capital; others, outstandingly Schumpeter, treated technical change, and the entrepreneurship needed to apply it, as fundamental to all explanations of growth.

Discussion was greatly expanded early in the nineteenth century by two writers, Ricardo and Malthus. Both were concerned rather with the limits to growth than with its initiation, and sought these in the finite quantity of available land. Ricardo reasoned that the best land would be the first to be put into production; subsequent inputs of land would be of lower quality and would yield less until a unit of land was reached that only just repaid the cost of production. As this 'margin' was approached, the cost of production per unit of output would rise and profits would be reduced. This 'law of diminishing returns' was thus capable of drying up the source and motivation of capital accumulation, and would yield a stationary state, with expansion at an end. Almost the whole produce of a country, after paying the workers, would then be the property of the owners of land and the receivers of taxes. Ricardo did not ignore technical improvements, but considered them as capable only of a temporary effort. Since he regarded agriculture as the key sector, improvements in the manufacturing sector merely led to a fall in their exchange value against agricultural products.[2]

Malthus introduced the question of population into economic growth theory more thoroughly than any of his contemporaries. In common with them, he assumed that population would grow as the

---

[2] Ricardo's concepts of 'economic rent' and the 'margin' are virtually identical with those discovered almost simultaneously by von Thünen, except that the latter was concerned with the costs of distance over uniform land, while Ricardo was unconcerned with distance and assumed land to be of unequal quality. But whereas von Thünen's was a static equilibrium model, Ricardo's theory was dynamic.

economy expanded, but he dissented with the view of some writers in the previous century who saw no limits to this process. He saw that population is capable of growing much faster than food production, and this led him to envisage the ultimate theoretical limits with which his name is especially linked. But Malthus's interpretation of development in the real world was much more optimistic. Given a proper balance between agriculture and industry, each sector providing a market for the other and sustaining 'effective demand', Malthus saw the process of capitalist accumulation as continuing uninterrupted for a very long period provided that population growth is restrained. He did not see any inevitable 'law of diminishing returns' and this freed him to look at institutional limitations, especially in the unequal distribution of landed property which could prevent land from being used optimally. In this connection, almost alone among the classical economists, Malthus looked abroad. Drawing on the work of Humboldt in Spanish America, he observed the existence of institutionally created poverty under the *hacienda* system, whereby much land was under-utilized while other land was already carrying a maximum population. The effect was to reduce 'effective demand', and hence deprive the economy of any spur to growth. This concept, neglected for a long period, was taken up again in the present century by J. M. Keynes.

All these early economists, and many of their successors, saw in *laissez-faire* the true avenue to growth. Unfettered, the capitalist system would work toward optimal production functions, combining the factors in the best proportions, and thus operate to the greatest long-run good of all. Such optimism became harder to sustain in the face of persistent working-class poverty, and the evidence of growing impoverishment presented by Friedrich Engels and other observers, and was decisively challenged by Karl Marx. Marx's first and fundamental contribution was to identify and separate the capitalist system from other systems of production. He then sought to resolve the conflict between the evident value of this system as an engine of expansion, and the poverty which it produced. Like his predecessors, he saw in capitalist expansion built-in limitations that would check its progress, but to Marx these derived from within the system itself rather than from external constraints such as finite land.

To Marx, the key to understanding capitalism lay in 'primitive accumulation', essentially a concentration of ownership in property, which separates workers from their own land and turns them into proletarians. Coupled with population growth, this concentration of ownership of the means of production creates an abundance of labour power, and makes it possible for the owner of land not only to employ labour, but to appropriate to himself the 'surplus value' of this labour's production over and above the minimum required to pay the labour force.[3] The creation of a 'reserve army of unemployed labour' keeps wages low, and facilitates a process of enrichment which thus permits the accumulation of capital.

But this process is competitive, and capitalists must invest in technical improvements in order to gain advantage and avoid being ousted and reduced to proletarian status. Using the improvements, labour becomes more productive, but capital is absorbed. Thus as the capital-to-labour ratio increases, the capital-to-output ratio will also increase. Profits will therefore decline, unless new techniques are introduced further to increase output per worker. This puts capitalists on a treadmill. In order to survive they must continue to accumulate capital in order to invest in new techniques, to increase the output per worker, and to widen the gap between this output and the wage rate in order to offset the declining trend of profits. This highly competitive process leads to the destruction of weaker capitalists and the progressive concentration of capital into fewer and fewer hands. It also has other consequences. Technological unemployment, and elimination of the small capitalist, enlarge the 'industrial reserve army' and make it possible for capitalists to force wages down toward the subsistence limit.[4] Capitalists also seek more and more widely for investment opportunities, and find these in foreign trade and investment so that the system spreads and

---

[3] In common with other classical economists, Marx employed the 'labour theory of value'; goods and services were valued in terms of the quantity of labour required for their production. In a labour-surplus economy, labour could be had for just that margin above the subsistence minimum necessary to induce labour to offer for hire; the surplus productivity of labour, multiplied by the use of capital, then accrued to the capitalist.

[4] Or below this limit, if such analysis is applied to many real cases in the world of the last five centuries. Theoretically, and employing a variant of the Malthusian principle, this would reduce the 'reserve army' and so bring capitalist evolution to a halt. An excellent allegory on such social Darwinism,

eventually becomes worldwide. But the process is self-destructive. Profitable investment opportunities are exhausted; competition leads to concentration into fewer and fewer hands and to the formation of monopolies; increasing oppression of labour leads at last to revolution. The system thus generates its own negation, and 'the expropriators are expropriated'.

All these schemes are only marginally concerned with the dependent economies. Even Marx saw these only as extensions of the capitalist core, and he said little about them; it was left for his successors to elaborate the role of territorial expansion in capitalist evolution. Marx had ultimately a revolutionary effect on economics, just as on politics, but already in his time the main thrust of economic theory had turned away from questions of aggregate growth, and toward the determination of price and the operation of the individual firm. Schumpeter only excepted, economists therefore left growth theory in a state based on the experiences of the industrial revolution, and did not return to it until the middle of the present century.

Most of this theorizing is irrelevant from the point of view of the developing and dependent countries: it had little or nothing to do with them. In so far as assumptions were made, it was supposed that the capitalist transformation would reach them in time — hand in hand with commerce — just as it was reaching the USA, Belgium, Germany and other Western countries from Britain. All this is entirely understandable in its day, but it is less easy to see why such naive optimism should have persisted through the decline and demise of *laissez-faire* capitalism down to the present day; the mechanism was discredited and abandoned, but the supposed consequences remain unaffected. Theory about the dependent countries and their people as such continued to have little to do with economic matters until the present century, and when it arose its origins were in Marxist thought. Meanwhile, as colonial rule spread over the face of

---

and on capitalist concentration with finite 'labour' resources, is perhaps to be found in a Russian science fiction story in which mechanical crabs consume metal to grow and reproduce. When the available metal is exhausted they consume one another, innovating to gain advantage, until finally only one enormous crab is left, and dies (Anatoliy Dneprov, 'The island of the crabs', in D. Suvin, *ed., Other Worlds, Other Seas: science fiction stories from socialist countries*, New York (Random House), 1970: 197–217).

the earth, the basic problems which engaged serious thought were again in the realm of ethics, just as in the time of las Casas.

The 'ethical' period, and the emergence of 'development'

The term 'liberalism' has meant many things to many people. The 'liberals' of early nineteenth century *laissez-faire* were also the men who forced China to accept massive imports of opium to balance her exports of tea; they liberated the slaves of the West Indies while permitting Ireland to sink into famine. Later in the nineteenth century liberals were in the forefront of the final expansion of empire, but among them were also men who mapped out a new set of policies toward dependent peoples, based on a sense of responsibility accepted by the metropolitan power.

Such a group emerged in the Netherlands in the 1890s, demanding an end to appropriations from Indonesia and some restoration of what had been taken. By about 1900, their views had won acceptance and became crystallized into a new colonial policy, termed 'ethical' by contrast with its antecedents; the term might as well stand for the succeeding half-century of emerging Western thinking in regard to dependent peoples and countries. The ethical policy in Indonesia called for decentralization, government welfare and infrastructure investments, greater government participation in the organization of production and especially research, greater encouragement to private investment, a reconstruction of the fiscal system, and greater respect for indigenous custom which began to be studied in fine detail and codified in the form of *adat* law.

Rather similar trends were emerging in British Africa, where territorial expansion had, by the 1890s, compelled the government itself to accept some direct responsibility for making the new acquisitions economically viable. Where this could be done through white settlement, this was encouraged; where it could not, direct encouragement began to be given to indigenous participation in the cash economy. Opposition continued to be suppressed, harshly at times, but a new conception of the rights of dependent peoples steadily surfaced. Active intervention was not universal: these were also the years in which territories once thought of as more important than Europe itself, in the Caribbean, lapsed out of mind into almost total neglect.

To read the literature of this period today is to experience a sense of remoteness from present reality almost more complete than that to be had from the nakedly exploitationist literature of earlier times. The 'ethical policy' of Brooshooft, van Deventer and their successors in Indonesia, the 'indirect rule' and 'dual mandate' of Lugard and his admirers in British Africa, were certainly inspired by 'lofty purpose' — that of associating the 'native' with the administration and development of his own country. But this was done with a racial arrogance that would seem to imply the most crude hypocrisy to all who have not witnessed these policies in action — as this writer has — in their dying phases since 1950. Liberals they certainly were. They stood in opposition to monopoly exploitation, to the claim of South African, Rhodesian or Kenyan whites to rule in perpetuity, sometimes even to the self-interest of metropolitan commerce. Many hundred pieces of colonial legislation defended indigenous against expatriate interests, yet the social distance between ruler and ruled grew wider as the pro-consuls became more and more self-congratulatory in their virtue, more and more deeply involved in the arts of colonial administration and management, and less and less in touch with the people whom they supposedly served.[5]

The ambivalence of the era is perhaps most clearly reflected in Lugard's famous concept of the 'dual mandate', under which the external power had a responsibility both to develop the resources of dependent countries for the benefit of the whole world, and also to advance the welfare and prospects of the dependent people themselves. Throughout the colonial period, as today, such twin aims were often found to be incompatible. In 1929, Britain achieved a

[5] Among the most striking documents covering this period is the collection of Margery Perham's essays and articles published between 1930 and 1949. Though there is a notable shift of emphasis through time, the paternalist tone is constant. Titles such as 'Our task in Africa' (1936), 'Educating Africa' (1938), 'Education for self-government' (1945) and 'The colonial dilemma' (1949) accurately reflect an ethos which even this wise and competent observer was unable to escape. Particularly interesting is a 1934 paper on 'Some problems of indirect rule in Africa' printed with its discussion. Bitter opposition from a lone Ghanaian was ignored by most discussants, but Miss Perham 'felt it was necessary to remind the educated natives who criticized indirect rule that there was a serious responsibility upon them to make a very careful study of it; to go into the hinterland, away from the towns, and realize what was being done there. Their opinions would gain in value when they learned to understand not only their own difficulties, but ours' (Perham 1967: 116).

significant advance toward modern 'development' goals with its colonial Development Fund authorizing grants and loans to aid agriculture and industry. By some this was heralded as a new beginning, but in 1934 an examining committee felt doubtful that a second condition of the Act was being observed: how far in aiding the colonies the grantors were 'thereby promoting commerce with or industry in the United Kingdom' (W. M. Macmillan 1938/1949: 220). Lord Hailey, whose influential *African Survey* was published in 1938, was dubious over all 'changes of direction' before the colonial Development and Welfare Act of 1940. At last, he felt, this Act put colonial development problems squarely before a British public that was 'now able to view the problems presented as being in line with those of the "depressed" areas in Great Britain itself, the treatment of which had become a matter of engrossing concern in domestic policies' (Hailey 1943: 16).

But many observers in the dying years of the 'ethical' period were as depressed by the results of the new policies as they were of the old. Among these was J. H. Boeke, who observed in 1934 that all the economic progress in Java since 1900 had brought little benefit to the Javanese people, who ate less well, received less for their produce, and could not afford to pay the taxes that had been substituted for compulsory labour and deliveries (Boeke, cited in Furnivall 1939: 403). J. S. Furnivall, whose own profound historical analysis of Dutch Indonesia stands as a landmark in the description of 'development', offers this comment on the varying directions of Dutch policy through one and a half centuries (Furnivall 1939: 392):

> Doubtless the Ethical movement as originally conceived was open to the criticism used against it, that it was Capitalism dressed up as Christianity; social reformers are usually charged with hypocrisy by critics. Raffles was regarded as a hypocrite by Van den Bosch [founder of the 'culture and consignment system']; Van den Bosch was painted in similar colours by the Liberal historian, Van Soest; the Liberals entered 'love for the Javanese' in their published accounts, but did not let it touch their pockets; and when the Ethical leaders hauled down the Jolly Roger and hoisted the Cross, they did not change the sailing orders. The whole history of the social and economic development of Netherlands India may be regarded as illustrating the theme that

economic motives dominate colonial policy, and that any colonial policy in application is effective only in so far as economic circumstances are favourable.

Mutatis mutandis, Furnivall's comment might stand for the policies of the whole period we have had under review. While there is an overwhelming consensus among objective modern commentators that the effect of colonialism has been either the relative or absolute impoverishment of the 'indigenous' economy, it is also true that colonial administrations in the modern period have had in the main honestly desired and sought the betterment of the people they served. Many scholars have believed with them that they were achieving this end. And as the inequality has increased, so also has the optimism of those whose activities were directed to the social and administrative fields. The paradox is explicable in several ways. We can presume hypocrisy on a monstrous scale; we can presume a remarkable degree of self-delusion and selective blindness; or we can take note of the fact that the reforming administrations and their allies were working and thinking on a long time scale, whereas capitalists were habitually working in a very much shorter term. It was thus possible to believe that the short-term evils were temporary, and would be overridden in time by long-term recon-struction of society and polity which was the stated aim of colonial reformers. But we must also note that this was a convenient philosophy, and that it has been proved fallacious. As we shall see, precisely the same paradox has been continued into the 'develop-ment' period of the later twentieth century.

Theorizing around exploitation: Hobson and the Marxists

It was only at the beginning of the present century that the macrotheory of economic and political systems at last began to take note of the dependent and colonial world as something other than a mere penumbra around the places where the action happened. Schumpeter (1919/1951) specifically dissociated imperialism from capitalism, the interests of which he saw as fundamentally opposed to the costs and distractions of expansionism. Imperialism, in his view, was an anachronistic product of surviving elements from the power system of the pre-capitalist era; though he saw that certain capitalists might find it to their advantage to ally themselves with imperialist interests. Essentially, however, the acquisition of overseas dominions was seen as motivated by strategic rather than economic reasons.

Others were more inclined to seek economic motives. A whole group of mid-nineteenth-century socialist writers were concerned with the injustices of the capitalist system, its oppression of the working class, its exaction of an 'unearned tribute', and its creation of persistent poverty. The contribution of these writers has been largely obliterated by the invective directed against them by the more revolutionary Marxists, who saw them as shrinking back from the logical conclusions of their analysis. Among them was Karl Rodbertus who, perhaps independently of Malthus, argued that a consequence of working-class poverty under exploitation was shortage of purchasing power and hence of 'effective demand' wherewith to sustain the capitalist economy. Hence it became necessary for capitalists to open up foreign markets for sale of their produce, and to cause their governments to use military power for foreign conquest to this end. This is the origin of the theory of economic imperialism (E. Heimann 1945: 136–8) later elaborated in a different theoretical context by J. A. Hobson (1902) and by Rosa Luxemburg (1912/1951T). Hobson was in no sense a Marxist; he was, however, a dissenter with the established economic wisdom of his day. After a visit to Africa in the heyday of British imperialism (R. Heilbroner 1972: 186–92), he offered a wider interpretation of his earlier unpopular views on the consequences of unequal income distribution in the capitalist system. The poor were too poor to consume; the rich could not consume because they had more than they required: the result was underconsumption, and the rich were *forced* to save and hence to expand production further. This created an impossible imbalance between production and consumption, solved by investment of the 'surplus' capital overseas and sale of the 'surplus' products in foreign markets. Capitalist nations are thus drawn into competition for new fields of conquest in which to employ their unemployable wealth, a competition leading to imperialist wars. It led also to the creation of a large *rentier* class at home living on colonial profits,[6] and accentuating the unequal

---

[6] In this vision of the interdependence of 'home' and 'colonial' economic and social structures, Hobson also anticipates an argument raised fitfully in recent years, and to which I call attention in chapter 7.

distribution of incomes which is its basic cause. Hobson, like the nineteenth-century under-consumptionists, saw the answer in more equal income distribution in the metropolitan economies and he was an early advocate of state intervention toward this end; elsewhere he also advocated measures to control the centralization of capital in the great 'cartels' or conglomerates that were already emerging in his day. Rosa Luxemburg reinterpreted the theory of economic imperialism in strictly Marxist terms. Denying that consumption can increase in a closed capitalist system, and hence that accumulation is also impossible, she sought the dynamic force of capitalist expansion in the extension of markets overseas. Only so long as such markets can continue to be brought into the expanding capitalist system can this system continue to thrive; the total incorporation of the world into the free-market system will thus bring its necessary processes of accumulation to an end.

But it was the view of Hobson rather than of Rosa Luxemburg that has survived through time, and this for a surprising reason. When V. I. Lenin turned during World War I to write his sketchy polemic on imperialism (Lenin 1917/1926T/1970R), he found more support in Hobson's work than in that of many of his fellow Marxists. He argued that imperialism represented the monopoly stage of capitalism, the period of concentration and centralization of capital coupled with a worldwide search for profitable investment opportunities, that should herald the final demise of the system. He saw clear evidence of the capitalist monopolies sharing out the world in the burst of imperialist expansion after 1880, while the conflict between these powers then approaching its climax constituted the phase of bitter internecine capitalist conflict. His emphasis on the export of finance capital is in sharp distinction to Rosa Luxemburg's emphasis on the search for markets, which is also a subsidiary element in Hobson's argument. But this 'internal contradiction' within the greater contradiction of interpretations of world expansion and 'development' was stillborn. Rosa Luxemburg herself perished, while Lenin's views quickly acquired the status of unassailable orthodoxy among Marxists. What should have been the opening of a vigorous and fertile discussion became ossified. In fact the data base of the Hobson/Lenin argument is shaky, for the most rapid increase in both portfolio and direct investment from Britain — by far the leading investor — in the late nineteenth century was in the 'white' portions of the empire, independent or soon to become independent, and in the southern countries of Latin America.[7] Among 'underdeveloped' dependencies, only India was a major recipient of British capital. Certain territories, such as North Borneo, Central Africa, the Solomon Islands and the Pacific phosphate islands, were certainly acquired either by, or with the vigorous urging of, monopoly capitalist companies — albeit that these depended initially on the small shareholder for finance — but elsewhere investment followed, rather than preceded, territorial acquisition. Robinson, Gallagher and Denny (1961) tend to support Schumpeter's view in concluding that most of the 'scramble for Africa' was motivated by strategic considerations, and followed from the 'necessary' intervention in a bankrupt and incompetent Egypt in the 1870s. But they do not face the basic issues.

Hobson and Lenin were right in some respects. The beginning of the modern period of mergers and conglomerate formation in capitalist business is found in these years. These oligopolies quickly became much more powerful and omnipresent in the overseas dependencies — colonized or not — than in the metropolitan countries themselves. The consolidation of a few highly integrated corporations, metropolitan-based but operating in the dependent territories, quickly brought monopoly capital into a position of control over dependent economies that commerce has never yet enjoyed at home.[8] As Marx would have predicted, this consolidation became especially rapid during the Depression years. But these changes, and the parallel reconstructions of capitalism in the metropolitan countries, did not lead to collapse; they led instead to a rebirth of the capitalist system in a new form. Marx's predictions were thus completely invalidated in this area, for reasons that are perhaps to be sought in the Depression years of the interwar period, and in the emergence of new economic theories that, translated into policy, were in time to facilitate the successful restructuring of international capitalist enterprise.

[7] Hobsbawm (1968: 122) describes Argentina, Uruguay and Chile at this period as 'honorary dominions' of the British Empire.

[8] See Brookfield (1972a) for a more detailed documentation of this process in the south Pacific region.

Economics, and the Great Depression of the 1930s

As we noted above, economics moved away from considerations of growth in whole economies after the early nineteenth century. Attention centred on the evolution of an elaborate theoretical system concerning the 'firm' and its behaviour under idealized market conditions and operated by unreal creatures called 'rational economic men'. With the outstanding exception of Joseph Schumpeter — whose contribution we defer for the present — no major economist of the first quarter of the twentieth century was closely concerned with 'development' in any context. None the less, a crude theory of trade cycles was evolved in the later nineteenth century, and provided the basis for policy recommendations made to worried governments who sought advice when a persistent slump appeared after 1920. By and large, economists were still imbued with the 'liberal' principles of *laissez-faire*, and they believed the cause of cyclic downturns in production and employment to arise from over-production of capital goods during the preceding boom, requiring a slack period during which capital would be absorbed and wages and prices would fall until it again became profitable to invest in the expectation of improved demand. Little could be done, and little should be done provided that Adam Smith's supposed 'invisible hand' could be relied upon to maximize general good from the assemblage of individual self-interest. If this failed, something must be amiss, and it was decided that wages were too high because they had been raised too far in the previous boom, and were prevented from falling as they should by the new factor of trade union pressure.

No one at the time realized what was really happening in the 1920s, and indeed it is only in long retrospect that the full ramifications of the system of causes through space and time are at last being appreciated. But it was evident that the situation was desperately serious, and that the 'free market forces' were being severely constrained. Massive unemployment and brutal reduction of wages could be utilized as remedies in dependent colonies — wages were cut 50 per cent at a stroke on some Pacific plantations — but efforts to force down wages in representative democracies were bitterly resisted, and the fear of revolution haunted employers and the authorities. The situation grew rapidly worse after the American stock market crash in 1929. Export-orientated and capital-goods industries suffered especially severely; trade between nations fell off catastrophically and unemployment in the 'advanced' countries swiftly mounted into the millions. In the dependent economies some forms of primary production were largely eliminated, and a great number of enterprises faced bankruptcy. The initial reaction of governments was almost everywhere the same: if possible reduce wages further; in any case balance the budget in order to retain financial stability; seek whatever trade advantage could be gained by tariffs and bilateral agreements; reduce imports, and cut prices — and by this means spread the disaster to other nations.

A small minority of voices called for a different policy, based on massive public works and supports to enterprise in order to absorb unemployment and reactivate investment. Few economists agreed. However, the new government in the USA adopted such a policy under the 'New Deal' in 1933, though on an insufficient scale to eliminate the problem. In Germany, a more thoroughgoing policy of economic stimulation was adopted by Hitler and enjoyed striking success even before government intervention was enlarged by massive rearmament in 1935. The Japanese, initially hard hit by trade restrictions, embarked on a vigorous policy of export expansion in southeast Asia and this policy extended quickly into military expansion to secure a commercial empire. More widely, governments found it necessary to intervene to save 'essential' industries from bankruptcy, supporting credit or the writing-off of debts against their better economic judgement. In their overseas territories, the French were far more active in this area than the British, who concentrated heavily on trading remedies, outstandingly the 'imperial preference' system introduced in 1932. Whether by such pump-priming, or from 'natural' causes, matters did indeed improve for a time. But in the second half of the 1930s, with recovery only partial, there was a new downturn which was reversed only by general rearmament. The Depression did not really end until after the adoption of full-scale war economies, with comprehensive government control, a couple of years or so into World War II.

Reluctantly, but inevitably, the need for government action in economic affairs was indelibly established during the 1930s; *laissez-faire* finally died. A new theoretical justification was required, and this was provided by J. M. Keynes's *General theory of employment, interest and money* published in 1936. This contribution, which restored macroeconomics to its classical leading role, has led to much else, and to policies that have dominated the development scene in the 1950s and 1960s; it is therefore necessary that we examine it in some detail.

Keynes's central argument was that employment is governed by the level of national output, and that this in turn is controlled by the volume of demand for consumer goods together with the volume of private plus public investment. In money terms, the output of an economy is equal to the income of that economy. The proportion of income that is not consumed constitutes savings; the proportion of output that is not consumed constitutes investment. Savings therefore equal investment. Only when all four elements are in balance is the economy in equilibrium, but because any non-equilibrium state means either want or waste, the economy must always be seeking such an equilibrium.

But *desired* savings and *desired* investment can only co-incidentally be in balance, because they are determined by quite unrelated considerations. The proportion of income that is saved depends on the 'marginal propensity to consume', that is on how much of each additional pound or dollar received people wish to spend. In the short run, this tends to be a fairly stable proportion of national income. An increase in savings therefore requires an increase in total income, unless consumption is damped down by deliberate action. The willingness to invest, on the other hand, depends on the anticipated yield of investments and on the cost of borrowing the money — the rate of interest. The anticipated yield depends on future expectations of sales and costs and hence varies according to the state of economic confidence. Given that marginal propensity to consume is relatively stable, the most variable element in the system is desired investment. It is the manner in which savings and investment are brought into balance that is the core of Keynes's theoretical system.

An increase in investment will generate employment, and thus increase total national income. A proportion of this is saved, being that part that is not spent on consumption. The amount that is saved depends on the 'multiplier' effect that Keynes adopted from earlier workers. This 'multiplier' derives from the re-spending of money by its first recipients, second recipients and so on, each of whom saves a proportion of what he receives. The rate at which the required savings are produced thus depends on the proportion that each saves, conversely on the marginal propensity to consume. Investment will therefore create new incomes which will enlarge the national income, increasing both consumption and savings at a rate which depends on the multiplier until a new equilibrium is reached. The same process operates in reverse if there is a shortfall in investment, so that national income is reduced and hence savings are reduced.

There is no reason at all why the equilibrium should be at a level of full employment: it can correspond with any level of employment. Employment is a dependent variable of forces generated elsewhere in the system. Adam Smith's 'invisible hand' is thus repudiated, for the free operation of the system may maintain for long periods an equilibrium at which many people are in distress. If the government wishes to achieve full employment, or to increase employment above prevailing levels, it must act to increase the national income. Government can increase savings — for the economy as a whole — by taxation, by disincentives to consumption or by incentives to save. But the most immediate results can be obtained from incentives to invest, coupled with direct investment by the government itself. A whole battery of control measures is available, by means of which the government can raise the equilibrium level of the national income, and effectively eliminate the cycle of boom and slump.

Keynes's 'general theory' has certain limitations. In modern times it has not helped governments deal with a combination of inflation with high unemployment. But more serious limitations arise when the logic is applied to partially commercialized economies. If there is insufficient productive capacity to meet an increase in demand, a rise in income will stimulate inflation more than consumption. Where incomes are very unequally distributed, an increase in investment will not necessarily generate savings of the form and quantity desired. Where the necessary apparatus of an integrated economy and financial system does not exist, Keynes's theoretical system cannot apply. The 'general theory' is in fact specific to the time and place of its formulation — a period of persistent under-utilization of resources in the 'advanced' economies. But the case for government intervention is more general, and the value of economic management was in any case empirically demonstrated. Keynesianism seemed to present a viable alternative to socialism, permitting capitalism to survive in partnership with the State, and the alternative was in fact accepted by many socialists. It would not be long before attempts were made to translate this equilibrium theory into a theory of growth, and to find in it prescriptions for economic growth in the less-developed economies; such moves provided the foundation for the post-1945 drive to 'develop the underdeveloped countries'.

The influence of Keynes has been very great, though *laissez-faire* had already died before he wrote, and greater public involvement would have come about without him. But Keynes, and the work on national income analysis which supported him and which he helped greatly to foster, performed certain unconscious disservices to economic planning, and especially planning in the dependent developing countries. The emphasis on aggregation at the national level encouraged the neglect of internal income distribution, economic structures and regional disparities. It also lent weight to an established fashion to compartmentalize economic problems within national boundaries, and to disregard interdependence of economies; the failure of the international trading system had already devalued interdependence in the minds of national planners. The revival of macroeconomics, at a critical time, thus had some rather unfortunate consequences. Keynes was not himself responsible for these errors, but they were made, as we try to show in the next chapter.

2: The virtues of growth

In the last three years of World War II the Allied governments and their people became almost unanimous in adopting higher productivity, greater welfare and democratic government as goals for the colonial territories. With the formation of the United Nations Organization in 1945 the intention of goodwill widened to include the underdeveloped world as a whole. In the years that followed there was some decline in enthusiasm, as the developed countries became preoccupied with the problems of their own economic reconstruction and devoted most available resources to this end. But the momentum was restored around 1950, and this time it continued, so that the philosophy of 'development' has become an integral part of world polity for the whole of a generation.

It is easy to attribute this new awareness to uncomfortable events: the Japanese conquests in 1942 and their formation of 'independent' governments in southeast Asia in 1944-5; the resistance to returning European rule in these countries, and the pressures toward independence that quickly grew irresistible in India, once released under the threat of war; the widening swells of anti-colonialism that surged across the dependent world from these Asian origins; the competition for support, resources and strategic advantage that began to emerge between East and West; the succession of discomfitures for Western policy that culminated in the Chinese communist victory in 1949. All this is true, but there were also underlying forces of another kind, and of longer history.

Perhaps we can identify three. There is a real sense in which the new concern flowed directly from the fifty-year-old 'ethical' policy in colonial affairs, sharpened by a realization of the inadequacies of early efforts. There was indeed altruism, and it should not be scorned. Secondly, there was a renewed sense of world interdependence as major efforts were made to rebuild foreign trade after dislocations of depression and war, to obtain supplies and to sell the exports of hard-pressed Western countries. A major consequence of this latter force was the 'Eur-Africa' movement of the late 1940s and early 1950s: the African colonies of Western Europe would supply the foodstuffs needed, and would buy the products of rebuilt industries, all within European currency areas. Some colossally uneconomic developments were perpetrated in the name of this policy, but it lingered through the French *loi cadre* of 1956 into the Yaoundé Agreement between France and its former colonies, and so into the present arrangements of many dependent economies with the EEC.

But we should look deeper yet if we are to understand not only the early post-war origins of this movement in Western countries, but also the persistence of the new mood. We might also look at the reconstruction of capitalism that had taken place between the wars, after the old capitalism had approached the brink of a Marxian disaster. The emergence of new and larger forms of organization was one aspect, but of equal importance was the partnership with the State, and the adoption of an economic role by the State—the whole movement given theoretical blessing by Keynes. There is nothing new about partnership between capital and the State, with well-defined roles for each despite boundary disputes that attracted disproportionate political heat in Britain and some other countries during these years. This partnership was again respectable, and it was also better organized than in earlier times. It was the job of the State to provide the infrastructure for capital, to ease its movement into new economic or geographical areas, and to take care of the necessary welfare investments that followed successful growth. If this was true within countries, it was also true internationally. Aid facilitated investment, and investment facilitated the use of aid. What now happened was not only a surge of aid in all its varied forms, but also a new and massive wave of overseas investment from the developed countries. As so often in past history, an alliance of economic power with idealism achieved dramatic results, no less effective in that the nature of the alliance was not fully appreciated for most of a generation.

Underlying the last quarter-century of 'developing the Third World', then, has been the steady and spectacular growth of the 'advanced' industrial economies themselves, a growth which has involved a new phase of economic expansionism and integrationism on a scale far exceeding anything that has gone before. The State economic partnership with the private sector, or the State capitalism that has evolved in the so-called 'socialist' system, has facilitated and almost guaranteed growth within countries. Economic growth now became once again a 'normal' condition, but with a certainty that it had never had before. And the institutional arrangements facilitating growth within the 'advanced' nations have been paralleled to some degree by new international arrangements: the International Bank for Reconstruction and Development and its affiliates; the Organization for Economic Cooperation and Development; the United Nations Conference on Trade and Development; the multinational corporations. The great surge is not only due to the dynamic of the revitalized economies of an enlarged 'core group of advanced countries', for the growth of world population, mainly incident in the 'less-developed' countries, has also provided an engine for expansion. But the quasi-religion of economic growth has had its origins in the 'long boom' experienced most joyfully in the West. In this chapter we look in outline at some of the economic thinking which has evolved in response to, and in aid of, the world economic expansion.

Growth in theory

Measures of economic performance

The new Keynesian emphasis on the central manipulation of whole national economies demanded much more adequate measures of national economic performance than were available before World War II. The concept of the 'national income' goes back a long way, and the first serious attempts to measure it were made even before 1914. But major advances were achieved in the late 1930s, and one of the earliest efforts of the United Nations was a drive — initially sponsored by Keynes — to create a vast improvement in national statistical services and back this with a system of international collection, standardization and reporting. By the late 1950s adequate national income data were available for a large number of countries and territories, and by 1970 few 'market economies' remained for which at least estimates were still unavailable. Since these indices have become of such importance for evaluating the economic performance of countries, and because they have now passed almost into everyday use, we must examine their construction briefly before advancing further.

Essentially, the aggregate income or product indices now used measure the final product of a country's economic activity,[1] the

---

[1] There is no reason why they should be confined to 'countries'. Indices can also be obtained for regions within countries, and this is increasingly done.

summation of the total flow of goods and services available at a given time. The method or methods of computation have been elaborated greatly over the years, through a process that has entailed a great deal of theoretical and practical discussion. Basic data readily available are often inadequate, and supplementary inquiries are often needed to fill out the data available from tax returns, censuses of production, customs and excise statistics, and the banking system. Very mixed data still have to be employed, ranging from precise totals to the grossest of estimates. For some industries, such as many of the service industries, there is no measure of 'product', and the sum of income has to be used as a surrogate. Auto-consumption, especially important in countries where there is a large population of peasant farmers, can only be estimated; some countries provide both 'monetary only' and 'total' estimates. It is normal to divide the national income or product into sectors, and then to obtain three final values which are distinct from one another — though often confused in the literature, and known by a variety of names.

A little thought will reveal that very different sorts of quantities are involved. Cash production of primary industry can be measured fairly readily; the estimate of 'household production' is clearly not much better than intelligent guesswork. But the 'output' of transport, commerce, government and other services is much harder to measure, being based essentially on incomes received in these sectors. The same data can be classified in other ways, according to whether they represent such classes as wages and salaries, income from enterprises, gross operating profits, income from property, and so on. They can also be classified by ethnic group of earners, by region, and in other ways.

Among the three final values, the *Gross Domestic Product* (GDP) is essentially the total earnings or product of the economy, and is more and more often the value used in international comparisons; generally, it is the only value possible for interregional comparisons within a country. The *Gross National Product* (GNP) is the proportion of the GDP that remains at home. From this the consumption of capital goods, measured in the main by depreciation or amortization at taxation rates, is deducted to yield the *National Income*. In order of magnitude, therefore, the GDP is larger than the GNP which is larger than the National Income. Normally in comparative tables, the values are divided by the population to yield *per capita* indices. In comparisons through time, index values of prices are often applied to the data in order to obtain comparisons at 'constant' rather than 'current' prices. But because there are problems in the use of index numbers, growth rates are best quoted at both current and constant prices. The effect of these adjustments can be considerable: thus the growth in GDP at current prices for Fiji from 1968 to 1969 was +9.1 per cent. Per head of population, however, it was +6.6 per cent. The growth in total GDP at constant prices was +1.2 per cent, and the growth in *per capita* GDP at constant prices was −1.0 per cent. One can 'prove' very different things by using the data in selected ways.

The weaknesses of such indices are obvious. They entirely conceal variations in the internal distribution of income, whether between individuals or places. The element of estimation is sometimes very large, especially where a substantial part of total production and services is either not marketed at all, or is not marketed through commercial channels. They suffer from all the weaknesses of any composite index, together with a number of additional weaknesses arising from their comparative use across a great many economies structured in different ways. But the gross differences between countries are of such an order in the modern world that these internal weaknesses are overshadowed. Furthermore, it is more and more possible to compute the GDP for subnational units, often of quite small size, and thus to obtain at least a good first approximation of internal differences in regional standards. Some scholars have also explored the possibility of estimating national or local income backward through time (Clark 1957; Zimmerman 1964). There is no doubt that a tool-kit of great value has been provided, and that its utility is by no means exhausted.

Models of growth

It is almost true to say that the economic theory of growth in the 1930s rested pretty much where Adam Smith, Malthus, Ricardo and Marx had left it in the previous century. However, the evolving theory of economic cycles contained growth theory in so far as interpretations of the boom phase where concerned, and Schumpeter's contribution in particular has provided some very useful insights to modern workers.[2] Furthermore, as Keynes himself

[2] We discuss Schumpeter's ideas in chapter 4.

realized, his equilibrium theory contained some necessary growth implications. If the fundamental engine is investment, and the objective of investment is the improvement of productivity; if an increase in employment demands a higher national income achieved through the multiplier effect of investment; if a shortfall of consumption due to a rising propensity to save can disequilibriate the system by demanding a long-run reduction in investment and can only be cured by measures having the effect of total income expansion; if all these things are true, then net growth is a necessary accompaniment of each restorative adjustment. In any event, the progressive capitalization of production through time has enormously expanded productivity, and would continue to do so.

But this was some way from a model of growth. The economic planners of the post-war era hoped to find in capital investment something like a development-vending machine: you put in the money, press the button, and get growth. But the problem was the button. Only the beginnings of a new body of growth theory had yet emerged in the aftermath of Keynes, but an immense amount of work was now about to be done in this area. In a real sense all this work rested on Keynesian concepts of the independent action of investment in the system, and of the importance of effective demand, but some workers from the 1950s onward introduced the classical concept of the 'production function'[3] into the discussion.

---

[3] It is best to explain this in an extended footnote. The production function is simply a statement that output is a function of the factors used in its production, i.e. in its simplest form:

$$0 = f(K, L)$$

where K = capital and L = labour (technology, land and entrepreneurship being collapsed into 'capital').

If the proportions of K and L are fixed, then the production-expansion path is rigidly determined: if 2 units of labour combine with 1 unit of capital to produce 1 unit of output, then 4 units of labour combine with 2 units of capital to produce 2 units of output. Alternatively, while is is possible to employ additional labour (or capital), there will be *no* increase in production unless the complementary factor is also increased in the required proportion. As we shall see in chapter 3, this is by no means as 'unreal' a case as we might suppose.

If the proportions of K and L are variable, then it is possible to substitute factors for one another while obtaining the same output. So long as the marginal product of each factor remains positive, the firm (or whole economy)

Hence the rather fine distinction often drawn in the literature between 'Keynesian' and 'Neo-classical' models of growth: the distinction is of greater importance to economists than to users of their work. Growth theory quickly became highly elaborated and often very esoteric: contact with the real world was not often established. Nevertheless, some of the basic assumptions contained in the growth models and their evolution became also the assumptions of economic policy; we must therefore spend a little time on them in order to understand what theory underlay the growth policies actually put into effect.

The beginning was in 1939, when R. F. Harrod proposed a growth model arising from the new thinking of the previous decade. He was followed in 1946 by E. Domar, whose unrelated model was so similar in many respects that the two are generally discussed together as the Harrod–Domar model of growth. They have two control assumptions. The first is a fixed ratio between a unit of capital injected into the system and the resulting value of output produced in a year.[4] The second is that the level of savings is also a fixed proportion of income. Given this situation, an investment at

---

has a considerable range of choice in its factor combinations. However, there will still be an optimal expansion path determined by proportionate cost of each factor.

Production functions have many forms. A common one used in growth theory has been the Cobb-Douglas function, where:

$$0 = K^a L^{1-a}$$

(usually with the addition of a constant to the right-hand side of the equation, differing for different economies).

In this case a and $1 - a$ are exponents which indicate the marginal efficiency of the factors (productivity of an additional unit). In the Cobb–Douglas case these two exponents total 1, meaning that an increase in income is equal to the marginal productivity of the factors times the respective increases in the quantity of each factor used. Returns to scale are thus constant; diminishing returns do not apply. The important property of this function (others also have this property) is that it permits capital and labour to grow at different rates.

[4] By implication, this model also relies on a production function with fixed factor proportions, so that the input of labour is controlled by the input of capital. The incremental capital/output ratio (ICOR) is discussed in more detail below, p. 35.

time t will generate additional income through the capital/output ratio and the multiplier at time $t + 1$ and the resultant fixed-proportion savings from the larger income will be invested to generate further growth at time $t + 2$, and so on. Economic growth thus becomes a function of the marginal propensity to save, which determines the amount of investment at t, and the output produced by the resulting capital according to the fixed capital/output ratio, at $t + 1$. The rate of growth is given by the savings ratio divided by the capital/output ratio, or s/C.

But whereas in Keynes's scheme the difference between the mode of decision involved in savings and investment could be accommodated fairly easily, in the Harrod–Domar growth model an initial error in entrepreneurs' expectations of the right level of investment is enlarged through the multiplier, given by the reciprocal of the savings ratio. So the expected demand at $t + 1$, on which investment decisions at t are based, may deviate substantially from the actual growth of demand which should be given by the growth in the labour force plus the rate of labour-saving technical progress $(n + m)$. If this fails, there will be excess or unused capacity in the system at $t + 1$, and the departure will be cumulative.

Some succeeding economists sought to resolve this problem through adjustment of the savings ratio, relying on varying the distribution of income between classes; capitalists have a higher propensity to save than workers. The discussion is complex, but the point of income distribution has been taken up in other ways of relevance to us. Others, the so-called neo-classicists, one of whose earliest members was R. Solow, proposed instead to abandon the fixed capital/output ratio, using a variable production function. Thus when the 'warranted' growth rate given by s/C exceeds the 'natural' growth rate given by $n + m$ the economy requires more labour than it can get; labour becomes more expensive in relation to capital, inducing shifts to labour-saving techniques. The capital/output ratio C is thus raised, and the volume of s/C is thus reduced to equal $n + m$.

While this may seem to contain rather more realism, in fact realism has not often been the intention of the growth modellists; no empirical process has been properly established. There has, however, been an important spin-off from this thinking, in such areas as the role of capital, the importance of capital/output ratios, the study of the multiplier as a means of evaluating new investments, measures to control the savings ratio, and hence consumption, and more generally a continued emphasis on generating growth. The importance of savings was especially underlined, and since poor countries can raise only a small volume of savings, they are unable to finance sufficiently high growth rates to overcome the depressant effect of population growth on *per capita* incomes. Hence the importance of international development assistance on the one hand, and of population control programmes on the other.[5]

The theoretical problem of getting growth started

Given the objective of enlarging total and *per capita* GDP/GNP/NI in a sustained manner, it soon became apparent that the growth theories omitted an element of vital importance to the problem of the developing countries. They started from a base of an already dynamic and wealthy economy. Early attempts to apply the monetary devices envisaged in the Keynesian system (which we have not discussed) proved disastrous; international development aid remained quite small until the middle 1950s; what did theory have to say about an underdeveloped country seeking to *initiate* growth mainly from its own resources? Among other problems, this was one question toward which economists turned their attention in the 1950s, and some fine, dramatic solutions were proposed, calling for 'waves of capital investment' spread across different industries according to the views of the economist concerned. The basic argument was that it was necessary to make a 'big push' in order to overcome the vicious circle of low production, small market, small savings, little capital, low production, and so on. The external economies of industry, the importance of establishing inter-industrial linkages, the 'lumpiness' of capital, the need to produce a bundle of new employment and a bundle of goods for the employees to buy — all these and other considerations which followed led

[5] Perhaps the most comprehensive treatment of growth theories readily available is the collection of papers (including those by Harrod, Domar, Solow and others not mentioned by name, referred to here) printed together with an excellent but rather demanding introduction in Sen (1970). Most of the more condensed treatments in the development literature are only partial, and often reflect the predilections of the author. However, for a simple non-technical discussion, that by Kindleberger (1965: 40-54) is perhaps particularly to be recommended.

toward an approach to the question of growth that became very influential.

From among a number of writers of the 1950s I select two for comment. Ragnar Nurkse (1953/1967R) was among those who favoured a 'balanced growth' approach, spreading investment across a wide field and enlarging the size and volume of the market. But he was much concerned with the problem of generating savings, and doubtful over the value of external aid. He emphasized very strongly the role of the State in controlling trade movements, enforcing savings through taxation, and in effect redistributing income in favour of entrepreneurs in the growth industries. He points out that a country importing capital rather than consumption goods is 'saving' in so far as some of the product of its export industries does not feed consumption. But to translate such savings into domestic savings is another matter, for it is likely that the unsatisfied demand for foreign consumption goods will be in part transferred to consumption of home goods, and not become available for an improvement in the savings ratio. This leads him to remark with apparent favour on the Japanese experience in the nineteenth century, where very heavy taxation on agriculture was used to support State investment, while manufacture and commerce were very lightly taxed, since they produced savings in the necessary concentrated form. He concludes with a plea for the encouragement of entrepreneurial saving in poor countries, since whatever the contribution of public finance and State investment in 'social overhead capital', it is from the savings of those who have money to save that the necessary venture-investment for economic expansion must be generated.[6]

W. A. Lewis (1954; 1955) had a different but related approach. He was concerned to elaborate a model applicable to the problems of countries with very large resources of labour in proportion to the scale of their economies. While the major thrust of his arguments concerns the problem of sectors and dualism, and hence is discussed in the following chapter, two aspects of his discussion are more

[6] This somewhat cold approach derives from the limitation imposed at the outset of his book, where he deliberately isolates the question of accumulating material capital, though agreeing that this is not a sufficient, but only necessary, condition of progress. However, it leads him to neglect of forces that we shall examine in later chapters.

immediately relevant. Like Nurkse, but much more specifically, he doubted whether savings could be generated in the subsistence sector; one has to look to the capitalists, because it is those who receive more who will save more. Furthermore, since the whole benefit of growth accrues to the capitalist sector in his model, for reasons we shall see in chapter 3, it is by reinvestment of profits that this sector generates its own expansion. If the capitalist is the State, the conclusion is the same. It would follow that widening income inequalities are a necessary prerequisite of growth: 'the central fact of economic development is that the distribution of incomes is altered in favour of the saving class' (Lewis 1954: 417).

This is necessary because gradualism is insufficient. Very large increases in saving and investment are necessary to escape low-level equilibrium. In the same place (p. 416) he argues that:

> The central problem in the theory of economic development is to understand the process by which a community which was previously saving and investing 4 or 5 per cent of its national income or less, converts itself into an economy where voluntary saving is running at about 12 to 15 per cent of national income or more. This is the central problem because the central fact of economic development is rapid capital accumulation (including knowledge and skills with capital). We cannot explain any 'industrial' revolution (as the economic historians pretend to do) until we can explain why saving increased relatively to the national income.

The discussion thus became more and more sharply focused on savings, following the Harrod–Domar approach. Underdeveloped countries were not, it was now agreed, underdeveloped because of a want of scope for investment; they were underdeveloped for want of capital; capital was lacking for want of savings, and savings were lacking for want of development. But there is a potential margin of savings capable of being released by one means or another, from one source or another. Some saw it well spread through the economy, others saw it as concentrated in the hands of a 'saving class'.[7] There

[7] There were those who doubted the value of the 'saving class' on the basis that it did not seem to save. It was not until some time later that it became widely appreciated that the savings of such people, in countries of very unequal income distribution, are in fact substantial — but often located largely abroad.

were differing views on how it should be mobilized: Nurkse noted, and many supported him in so doing, that the marginal propensity to consume rather than save is high in developing countries. Forced saving of one kind or another seemed by many observers to be required.

The measurement of required savings: a digression

It was obviously insufficient to pull some estimated savings ratio out of a hat: something rather better was required if the new realization of the importance of savings was to have planning application. On the basis of a characteristically thorough effort at data collection, Colin Clark estimated as early as 1953 that an investment ratio — accepting savings as being synonymous with investment — of 4 per cent of national income would be required simply to provide work for a growing population enlarging itself by 1 per cent *per annum*. A 3 per cent annual rate of population increase would thus demand annual investment at a rate of 12 per cent of national product simply in order to stand still. Hans Singer arrived at a range of estimates for different conditions on the basis of theoretical deduction.[8]

There now ensued a spell of quite profound research into the capital/output ratio, or, as it now came to be called, the 'incremental capital/output ratio' (ICOR) of whole national economies, and of sectors within economies. This was the critical figure needed in order to evaluate the savings required in all the growth models, and is expressed, as we recall, in terms of the amount of investment required to produce target increases in *per capita* income.[9] There are great problems of determination, for the data requirements of accurate estimation are rigorous.

The meaning of the ratio is as follows. A ratio of 1 : 1 would mean that only 1 unit of investment is required to produce each year an additional unit of output, or, the net rate of return for the whole economy is 100 per cent *per annum*. On the other hand a ratio of

[8] The papers of Clark and Singer cited here are reprinted in the very useful collection by Agarwala and Singh (1958/1963R). Lewis's 1954 paper is also in this collection.

[9] A particularly full presentation is given by Higgins (1959: 642–53) and, slightly less fully, in the revised edition (1968: 389–94). What follows here is based on this source.

5 : 1 means that 5 units of investment are required to produce 1 unit of output a year; the rate of return is 20 per cent. Quite apart from the estimation problems, there are problems with time: some forms of investment offer a much quicker return than others. Generally ICORs are found to be greatest (poorest) for basic infrastructure investments, much lower for investments in manufacturing industry, and least (best) for investments in services. It follows on *prima facie* grounds that as an economy 'advances' to higher levels of productivity and consumption, the average ICOR should decline.

Taken in the aggregate, ICOR values for whole economies fall within a range of 1.5 to 7.5. Some data given by Higgins exhibit better than words the meaning of these values:

Country ICOR	Percent rate of growth of national income, given an investment level at a constant 10 per cent of NI	Investment percent of NI required to yield a constant growth rate of 4 per cent in NI
1.8	5.5	7.5
3.0	3.3	12.0
4.2	2.4	16.8

The magnitude of variation in the levels of required investment to yield a modest constant growth rate is striking; this appears, however, to reflect a real world situation in which investment rates vary from as low as 5 per cent to as high as 35 per cent of GNP. It will be apparent that a small error in ICOR estimation can have a very large effect on estimated capital requirements, and lead to total failure of prediction. The ICOR has to some extent been overriden by the use of other and more complex measures since the time we are considering, but it is none the less useful to understand its meaning and its problems. Work based on very simplistic assumptions concerning this value has had a long-lasting influence in development studies.

Growth as a doctrine: the work of W. W. Rostow
Movements tend to feed on themselves. The rise of growth theory generated measurements of national economic performance; improved data fed the further elaboration of theory. The body of

measures that we have discussed has now passed quite ineradicably into general use for the purposes of international and through-time comparison, and with them a basic concept of material productivity as an indicator of economic welfare.[10] Right through the 1960s the concept of aggregate growth dominated policy. And one major reason for its dominance was not the erudite body of theory we have briefly noted, but the work of an economic historian who set himself up as a latter-day anti-Marx. W. W. Rostow evolved his historical scheme through several publications from 1952 onward, and in 1960 published his *The Stages of Economic Growth: a non-communist manifesto* from, of all places, the august house of the Syndics of Cambridge University Press. Through its influence on a whole new generation of students of change, this publication is a major event in the prolonged obfuscation of the real issues contained in 'development'.

Basing his work on the long-period data available for only fifteen countries, and outline data available for some others, Rostow maintained that all societies in the world can be located at some point along a progress marked by five stages: 'traditional society', 'preconditions for take-off', 'the take-off to self-sustained growth itself', the 'drive to maturity' and the 'age of high mass-consumption': only the United States has yet reached the end of this road. The core of this interpretation is the identification for each country of a critical two decades or so, during which a transformation took place to convert the society into one in which growth is 'more or less automatic'. This is the 'take-off', and the conditions required are identified as follows:

(a) The rate of productive investment rises from about 5 per cent of national income to over 10 per cent.

---

[10] For example, the GNP *per capita* of Japan surpassed that of the United Kingdom for the first time in 1972. Therefore, the Japanese:

> have begun to justify a comparison with west European standards, if not yet American standards, in their enjoyment of private goods, such as clothes, food and cars and television: and it is worth remembering that their faster growth is closing the remaining gap in this field more rapidly than in some of the others ... The Japanese are rich, and rapidly getting richer, by the basic test of total production of wealth. (*The Economist* 246 (6762), 31 March 1973: Survey, p. 27)

(b) One or more substantial manufacturing sectors emerge to become 'leading sectors' in growth.

(c) The political and social framework is modified to exploit the impulses in the modern sector, and thus give growth an ongoing character.

Although Rostow was meticulous in his attention to the institutional changes, and elaborated the 'leading sector' concept[11] in later writing, his argument relies at base on the theory of growth. On slender evidence, he assumed an ICOR of 3.5 in the early stages of economic development, together with a population increase of 1.0–1.5 per cent *per annum*. A lift in the savings ratio to above 10 per cent was determined thus, and everything else followed. It was as simple as that. Rostow was not alone in his assumptions: others were assuming ICORs of 3.0 or 5.0 on equally slender grounds, and calculating accordingly. But Rostow's writing, and his basic idea, were extraordinarily persuasive. It seemed to give every country an equal chance; it 'explained' the advantage of the developed countries; it offered a clear path to progress — without spelling this out in detail; it identified the requirements for advance with the virtues of the West; it suggested comfortingly that the communist countries were in fact following Western recipes, with a difference; it debunked the historical theories of Marx. As Rostow ably demonstrates in his lengthy appendix to the second, 1971, edition of *The stages*, his approach was of sufficient generality to absorb much of the criticism levelled against it. The concepts of 'take-off' and 'sustained growth' in particular have passed quite firmly into the literature, outliving the historical criticism which disproved their identification in country after country. Moreover, his book was very widely read, unlike the writings of the economists themselves, so that the 1960s can almost be described as the Rostow period in the history of development studies.[12]

[11] This is not new, but an elaboration of a notion long present in economic history. It has certain direct links with the 'staple' theory of economic growth which we discuss in chapter 4.

[12] The literature of this period is replete in references to Rostow, most especially in the writings of non-economists who often took his 'stages' as gospel. Some geographers are included in this number. An extreme example of his influence, which might perhaps be apocryphal, is a story told of a

It is not surprising that so seminal a work should also have met with a great deal of criticism. In the 1971 second edition Rostow sets out to answer his critics. On essentials he is unrepentant, though he gives several of his critics a very full and well-documented discussion. He believes nonetheless that the essential identification of the 'take-off' — in which he relies more specifically than in the first edition on W. A. Lewis — is correct. In this connection, he cites more recent data on gross investment rates and 'industrial modernization' through time in a number of countries, and tentatively classifies them according to their position of readiness on the way to development. Japan, Mexico, Trinidad and Venezuela, among others, have attained take-off speed and might be airborne; Peru, the Philippines and some others are racing along the runway; among those revving their engines is South Vietnam. It becomes rather clear that Rostow on the one hand, and observers who reject his strait-jacket on the other, are talking about very different phenomena when they use the term 'development'.

Growth in action: the 1960s

The drive to achieve development

Whatever can be said about Rostow's version of history, the date of its publication coincided with something very like a 'take-off' in the drive to achieve development of the 'Third World'. A sufficient body of theory, experience and expertise was now accumulated; a decade and a half of writing and speaking had prepared public opinion in all countries; the West had achieved its own recovery and was in an expansive phase and mood. Then there occurred a series of events that sparked off a new sense of urgency.

By 1960 the process of decolonization was accelerating rapidly, and the composition of the representative international organizations was changing. New competition had now appeared

---

conference of anthropologists met to discuss the 'anthropology of development'. Someone expressed surprise that no economist was to be found among the invited participants. The answer came that there was no need: copies of Rostow's *The stages* were readily available at the conference bookstand.

from the Soviet Union, where an outward-looking government was reaching beyond the territorial confines of Stalin's empire. The Suez debacle, and a series of more or less successful nationalizations, had revealed the new options open to formerly dependent countries. The Congo imbroglio made the perils of gradualism brutally clear, and had its effect on policy as far away as the South Pacific. And closest to the economic heartland, the unexpected success of the Cuban revolution and the excitement which it generated led to a sudden fear that the whole of Latin America might be on the edge of revolution.

In this period of challenge, a new organizational structure for development was ready, and its statistical findings added fuel to the fire of urgency. In 1956 the International Bank for Reconstruction and Development decisively shifted its lending policy away from the developed countries toward the underdeveloped, and its loan requirements brought into being a series of development plans, and the inquiries on which they were based. The United Nations statistical agencies had a major success in their drive to achieve a vast improvement in worldwide statistical coverage for the census years 1960 and 1961. The data were not encouraging. There was some evidence that the rate of growth in GDP was actually slowing down in the 'developing' world. In less-developed countries as a whole the growth of total GDP was at a rate of 4.6 per cent *per annum* in 1950–5, 4.5 per cent in 1955–60 and only 4.0 per cent in 1960–3. On a *per capita* basis the trend was made much worse by the accelerating growth of population: it was 2.5 per cent *per annum* in 1950–5, 2.1 per cent in 1955–60, and only 1.5 per cent in 1960–3. Agricultural output was only just keeping ahead of population increase; the share of the developing countries in world trade had declined steadily for several years, and whereas their export earnings had grown little their import bill was rising rapidly. Foreign capital accounted for about one-quarter of all investment in these countries, and without its contribution there might well have been an actual decline in *per capita* national product in several countries (G. M. Meier, *in* Robinson 1971: 18–37).

All these disturbing trends had to be set against the seemingly satisfying doubling of the aggregated national income of the developing countries in the twenty-year period following World War II. Though not all the adverse trends were yet apparent at the beginning of the 1960s, it was clear enough that the efforts up to that time had been too little and too slow. It was also not yet clear that economic growth, by itself, was insufficient as a prescription for development and this did not become clear for another decade. Whatever else they had achieved, the economists of the 1950s had done an extraordinarily good job of selling their profession. Many people believed, and many economists themselves believed, that they had the answers to the world's ills. There was also an unconscious Madison Avenue touch: fine-sounding phrases like 'take-off', 'sustained growth', the 'big push', 'balanced growth', 'steady growth' and the 'critical minimum effort' held all the charm of a primrose path after a long winter. Politicians were now about to add their own phrases to the collection, with such innovations as the 'Alliance for Progress' and the 'First Development Decade'.

The First Development Decade

In 1961 resolution 1710 of the General Assembly of the United Nations inaugurated a programme for the 1960s in which 'to attain for each country a substantial increase in the rate of growth, with each country setting its own target, taking as the objective a minimum annual rate of growth in aggregate national income of 5 per cent at the end of the decade'. This was to be aided by an improvement in official and private financial flows from the developed countries (DCs) to the less developed (LDCs), to equal 1 per cent of the former's GNP. Comprehensive aid was to be offered in the formulation of development plans to meet these ends.

The rather mixed effort by the developed countries, and the more wholehearted work of the various UN and related agencies, are recounted in great detail in UN and other publications. A few of the DCs have reached or surpassed the 1 per cent aid target throughout the decade, but the average DC flow peaked at 0.95 per cent of their GNP in 1961, declined to only 0.71 per cent in 1966 and then recovered to only 0.78 per cent at the end of the decade. Official development assistance declined almost consistently from 0.53 per cent of average DC GNP in 1961 to only 0.34 per cent in 1970. Private capital flows, by contrast, have risen from a low point of 0.23 per cent of DC GNP in the early sixties to reach 0.38 per cent in 1970.

Notwithstanding this disappointing performance and repeated

TABLE 1 GNP growth rates at constant prices in the 1960s, by regions

	1960–1965		1965–1970		1970	
	Total % p.a.	Per capita % p.a.	Total % p.a.	Per capita % p.a.	Total % p.a.	Per capita % p.a.
Less-developed countries						
Total	5.3	2.8	5.9	3.3	6.2	3.6
Latin America	5.3	2.3	5.8	2.7	6.9	3.7
Middle East	8.4	5.4	8.0	5.0	7.4	4.4
South Asia	3.3	1.0	4.7	2.3	4.1	1.7
East Asia	5.4	2.6	7.3	4.5	7.3	4.5
Africa	4.3	1.9	4.7	2.2	5.4	2.8
South Europe	7.3	5.8	6.6	5.0	6.5	4.9
Developed countries						
Total	5.2	4.0	4.5	3.5	2.7	1.8
Western Europe	5.0	3.9	4.6	3.7	4.8	3.9
Canada	5.5	3.5	4.5	2.8	3.3	1.8
United States	4.8	3.3	3.3	2.1	−0.4	−1.5
Japan	10.0	8.9	12.1	11.0	10.9	9.8

Notes: 1. Data as given in source; separation between 1960–5 and 1965–70 not included.
2. Southern Europe LDCs are Gibraltar, Greece, Malta, Spain and Yugoslavia.
3. Data do not include 'centrally planned economies', i.e. the communist countries.

Source: E. M. Martin, *Development Assistance: efforts and policies of the members of the Development Assistance Committee: 1971 Review, Paris* (Organization for Economic Co-operation and Development), 1971: 116.

failures to fulfil promises, the LDCs taken as a whole not only achieved but surpassed the target rate of aggregate growth. Table 1 shows the performance in more detail, and compares it with that of the DCs.

In the LDCs as a whole there is clear evidence of an 'improving' trend, with growth rates higher than those of the DCs taken as a group toward the end of the decade. Broken down into regions, however, it becomes clear that this 'good' performance is heavily weighted by the Mediterranean countries, East Asia and Latin America: Africa and South Asia — dominated by India and Pakistan — reveal a much less sanguine picture. Among the DCs, the high growth rate of Japan is especially noteworthy; toward the end of the decade, Japan became the second largest source of financial flows to the LDCs, after the United States. The latter is consistently the 'poorest' performer among the DCs, and in 1970 we see a clear hint of trouble that was to come.

But growth rates tell us little, notwithstanding the emphasis given to them in the development literature, and in statistical presentations. Table 2 examines the data in real terms, and exhibits especially the enormous disparity between the developed and the developing countries (here excluding Southern Europe). Notwithstanding the higher growth rates in the LDCs, the gap between developed and developing has widened during the 1960s in absolute terms. It is noteworthy that three-quarters of the total world economic product, by current methods of valuation, comes from North America and Europe; 'growth' means a great deal more when measured against these already large national products than when measured against the comparatively tiny output of the 'developing' countries.

Table 2 also gives some indication of the origins of aid: no data on aid from China are included in this table, but in 1970 its value suddenly appeared as larger than that coming from the USSR. But much aid is spread very thinly, commonly amounting to no more than 2 to 5 dollars per head of the recipient country's population, and only rarely exceeding 5 per cent of GNP. Most of the really notable concentrations of DC/LDC financial flows are from metropolis or former metropolis to colonial territory or ex-colony. This is the mark of the very last days of the old 'ethical' colonial policy. Thus Australia is one of the major contributors of 'official'

TABLE 2 Data on GNP for regions and selected countries, and on DC/LDC transfers in the 1960s

	A. National Income Data					B. DC/LDC Transfers 1969 (official)	
	GNP						
	Gross		*Per capita*				
Market economies only	*1960* $ *bn*	*1969* $ *bn*	*1960* $	*1969* $		*From market economies* $ M	*From 'centrally planned' economies* $ M
Developed countries	858.0	1727.0	1360	2480		−7208	−776
Developing countries	171.0	323.0	130	190		+7208	+776
Africa	33.0	60.0	120	170		+1661	+184
Ivory Coast	0.5	1.3	167	303		+37	n.a.
S. Africa	6.4	13.8	387	683		—	—
Madagascar	0.5	0.8	95	122		+18	—
North America	495.0	914.0	2490	4080			
Canada	33.5	64.7	1870	3068			
USA	462.3	838.2	2559	4137			

South America	*60.0*	*120.0*	*290*	*540*	*+1329*	*+55*
Brazil	13.6	27.4	196	296	+182	—
Peru	1.9	4.3	191	323	+14	+30
Middle East	*18.0*	*39.0*	*220*	*390*		
Israel	1.8	4.1	859	1459	+59	—
Iraq	1.3	2.5	192	274	n.a.	+281
E. and S.E. Asia	*68.0*	*122.0*	*90*	*120*	*+3892*	*+537*
India	29.9	46.2	70	88	+870	+32
Indonesia	7.1	11.5	76	98	+363	—
Japan	79.2	144.1	421	1410	—	—
Pakistan	7.2	14.7	78	132	+377	+75
Europe	*297.0*	*616.0*	*970*	*1850*		
EEC (pre-1973)	*174.0*	*388.0*	*1010*	*2070*		
France	54.9	127.1	1202	2525		
Italy	31.9	76.6	644	1441		
EFTA (pre-1973)	*108.0*	*189.0*	*1150*	*1890*		
Portugal	2.3	5.2	270	554		
United Kingdom	66.8	101.4	1277	1826		
Greece	3.3	7.9	399	891		
All market economies	*1029.0*	*2050.0*	*520*	*860*		

Source: UN Statistical Yearbook, 1971.

aid, but principally to its colony of Papua New Guinea.[13] The only non-colonial territories in receipt of aid at a rate higher than $19.50 *per capita* are Congo (Brazzaville), Gabon, Guyana, Israel, Jordan, Laos, Panama, Singapore, Tunisia and South Vietnam. It will be clear that the 'aid' received by several of these countries is by no means wholly attributable to 'development'.

The case of Latin America

A closer look at a major region will help clarify the nature and effects of the development drive in the 1960s. A specific programme, dominated by the United States as donor and policy director, was set up in 1961 at the Punta del Este conference. This 'Alliance for Progress' was drawn up in the shadow of the Cuban revolution and the Bay of Pigs disaster; fear of revolution led to the very specific incorporation of a series of recommendations on income distribution, land reform and social progress in addition to the more basic objectives — an acceleration of GNP growth to a 2.5 per cent rate coupled with a heavy emphasis on industrialization and trade policy. The land reform drive was especially important in view of the gross inequalities of land tenure that are such a feature of the continent. A series of reports was commissioned from the Comité Interamericano de Desarollo Agricola (CIDA — the Interamerican Agricultural Development Committee); we shall make more use of them in a later chapter. However, enthusiasm for land reform quickly cooled as a potentially viable alternative appeared — that of intensifying production on the large estates as a 'faster' road to growth in the whole economy, and thus, incidentally, raising the incomes of the 'saving class'. In 1965 this 'productionist' school of thought received solid support from none other than W. W. Rostow, at that time rising rapidly in Washington circles, who felt that 'private enterprise should have real scope for initiativeness . . . and a way of demonstrating to all the peoples its inherent virtues' (*cited in* Petras and LaPorte 1970: 259). In 1973 an official survey of the

---

[13] In the remaining French overseas territories, official aid *per capita* of the territorial populations ranges between $140 and $600 (Cayenne). The US Trust Territory of the Pacific Islands receives about $500 *per capita*. The Netherlands overseas territories are also major recipients, but while the remaining British overseas dependencies are generally above the average of *per capita* aid receipts, they range much lower than other colonial dependencies.

first decade of the development programme (OAS 1973: 241-2) confined itself to noting that few land redistributions had been accompanied by the necessary provision of new services, and that interest had declined as reform had yielded rather poor results.

Table 3 provides a summary of the first decade of the 'Alliance' in nationally aggregative terms. Growth has been rather variable, both through the decade and between countries, and it is interesting to note a minimum correlation between this variability and the fairly high levels of fixed capital formation, or investment coefficients, which run well above the levels experienced in Europe and North America during the first half of this century. Between countries, the most noteworthy features of the table are first, the sharp contrast between Argentina and Uruguay on the one hand and the rest of the region on the other; second, the striking growth in volume recorded by the Mexican economy; third, the stagnation of Haiti, which has an economy structured more like that of some south Asian countries than the rest of Latin America.

The interest of this table increases as we move to the right. Except in Argentina and Uruguay, the contrast between the shares of product and of employment in the agricultural sector are very striking: the variable but substantial shift out of agriculture corresponds with the massive urbanization in progress in the continent; nonetheless, the divergence between the structure of production and that of employment is continuing to widen in Latin America. We shall return to this question in the next chapter. Of particular concern are the two right-hand columns, which exhibit both generally low levels of consumption even in the more 'developed' countries, and especially the evidence of enormous income disparities in the incomplete data of the last column. This situation is not greatly changed: large parts of the Latin American population have not benefited at all from the overall economic improvement that has taken place.

It is when we view the situation in general terms, however, that the most devastating conclusions emerge from this macro-microcosm of the First Development Decade. Latin America has achieved substantial growth, at an average annual rate close to 5.3 per cent in gross terms; several countries have achieved significant increases in wealth *per capita* despite an average annual population increase in the whole continent of 2.86 per cent. There has been a major

TABLE 3 Sundry data on economic progress during the 1960s for Latin America

Selected countries ranked according to per capita GNP in 1970	Per capita GNP, 1960 $	Per capita GNP, 1970 $	Growth rate of per capita GNP, 1961–70 % p.a.	Total GNP, 1970 $ bn (US bns)	Mean fixed capital formation as % of GNP, 1961–70 %	Agricultural sector as % of GNP, 1969 %	Agricultural employment as % of all employment, 1969 %	% change in agricultural share of total employment, 1960–9 %	Per capita consumption at 1960 prices, av. 1967–9 $	Per capita income of lowest 20% of earning population, c. 1960 $
Argentina	758	934	2.1	22.7	20.2	15.2	19.1	−3.5	676	203
Uruguay	683	677	−0.1	1.9	12.6	20.9	19.9	−3.3	523	–
Venezuela	589	666	1.3	7.2	16.6	7.8	34.2	−7.6	371	77
Mexico	438	622	3.6	31.6	18.1	12.8	54.3	−7.1	471	70

Chile	491	590	1.9	5.8	16.0	10.1	26.9	-4.4	490	—
Panama	359	566	4.6	0.8	17.8	20.1	47.0	-3.1	431	86
Costa Rica	364	469	2.6	0.8	20.2	22.4	52.5	-3.2	401	114
Peru	291	360	2.1	4.9	18.7	18.2	52.2	-6.0	298	—
Colombia	298	355	1.7	7.9	16.8	30.3	48.2	-5.9	292	77
Brazil	263	350	2.9	32.6	16.5	19.9	52.2	-5.6	259	40
Guatemala	241	302	2.3	1.6	11.8	27.3	68.0	-3.3	283	—
Ecuador	241	284	1.7	1.7	11.9	31.7	55.8	-3.3	229	—
Paraguay	237	264	1.0	0.6	16.0	34.2	56.1	-5.0	235	—
Bolivia	142	196	3.2	0.9	19.5	23.1	56.7	-4.7	152	—
Dominican Republic	183	187	0.3	0.8	16.4	24.8	64.8	-5.0	200	—
Haiti	85	79	-0.7	0.4	(5.0)*	45.9	81.2	-0.7	—	—
					*1969 only					
Total/Mean										
All Latin America	368	467	2.4	124.5	19.6	17.3	—	-5.0	—	—
Source of data	1	1	1	1	1	2	2	2	2	2

1. Organization of American States (OAS), *El Desarrollo de América Latina y la Alianza para el Progreso*, Washington, 1973.
2. UN Economic Commission for Latin America (ECLA), *Economic survey of Latin America 1970*, New York (UN), 1972.

improvement in the average level of savings; at the end of the 1960s it had reached about 17.5 per cent of GNP, distinctly higher than the average in the LDCs as a whole, and it has risen further since that date. There has been substantial aid and especially foreign investment, which has assisted in particular the growth of the manufacturing sector and facilitated notable improvements in the efficiency of this sector. But it is all insufficient. Income inequality is widening; unemployment remains persistently high and great numbers of people are destitute, or living only at a most basic subsistence level. And the total wealth of the continent remains pitifully low. At constant 1960 prices, the total GNP of all Latin America is not much above one-half that of the United States in the 1920s; currently the aggregate product of the economy of the State of California alone exceeds that of the whole Latin America region. There is no question of 'catching up' at present rates of progress; even to raise productivity and income levels in the rest of the region to the more modest relative 'affluence' of Argentina involves 'growth' on a scale enormously larger than anything achieved to this time.

The Second Development Decade, and second thoughts

Chastened, but not yet discouraged, the UN General Assembly adopted a new set of development resolutions in 1970 to launch a second 'development decade'. Growth remained central, with a target average of 6 per cent *per annum* in gross terms, 3.5 per cent in *per capita* terms, but this aim was accompanied by a series of 'strategy' resolutions concerning the need to reduce regional, sectoral and social disparities, to expand exports faster than imports, to promote manufactures and raise the level of aid. The 1 per cent of DC GNP target was maintained, but it is now hoped to raise official development assistance to 0.7 per cent, about double its 1970 level.

The chances of achieving the last-named targets seem minimal as viewed from 1973, but the growth targets seem not only attainable, but even insufficient to many observers. For Latin America, at least:

> a target of 6 per cent is not high enough if Latin America is to make progress in overcoming the serious economic and social problems faced by the countries of the region. It is not just a question of raising the growth rate, but of laying the basic institutional foundations of a structure that will increase the

social impact of development by absorbing labour in productive activities, ensuring a more equitable distribution of property and income, and resolving the problems of sectoral imbalances and backward regions within countries ... the annual growth rate must be raised to 8 per cent by the end of the 1970s and sustained at that level in the 1980s. (ECLA 1971: 9, 12)

The argument is that a high growth rate will offer the freedom to make other necessary changes, and that this is feasible. In general, targets are being pushed higher: manufacturing in the LDCs, for example, is designed to grow at 8 per cent, and it is hoped that agricultural expansion will facilitate such growth by raising levels of demand. The whole trend of thinking is toward more vigorous economic expansion.

Much, however, depends on trade. At least in its statistics, the first development decade was saved from total disaster by a surge of world trade in the last three years of the 1960s. The foreign exchange earnings of the LDCs increased from \$40 billions in 1967 to \$55 billions in 1970, and an important component in this growth was the exported output of the new manufacturing industries in certain of the LDCs. Realization of the importance of trade has made international trade policy very significant in discussion. The 1968 UNCTAD conference secured promises of a general reduction in tariffs on imports of manufactures and semi-manufactured goods from developing countries.

Events since 1970 have transformed the situation in ways that are only starting to become clear at the time of writing. Progress toward the elimination of international trade barriers has been very slow, and there have been contrary trends. The third UNCTAD conference at Santiago, Chile, in 1972 demonstrated the force of growing opposition between the interests of the wealthy trading nations and the poorer. Then in 1973 the collective power of the oil-exporting countries, which has been emerging for several years, was dramatically demonstrated in both political and economic fields. By imposing what is, in effect, a large new tax on oil they have restructured the pattern of world trade and financial flows and, in so doing, brought to an end the simple distinction between rich lands and poor that has dominated international aid and development policies for a generation. A new and more complex situation is emerging in its place.

The wealth of the West is certainly not destroyed, notwithstanding some gloomy views, for this wealth is measurable in many other terms than simply the balance of payments and the GNP. The oil countries have not suddenly become 'developed'. But a redistributive process that the UN Development Decades have not achieved and were not going to achieve has been sharply redirected. The large oil surpluses create major new opportunities for those countries which have a sufficient body of resources to absorb massive investment, and convert several of the oil countries into potential donor nations and investors. Certain of the non-oil countries also benefit, for they have established production of materials substitutable for oil in some of its uses — for example, natural rubber. But others are in a desperate plight in 1974. India, Sri Lanka and Bangladesh are among the hardest hit, but a great many smaller countries are also grieviously affected by a change in the terms of trade which hit them not only through oil imports, but also essential fertilizers and petrochemical products.

The problem is no longer simply one of growth, but of a major restructuring of international specialization. The GNP also is devalued, now that some of the most 'developed' countries no longer stand at the head of the table of GNP *per capita*. A shift in emphasis that has been growing in strength for several years is now becoming marked. Poverty, employment, redistribution, the incorporation of the so-called 'informal sector', and the problem of regional inequality are now given pride of place alongside growth. We shall not trace out all of these in this book, which is more concerned with the received wisdom from the recent past than with the edges of new advance, and speculation. It is necessary that we explore the other streams of thought that have arisen during the 1950s and 1960s if we are to be in a position to build a more soundly based paradigm for a new development science in the future.

3: Dualism, sectors and modernization

Dichotomies, or polarized constructs, are basic to the simplest structuring of human perception into comprehensible order. Inevitably they grow into stereotypes: things that are. Even though they may be further subdivided, argument often returns to the simpler method — 'as if' there were only two classes. When we reject one dichotomy, we often do so only to fall into another. They seem real, and are real at a certain level of analysis; if we adopt a phenomenological approach they become fundamental. Orwell's famous reduction of the revolutionary creed of *Animal Farm* into the slogan 'four legs good; two legs bad' sums up something that is widespread not only in human perception and human politics, but human science as well. The world looks simpler in binary, and social science and the development field are no exceptions.

This chapter is about dichotomies in the theory of development. In a sense the next chapter continues the same theme, for a part of the theory of regional development also employs dichotomous reasoning. Here, however, we are concerned with dichotomies that are not conceived or elaborated in any spatial context, though they certainly have spatial implications. The theme is one of the two fundamental elements in development theory, the other being that of transition, or growth. 'Development' and 'underdevelopment' themselves constitute a dichotomy, and they are linked by a transition. To help analyse the problem thus delineated we have further dichotomies: the dual economy; agricultural and industrial sectors; tradition and modernity, linked by the transition of 'modernization'. These three sets of dichotomies are closely interrelated conceptually so that argument within any one of the three themes can shift readily into the others. In what follows I try to illustrate this interrelation. But I also hope to show that the themes of dichotomy and transition have bedevilled clarity of thought and have permitted a great deal that is important to remain obscure.

Dualism

From observation to argument: 'classic dualism'

It is a matter of simple observation that the economies of a great many developing countries are organized in two parts, structurally and behaviourally so different that they deal with one another largely on a basis of trade — almost as though they formed two different societies and economies. Characteristically, the one is organized in small units employing interpersonal relationships and the family system to a high degree, has no centrality and is — in system terms — a complex or heap. The other is, at least at the centre, organized in large units, interconnected by a web of control that ultimately leads into the hands of a very few, and its dealings are based on contractual relationships: again in system terms, it has a high degree of summativity.[1] The organization, methods of operation and interpersonal behaviour within the two systems differ so sharply that there is often an almost total mutual incomprehension.

In a formal sense, the notion of the dual economy and society originated with J. H. Boeke in writings that go back to about 1910: it was first specifically introduced into English by Furnivall (1939) and then in translations of Boeke's works (especially Boeke 1953). Boeke argued simply that Western economic principles are invalid for Indonesian society, so that in a colonial economy two sets of economic principles are required; the central problem in understanding a tropical dependency, he argued, arises from the contact between the two social and economic systems. The Western or Westernized element in the economy is materialist, rational, individualist; much more than in European countries themselves, it is the epitome of exploitative and unyielding capitalism. The Eastern element, by contrast, is pre-capitalist, characterized by a prevalence of self-employment, fatalistic, unresponsive to variations in prices

---

[1] This organizational approach to the definition of dualism is further elaborated in Brookfield with Hart (1971), and Brookfield (1972; 1973). However, the treatment given the whole topic below departs rather radically from that given in these earlier writings, and reflects a process of rethinking that has been cumulative through the past three or four years.

and wages to the extent of being characterized by 'backward-sloping supply curves of effort',[2] and is not profit-orientated.

But this sort of contrast was not a new observation except in the context of colonial societies. Malthus based his opposition to the Poor Laws of his day on the contention that English society was divided into two classes, the one productive, useful, acquisitive; the other indolent, uncaring for the future, wasteful and unproductive. He was concerned that support provided for the latter would encourage growth in their numbers, dissipation of the hard-won gains of those taxed for support of the poor, and hence lead only to an increase in 'aggregate misery'. The context was different from Boeke's, but the basic observation is closely similar. Marx's somewhat later approach was historical (Marx 1939–41/1964T): he was concerned with the 'pre-capitalist economic formations' from which capitalism had evolved, and in a famous passage contrasted the basic motivation under 'production for use' with that under 'production for gain':

> Thus the ancient conception, in which man always appears (in however narrowly national, religious or political a definition) as the aim of production, seems very much more exalted than the modern world, in which production is the aim of man and wealth the aim of production (Marx 1939–41/1964T: 84)

Marx goes on to elaborate the manner in which the 'primitive' possession by labour of control or access to the 'objective means of its existence' — that is land, and other resources — is dissolved, permitting the accumulation of property and the creation of a proletariat. This occurs through 'exchange', under which goods and labour acquire value in relation to each other, independent of the 'objective conditions'. Marx did not attempt to project this analysis into situations where an alien economic system of different nature was implanted into an 'archaic' society: to him the presence of different classes and economic structures in a single country was

---

[2] This is to say that an improvement in price will only stimulate increased output up to the point at which wants are satisfied. A further rise in price beyond this point will cause a reduction in output (or input, or risk-taking), since wants can now be satisfied with less effort. The essence of the argument is that wants are, at least in the short run, static.

to be explained by the common evolution of each in relation to each other.

A. V. Chayanov (1925/1966T) carried the analysis of production for use an important stage further in work written during the 1920s, and provides a valuable bridge between Marx and Boeke. Marx was content that under 'primitive' conditions the worker had full access to the means of production, and produced only to satisfy his own needs. Chayanov covered similar ground, but on the basis of a great body of statistical evidence and a generation or more of thought about the economics of peasant societies. He was not concerned with evolution or transformations; this gave his analysis a static quality which was his own undoing in 1930, and certainly led him into historical error, but it also permitted him a greater depth of analysis within his own limited frame. He began with the functional interdependence of the several 'moving parts' in the capitalist engine: price, capital, wages, interest and rent. If one is not operative, the whole system of analysis becomes useless. He then notes that in a 'natural economy' human economic activity is geared toward the satisfaction of needs of each producing and consuming unit; comparative profitability does not arise, and nor do wages. What is important is the amount of labour effort which the producing and consuming family or group is prepared to expend on the satisfaction of its needs: it is assumed that beyond a certain minimum, labour is drudgery, and the rational calculation is thus a trade-off between needs and the drudgery of self-exploitation. This would seem to lead straight into Boeke's 'Eastern' behaviour, or to Malthus's indolent poor. The conclusions are identical:

> the family's single indivisible labor product and, consequently, the prosperity of the farm family do not increase so markedly as does the return to a capitalist economic unit influenced by the same factors [improved methods, higher intensity, better access to market, etc.], for the laboring peasant, noticing the increase in labor productivity, will inevitably balance the internal economic factors of his farm earlier, i.e. with less self-exploitation of his labor power. He satisfies his family's demands more completely with less expenditure of labor, and he thus decreases the technical intensity of his economic activity as a whole. (Chayanov 1925/1966T: 8)

It follows from Chayanov's argument, just as it does from Boeke's, that quite different theoretical systems are required to explain the different economic forms, and that a single 'capitalist' economics is an error.[3]

I have spent longer on the 'classic dualism' of Boeke than is normal in discussions of this topic for reasons that are perhaps already apparent: the contrast observed in widely different contexts by Boeke, Malthus, Marx and Chayanov, and remarked on countless times by other writers and by Western businessmen and planters in every bar in every colony there has ever been, is real. It is real as an empirical phenomenon, and to say this is not to accept any particular explanatory theory. But its existence may not be disregarded simply because it does not square with one's basic premise

---

[3] This is a very fundamental issue, not unique to economics. I have made two unsuccessful efforts to resolve it in relation to geographical work in developing countries. In a paper written in 1970 and not published, but quoted too often for my comfort, I came very close to arguing for two distinct approaches to geographical inquiry; an expansion of this paper (Brookfield 1973a) was more ambivalent on this question. As Harvey (1973) points out, the real problem is with one's methodology and its underlying purpose. If one is adopting an empirical or empirical-theoretical methodology — as has been my wont — one is inevitably concerned with analysis of the *status quo* (though I would not accept Harvey's contention that one is necessarily wedded to the *status quo* in so doing). In this case we do arrive at different theoretical systems, and the argument for so doing seems incontrovertible. If one is adopting logical positivism, or deduction from a set of premises, there is only a single line of analysis, and this is the whole thrust of what was until lately the 'new geography'. Harvey argues that Marx's 'structural functionalism' is concerned with 'totalities' and with their transformations, and avoids both errors. See also E. J. Hobsbawm's introduction to Marx (1939–41/1964T).

In the present instance, we see at one point Chayanov expanding a basic element of Marx's argument, but in an empirical-theoretical context, i.e. proceeding inductively. This led Chayanov to argue very conservatively in relation to the development of Russian peasant economy. But the central weakness is perhaps put in perspective by Marx himself: in the passage from *Pre-capitalist economic formations* quoted above, Marx goes on to say:

Hence in one way the childlike world of the ancients appears to be superior; and this is so, *in so far as we seek for closed shape, form and established limitation.* (1964T: 85, my italics)

Marx was, in fact, seeking to comprehend transformations, and his whole argument is concerned with the dissolution of this 'primitive' happy condition.

that all men are acquisitive, rational economic men under the skin, or because the form of analysis is at variance with one's view of scientific method. It has become the fashion to deride Boeke on such grounds. In his place, economists have attempted to set up normative models of dual economy that are supposedly 'value free'. These too have come under attack, and on the very grounds that the economic dualists sought initially to avoid: that of an underlying, even value-loaded purpose. But their efforts should be viewed on their own terms: they have made a valuable contribution toward greater understanding.

Economic dualism: reasoning from premises

The essence of the theory of economic dualism is the attempt to combine in one system theory for an advanced and for a backward economy. The former is assumed to be capital-intensive and mainly industrial; the latter is assumed to be labour-intensive and overwhelmingly agricultural. These 'sectors' correspond roughly with the 'Western' and 'Eastern' of classic dualism. Terminology has varied from author to author: here we shall use 'industrial' and 'agricultural', qualified as necessary. In many formulations there is also an underlying assumption that population growth at early stages is directly related to incomes: this is pure Malthus. Even Malthus's two-class dichotomy creeps in, for it is also implied that the advanced, industrial sector escapes the Malthusian trap and that economic growth and improvement become established once a sufficient part of the population is transferred from one sector to the other.

The primitive statement of economic dualism is the already cited paper of W. A. Lewis (1954) on 'Economic development with unlimited supplies of labour'. Though not formally a dual-economy model, Lewis's formulation concerns two coexistent sectors and the conditions governing the supply of labour to the growing industrial sector from the agricultural. He assumes excessive numbers and hence disguised unemployment in the agricultural sector so that a large volume of labour may be abstracted without loss of agricultural output. Under these conditions, the wage rate required to attract labour into the industrial sector need be only slightly above the productivity per man-hour in the agricultural sector. Until the growth in demand for labour soaks up the whole surplus supply, workers remain available to the industrial sector at a constant and minimal real wage. This argument follows Marx almost precisely, and the agricultural sector thus serves simply as a location for Marx's 'reserve army of the unemployed'.

All the surplus product above the wages of labour thus accrues to the industrial class, who also get the entire benefit of expansion. This situation is ended when the rate of industrial expansion draws so much labour out of the agricultural sector that a shortage finally develops, or if the expansion of production in the agricultural sector is constrained so that shortages of food develop, thus leading to price rises — a change in the terms of trade against the industrial sector. There is then an increase in the marginal productivity of labour in the agricultural sector, so that the minimum wage required to attract labour out of that sector will have to rise. Alternatively, the same result may be achieved by technical improvements or other innovations which will raise productivity in the agricultural sector.

Lewis's model leaves a great number of open ends. Some of these were closed by the model of 'factor-proportions dualism' developed by R. S. Eckaus (1956/1958R) and simplified by B Higgins (1959/1968). This model relies quite simply on contrasted production functions between the two sectors.[4] In the industrial sector, development is capital-intensive, and factor proportions are relatively fixed, or are assumed by entrepreneurs to be so. Given these 'fixed technical coefficients', an increase in employment can only be generated by a rigidly proportionate increase in capital investment, and any surplus labour offering cannot be absorbed without a corresponding increase in the supply of capital. In the agricultural sector by contrast, coefficients are variable, meaning that a wide range of techniques and factor combinations can be employed to yield the same output; the proportions actually used will then be adjusted to the relative availability and price of labour and capital, the latter including improved land. Placing the two sectors in juxtaposition, then, and given a population explosion — or a 'population multiplier' of development — we will have a situation

---

[4] Higgins uses the term 'rural sector', including handicrafts, small-plant industries, and the whole trading complex that some call the 'bazar sector' together with food production. The 'industrial sector' includes plantations, and other forms of industrial agriculture, as well as mines and industries.

in which the absorptive capacity of the industrial sector is limited, so that the increasing supply of labour is channelled into the agricultural sector, where it can be absorbed by the use of more and more labour-intensive methods. There is thus no incentive to capitalization in the agricultural sector, and the gap in productivity of labour in the two sectors widens as the economy grows. There is no need to appeal to contrasts in motivation; the whole phenomenon can be explained in normative economic terms.

As presented, this is a vicious circle of a most intractable kind. It is further elaborated for the agricultural sector by C. Geertz (1963a) in his famous generalization of rural Javanese colonial experience as 'agricultural involution'. As more and more labour is absorbed, the threshold level for a labour-using innovation grows closer and closer to zero return, so that capital investment becomes more and more a matter of micro-detail, at extremely low marginal yield. To reverse this trend requires an improvement in the man-land ratio by shifting labour into industry on a massive scale, but here capital is inadequately available. The separation of the two sectors in scale and organization becomes increasingly marked.[5] Since the trend of industrial innovation is toward increasingly capital-intensive operations, requiring less and less labour per unit of capital, the effect of industrialization without agricultural revolution is progressively more productive of dualism.

Models of economic dualism are growth models, and this characteristic has become more pronounced in the 1960s. We recall from the previous chapter that the 'fixed factor proportions' growth model stems from Harrod (1939) and is termed 'Keynesian', while the 'variable factor proportions' model is termed 'neo-classical'. In one sense, therefore, Eckaus and Higgins have simply juxtaposed the two approaches; Lewis, on the other hand, drew on Marx and Malthus and termed his own approach 'classical'. Except in the allocation of a common supply of labour, however, the interrelation and transformation of the two sectors formed no part of the efforts of the 1950s; modelling of this interrelation became the main thrust of a group of growth-economists of the 1960s, outstandingly J. C. H.

[5] Geertz's empirical generalization is very well known to geographers, and it is therefore important that the underlying theory also be better understood. Perhaps the clearest presentation by Higgins of his model of factor-proportions dualism is in his introductory essay to Geertz (1963a).

Fei and G. Ranis (1961; 1964) and D. W. Jorgenson (1961; 1969).

The model of Fei and Ranis was a far more ambitious attempt to explain a dual economy than its predecessors. It is summarized, adequately but critically, by Higgins (1968: 309–18), and is reviewed more sympathetically by Jorgenson (1969). Basically, Fei and Ranis rest on Lewis in treating the labour force of the agricultural sector as a 'reserve army of the unemployed' containing a surplus that can in the first stage be drawn on without negative effects on agricultural sector production, and hence at a constant real wage level. Beyond this, however, they explore not only the labour interrelation of the two sectors, but also the consumption of goods produced in each sector by members of the other, and investment by 'dualistic landlords' who have holdings in both sectors and hence act as agents for the growth of the industrial sector. Variable rather than fixed factor proportions are assumed in the industrial sector so that growth may be supplied by accumulation of either or both capital and labour, and all technical innovation is assumed to take place in the industrial sector. The model is one in which 'development' requires a shift of productive capacity from the agricultural to the industrial sector at a rate faster than the growth of the economy as a whole. Both Higgins and Jorgenson criticize many of the assumptions, the former particularly doubting the freedom of the industrial sector to absorb labour without a corresponding increase in capital.

Jorgenson varies the assumptions somewhat in what he describes as a neo-classical model. The marginal productivity of labour in agriculture is always positive, so that labour is never available to the industrial sector at a constant real wage and all abstraction of labour from agriculture causes loss to agricultural output. The real wage thus rises continuously with development. Some differences of development path emerge, but Jorgenson is not seeking to map out a development strategy. Although he claims some empirical verification, mainly from Japan, his elegant model is a contribution to theory.[6] Others have modelled with different assumptions, both demographic and economic; doubtless the fun of such elegant play

[6] One of the conclusions of his model, that since development abstracts continuously from the agricultural sector, the 'intersectoral terms of trade' move continuously against the industrial sector, runs directly counter to reality.

will continue to sustain effort in this direction. It does no harm provided that no one believes it to be an analysis of reality, but unfortunately this is not always the case.

Economic dualism: testing and modification

The problem of economic dualism is the problem of theoretical economics as a whole. A set of behavioural assumptions made about the real world is used through logical argument, geometry and mathematics to shed light on processes observed to be operating in the real world. However elegant the logic, however parsimonious the explanation, the conclusions can only have real world validity in so far as the assumptions are realistic and the calculus employed corresponds to real processes. By contagion, this is equally true of the 'new geography' as D. Harvey (1969) demonstrates brilliantly, but the difference is that whereas few 'new geographers' believe that their play does more than cast illumination on what was formerly obscure, a whole generation of economists has believed that they were finding real and conclusive answers capable of being mapped directly into development plans. Many policy makers have shared their belief. The fact that the infinite complexities of reality are being enormously simplified has always been perceived, but it is only in the last few years that the limitations implicit in this simplification have been widely appreciated.

There is an especially serious problem with economic dualism. The method is essentially to set up ideal types based on assumptions drawn from observation of real-world dualism. At best, these ideal types can do no more than generalize modal behaviour in a bi-modal reality. This is of great value, if and when the generalizations actually correspond to modal realities. But when the interrelation of two sectors is then analysed, the whole population is divided on the basis of the characteristics, real or supposed, of two modes in a very complex distribution. The approximation to real world conditions is inevitably moved a stage further from reality. The problem is that this is virtually inescapable if the modelling is to be of any use, for the two 'modes' acquire meaning and significance in relation to one another, and many argue that the mutual interaction reinforces the modal characteristics themselves.[7]

[7] Some go further and argue that all that we recognize as dualism is wholly a creation of this interaction, the modal characteristics themselves being brought into existence, in the form described, only by a larger single process of colonial or neo-colonial exploitation. I expand this view in chapter 5.

Any method of analysis based on ideal types depends at base on the accuracy with which the ideal types are delineated, and on the completeness of the delineation. In regard to the industrial sector, the growing body of input-output data now available, and modern appreciation of the significance of size and structure in the firm, make possible a realism that it is unfair to seek in the writings of more than a decade ago — the period with which we are mainly dealing. However, attempts to refine the characteristics of the industrial sector as an ideal type were made in this period, and they deserve notice.

R. E. Baldwin (1956/1964R) made an early attempt to separate the consequences for historical development in the United States of two contrasted farming types — the plantation and the family farm. This was a contribution to the theory of export-based growth, and I discuss it in this context in chapter 4. However, Baldwin carried the same form of analysis into developing-country work, and used it empirically to test the factor-proportions approach to economic dualism. In an historical study of Zambian development since 1920 (Baldwin 1966) he took as the central question the failure of the rapid growth of mines and plantations to generate much 'spread effect' through the economy as a whole. The benefits of growth reached only a restricted part of the population, and growth in the agricultural sector has been small. Baldwin discounted any resistance to change on the part of the agricultural sector. On the contrary he found evidence of ready response to economic stimulus, both in offer of labour and in production to meet the industrial sector demand.[8]

This being so, he turned to a closer examination of employment and income distribution in the industrial sector. When 'development' began, the cost of unskilled labour was very low in Zambia, the 'opportunity cost' in money terms being negligible. But there was no locally available skilled labour for mines, or for supervisory work on

---

[8] Though this market production was nowhere intensive, it was very widespread. M. P. Miracle (1962) shows how the Copperbelt towns were supplied with market produce from distances as great as 1200 km. Something akin to a Thünen ring pattern evolved. Vegetables were grown in an inner ring, forest production of firewood came from a second ring 80-100 km out, while weight-reduced crops were derived mainly from the remoter areas. The distances involved emphasize the low population density, which was an important part of the environment of the 'spread effects'.

plantations. It was cheaper to import skilled workers than to train local personnel. Once this pattern was established, it became entrenched by custom, and by the restrictive practices of the skilled workers' trade unions; only gradually were local workers able to force entry into the higher paid occupations, or take advantage of other opportunities requiring a modicum of capital.

An important element in the situation was the contrast in labour coefficients between the leading, mining sector, and the less significant plantations. Mining quickly became capital-intensive to a high degree. Plantations remained labour-intensive, but although they were thus better adapted to the factor-endowment of the country, they offered only limited scope for workers' advancement to higher-paid occupations. Ultimately the mines did offer opportunities for individual advancement, but these were few in number because of the structure of the industry, and because no local industries were set up to use the output of the mines.[9]

[9] In preparing my own study of the Melanesian islands (Brookfield with Hart 1971) in the late 1960s, I was confronted with the evident inapplicability of Higgins's factor-proportions approach, first because it relied on a population explosion in order to generate surplus labour in the agricultural sector, and secondly because of the assumption of fixed technical coefficients in the industrial sector. Neither was valid: dualism as I then interpreted it became established under conditions of stable or declining population, a persistent feature of 'industrial' enterprise has been shortage of labour, and I had strong qualitative evidence to suggest that the intensity of use of labour on plantations varied inversely with the cost of labour, whether this was measured between territories, or within any given territory through time.

In order to test the latter hypothesis I began in 1968 to collect data on plantations, and Ms Hart collected more. We gathered data on some 25 plantations, which seemed to confirm my hypothesis. However, up to the time when I left Australia and this work was terminated, it was possible to standardize data fully on only 13 plantations for statistical testing.

A least-squares regression on these few data gives the following:

$$y = 5.52 - 0.0126\,x$$

where y = workers employed per 10 tons of copra produced ($1000 at a plantation-gate price of $100/ton; range is 1.5–8.0)

x = annual cost to the plantation of one worker, in dollars (range is $130–$410).

The coefficient of correlation, $r = 0.546$. The trend therefore just fails to be significant at the 5 per cent level. (Critical value of $r = 0.553$.)

On the basis of this calculation the labour coefficient would fall by 1.26

Despite export growth, then, neither mines nor plantations provided any significant number of Africans with incomes sufficient to transform consumption patterns. Effective demand was insufficient to provide more than limited stimulus to agricultural sector production, and Baldwin concludes that significant overall expansion must await the improvement of rural incomes by means designed directly toward that end.[10] Though the factor-proportions approach is supported in so far as the industrial sector is concerned, it is also refined by giving weight to differences within that sector, while the maintenance of dualism as a whole is seen to be due to want of effective demand sufficient to generate agricultural sector transformation.

Baldwin's conclusion, and that of other analysts, is that even if 'fixed technical coefficients' obtain in the industrial sector, this is insufficient explanation of the failure of a leading industry to generate transformation in the agricultural sector; for this it is necessary to look more deeply, and not to rely on some version of the 'reserve army of the unemployed' to explain the failure. H. Myint (1964) also stresses the low-wage policies of mines and plantations, the product of an initial form of exploitation which has become institutionalized. He additionally emphasizes the contrasting accessibility of funds for industrialists on the one hand, and the rest of the population on the other, and regards the resulting 'financial dualism' as critical, preventing the agricultural sector from gaining the means of escape. This is a common view, and it has led in modern times to the creation of a large number of new credit institutions in developing countries. Whether as a result of the policies of these institutions, however, or from the deeper cause of

---

workers per 10 tons of production for each $100 of annual labour cost. But the data are not a proper sample, and are biased in favour of company plantations which have the requisite quality of accounting. Also the 'sample' is too small. An adequate test of the hypothesis would demand a much larger programme of data collection. Nonetheless, the assumption of 'fixed technical coefficients' is not sustained.

[10] Baldwin's analysis is incomplete in that he gives only small weight to the repatriation of profits and savings by companies and expatriate employees, the retention and reinvestment of which might have generated a greater transformation.

insufficient opportunity for open-ended entrepreneurship where this would require entry into a tightly structured commercial system (cf. B. R. Finney, 1973), these new credit-granting organizations have generally achieved rather limited results.

With regard to the 'agricultural sector' itself, an analysis of the literature would suggest that very little can still stand of the body of behavioural assumptions that have been made. It may be helpful to spend a little time on this question. The doctrine of backward-sloping supply curves of effort has been attacked by many writers, and numerous empirical studies have pointed to the quick responsiveness of peasant farmers and even 'primitive' farmers to price incentives. The Malthusian proclivity of peasant families to enlarge as soon as the lid of poverty is lifted a little has been both questioned and, where something like it can be demonstrated, rationalized as being a search for the security in old age that only a numerous family can bring in the absence of national welfare systems or company pension funds. In any case, the partial acceptance which family planning programmes have enjoyed is evidence enough that at least a minority of peasant families are readily aware of the countervailing advantages of having fewer mouths to feed.

But it is possible that the critique of behavioural assumptions about the agricultural sector has been carried to excess by some critics. K. Griffin (1969) for example, opens his *Underdevelopment in Spanish America* with a bitter attack on, and lampoon of, the whole theory of economic dualism. There is an underlying reason for his bitterness, which we shall come to shortly, but in the course of his onslaught he attacks the assumptions that members of this 'traditional' sector do not maximize, are largely unemployed or underemployed, and will not or cannot save — thereby risking the implication that they are maximizers, are fully engaged in productive activity, and are frugal. These things may be true of some peasants as individuals, but it is carrying matters too far to impute such behaviour to peasants as a whole. After the work of Julian Wolpert (1964), few geographers would look for maximizing behaviour in any farmer anywhere; enough empirical studies have accumulated to show that where they have adequate resources and can make do on, say, twenty hours of work a week, many farmers will do just this; the same empirical studies, largely by anthropologists, carry abundant evidence of a high marginal propensity to consume rather than to save, and of 'conspicuous consumption' which, even if it has a social purpose in terms of the acquisition of prestige and influence, is nonetheless far removed from the behaviour of Economic Man.

Fisk (1962; 1973; Fisk and Shand, 1969), incorporating latterly the work of Nakajima (1969), reaches his way toward a more rational explanation of this behaviour. In an elegant model, relying at base on Chayanov's insistence on the drudgery of self-exploitation, Fisk argues that farmers will suffer the disutility of work only up to the point at which their utilities are satisfied, being an adequate level of consumption for all purposes whether achieved by subsistence production, cash production, or a combination of the two. A farmer with abundant resources can achieve this with little effort, that is with low intensity of input. A farmer lacking in resources must work much harder, employ skills and enterprise, and so work more intensively in order to achieve a comparable level of satisfactions if he can. It is the latter, not the former, who will most readily seize at new opportunities for income. The surplus of utility remaining after deduction of the disutility of work is already small for such famers; new income-producing activities may require or seem to require less disutility than the subsistence activities which they replace. On the other hand the low-input, affluent farmers have abundant utility remaining after reaching their satisfaction level, and will see little benefit in undertaking new activities entailing much greater disutility than before. If, as Nakajima (1969: 166) argues, the objective of the peasant farmer is to maximize his utilities — or rather his utility after deduction of the disutility of work — then the 'affluent' farmer will not be tempted by price incentives unless his pattern of utilities is changed, that is unless new needs are perceived as a result of exposure to living standards higher — or thought of as higher — than his own.

These considerations are also relevant when the interrelation of the two sectors — or modes — comes to be analysed. We have noted that the majority of dualists, even if they admit of technological improvement and commercialization in the agricultural sector, regard the principal source of improvement as being a transfer of workers into the more productive industrial sector. A reduction of intensity, a conversion of agricultural sector production to more extensive, mechanized methods, is then seen as the main avenue for improvement of agricultural productivity. All this is in line with the

Western model of development. But even before the innovations of the much-debated 'green revolution' became apparent, or before the now-evident possibilities in what was once thought the 'desperate' situation in rural China were exploited, there were the historical examples of high productivity by the use of both labour-intensive and capital-intensive methods in some countries of Northwest Europe, and on some now neglected islands in the West Indies. These, as today the high production obtained from tiny landholdings in Singapore, or on land made from the sea beach in Hong Kong, were commercially motivated. In an interesting revision of population theory in its agricultural context, Ester Boserup (1965) has proposed that population pressure on resources is a principal spur of agricultural intensification, which yields lower returns per unit of labour but higher returns per unit of land, than less intensive methods. In her view, population is the independent variable; agricultural intensity the dependent. She thus inverts the Malthusian argument, and so presents an alternative path to Geertzian involution,[11] as I have tried to show in the very different context of explaining intensive systems in the pre-colonial Pacific (Brookfield 1972b).

Ms Boserup's theory was of the very long term; commentaries have mostly used either historical or comparative evidence. But the conclusions of one more immediate test are interesting. A. M. Maude (1973) has used data from a survey of population, land tenure and agriculture in Tonga in order to seek evidence of Boserupian intensification in a case where rapid population increase on limited land has already brought about major changes in the environment of farming. He finds no evidence of intensification in subsistence farming, or of its need being yet perceived, but he also finds that there have as yet been only incipient ecological consequences. On the other hand he does find intensified practices innovated among the most commercialized farmers, specifically for their cash crops, the spur being increased returns from very limited land.

---

[11] In its general theoretical application, which is not Geertz's own contribution. Geertz developed his theory in the quite specific context of Javanese wet-rice cultivation, where population pressures and external pressures were both extreme, and where no known higher technology capable of yielding more output was available.

Dualism revisited

The effect of a few dashes of cold empirical evidence is somewhat damaging to the assumptions made about economic behaviour in the two sectors required by most attempts to explain dualism. Something remains, for it is evident that the trend toward capital-intensive practices is very much stronger on the one side than on the other, with major consequences for employment capacity and income distribution. The problem of dualism may therefore be changing its nature, and whereas its origins may be structural and related to the policies of colonial authorities and expatriate entrepreneurs, the persistence of the condition may indeed have more to do with production functions and factor proportions than it had in the past. But the point must be emphasized that a phenomenon called 'dualism' exists, whether or not we have been able to explain it in satisfactory terms. The denigration of theory does not wipe out the observation which brought the theory into being. What the critics are complaining about most seriously is the state of mind that goes with dual economy theory: the encouragement of large-scale enterprise, and the neglect or the setting of inadequate goals for the small-scale operator on the 'agricultural' side. They are also complaining about interpretations which treat the problem as the fault of 'backwardness' in the agricultural sector, and conveniently ignore the forces which have stood to gain from dualism — the metropolitan enterprise and a privileged minority. This is the sort of dual economy theory about which Griffin and others grow bitter: the exploitative characteristics of dualism are quite insufficiently stressed in the literature. But dual organization of economic activity, combining both large-scale and small-scale enterprises, utilizing the potential of both labour-intensive and capital-intensive structures, may even be employed advantageously, as the modern history of Japan and still more the current 'walking on two legs' policy of China have been able to demonstrate.

In a recent paper with the title used for this subsection, H. W. Singer (1970) has, for the moment, the last word on this subject. As he sees it, the viciousness of dualism lies in the superiority of one sector and the inferiority of the other, the coexistence being chronic, without change leading toward equalization of conditions for the members of each; the interrelation is such that the superior element does little to pull up the inferior, and may even serve to pull it down. He identifies a potent cause in the growing concentration of modern technology into a few hands, both internationally and internally within countries, and to changes in that technology which favour its use only in the 'superior' economic activities. He sees the consequences of this trend to be expressed most starkly in the growing employment crisis of many developing countries, where 'real' unemployment levels as high as 25 per cent are now common and the situation is worsening. In common with W. R. Armstrong and T. G. McGee (1968/1971R) he sees the resulting 'involution', in the form of division of jobs among many people, as becoming more an urban than a rural problem. In other words the evils of the agricultural sector have now invaded the domain of the 'industrial' and have become worse in the process. But this raises the question whether we can any longer speak of 'dualism', but rather of a whole process in which the sector approach is increasingly irrelevant, and which is more amenable to analysis of an entirely different order.[12]

The two-sector problem

The urban-industrial bias

By convention, dualism is a value-loaded subject, but the problem of allocating development effort between sectors is discussable in 'neutral' terms. This is hardly so, however, for there are close links between the two debates, especially when the discussion is carried on at the level of the simplest — or principal — dichotomy: that between agriculture and industry. Until very lately it has been an almost universal assumption that a country dependent mainly on agricultural production, and with a high proportion of its population

---

[12] Mention should also be made at this point of a different application of the dual economy concept which is coming increasingly into vogue. It is being applied to the contrasted scales of operation within the economies of developed countries, outstandingly the United States. R. T. Averitt (1968) distinguishes between the 'center economy' of increasingly large enterprises, mainly in manufacturing and trade, and the 'periphery economy' of small firms. There are many similarities with the form of dualism that we have discussed here, but in this instance there is no doubt that the structure has evolved rather than been imposed or created by some inevitable process based on behavioural differences. The comparison is instructive, but it is best deferred until we return to the question of structure and process in economies in chapter 6.

in agriculture, is 'backward' and that the path of progress is to get people, capital and a far higher share of total production into industry and towns. This argument follows directly from the historical experience of Europe and North America; equally it follows from the hothouse pattern of development followed by the Soviet Union. It is only in the most recent period, and outstandingly in China, that a viable and perhaps even preferable alternative has emerged into the sight of planners and writers on development.[13]

There are multiple reasons for the urban-industrial bias which grew and flourished despite the constant sniping of a minority of critics. It is an historical fact that the powerful nations of the last 150 years have been the industrialized nations; the policy makers of developing countries have seen in industrialization a means of catching up and of reducing their state of dependency. Such thinking gained enormously from the experience of the late industrializers, Japan and the Soviet Union. It gained also from an embittered belief that any sort of 'expert' persuasion to concentrate on improvements in primary production and marketing was motivated by a wish to keep developing countries in a state of economic subservience. Thus K. Nkrumah (1965: 7 and 9):

> There are, however, imperialist specialists and apologists who urge the less developed countries to concentrate on agriculture and leave industrialization for some later time when their populations shall be well fed . . . . But even to make agriculture yield more the

[13] Industrialization was regarded as the golden remedy for 'underdevelopment' for more than a generation. In the early 1940s P. N. Rosenstein-Rodan (1943/1958R) argued that industrialization is '*the* way of achieving a more equal distribution of incomes between different areas of the world by raising incomes in depressed areas at a higher rate than in the rich areas'. Later W. A. Lewis and Raul Prebisch (1949/1950T/1962R) called for industrialization of the Caribbean countries and Latin America respectively as by far the best opportunity to capture the advantages of technical progress. In the 1960s we had a more questioning approach but

> It goes without saying that everybody in developing countries wants to industrialise swiftly. Industry glitters with promise. Nothing else seems to hold out much hope of fulfilling the expectations of new nationalism, winning economic independence and raising average prosperity dramatically; nothing else seems drastic enough to cast off the millstones of population increase and falling prices for primary producers that, in spite of their doubled efforts, have made them worse off than before. (R. Robinson, *ed.* 1971: 65)

aid of industrial output is needed; and the under-developed world cannot for ever be placed at the mercy of the more industrialized . . . we are convinced that we shall be able to adjust the balance in our favour only by developing an agriculture attuned to our needs and supporting it with a rapidly increasing industrialization that will break the neo-colonialist pattern which at present operates.

The coincidence of such political arguments with the persuasion of economic growth theory proved decisive. We recall the emphasis on capital as the engine of growth, on the lower (more favourable) ICORs of manufacturing industry investments, compared with investments in basic infrastructure such as were required for agricultural expansion. We recall also the weight given to the emergence of manufacturing sectors in Rostow's stages, and the whole thrust of the theory of economic dualism. It is therefore hardly surprising that growth targets and the supporting development plans should have placed heavy weight on industrialization.

The arguments are rather well summarized in the Report of the Cambridge Conferences of Development, held at intervals through the First Development Decade (R. Robinson 1971: 65–84). The opposing views, in so far as they relate to the inter-sectoral dispute, are summarized below.

Industry or agriculture first?

The argument for an industry-first strategy depends on the demonstrated or supposed ability of industry, and especially large-scale industry, to raise national income *per capita*, create investment capital, and save foreign exchange through import substitution, much faster than any other method. In almost every industrializing country, the rate of growth of industrial output exceeds the rate of growth in other productive sectors. It is also argued that the social reorganization accompanying industry forces the reconstruction of society as a whole — this was a basic argument for Russian industrialization in the 1920s. For these reasons, industry can draw the unemployed and underemployed off the land, gainfully occupy them, and so create a market for the produce of an agricultural sector relieved of so many unproductive, or less productive, mouths to feed: this is an argument applied especially in the Asian situation; in Pakistan, for example, the rate of increase in GNP contributed by industry and basic services has been more than three times that contributed by agriculture. It is argued that present rates of population growth are such that future entrants to the workforce already born cannot possibly be absorbed into agriculture; industrial expansion is essential if they are to be employed. It is further maintained that new exports of manufactured products can and should be developed, and that these will enjoy some competitive advantage over developed-country manufactures in view of lower costs; not only are the glittering examples of Hong Kong and Singapore in mind, but also the rebirth of Indian textile exports and the possibility of developing regional markets through 'common market' arrangements. Shortage of capital is recognized as the major check to industrialization, while another lies in the tariff barriers of a great many potential importers; both, it is argued, are capable of considerable easement. But the strongest argument of all follows from the wider case for accelerated economic growth; if this will provide the resources with which to develop the whole economy, spread welfare and alleviate poverty, then the means which will accelerate aggregate growth the fastest are the means that should be employed first. And these, on the basis of a mass of empirical evidence, are to be found through industrialization.

The contrary, agriculture-first argument, rests fundamentally on the Malthus-via-Keynes thesis of effective demand. If output per head in agriculture is raised this will produce the large and increasing demand for manufactures without which industrialization cannot succeed. Raising output per head will also release workers for industry without loss of agricultural output, and will also make capital available for industrial expansion.[14] Industry, being capital-intensive, does not provide adequate employment and this can only be generated on a sufficient scale in agriculture. The fastest road to successful industrialization is therefore through agricultural expansion. These are arguments clearly weighted toward countries with relatively low man-land ratios, in crude terms to Africa and perhaps Latin America rather than Asia.

In general, the pro-industry argument is still preferred, though

[14] This is in contrast to the view of emigration from agriculture taken by the industrialists. We see the significance of the 'classical' (Lewis, Fei and Ranis) and 'neo-classical' (Jorgenson) approaches to the theory of economic dualism in these opposing arguments.

disenchantment with the results of industrialization policies have led to a strong revival of the agricultural thesis. Although fuller explanation of this disenchantment belongs further forward in the argument, when we come to discuss the question of interdependent development in chapter 6, some of the reasons can most usefully be presented here.

The wrong sort of industrialization?

After an initial burst, the pace of industrialization has slackened in a great many developing countries. The easiest road to industrial expansion has very often been through import-substitution industries, the market for which is circumscribed. These industries have not always led to a diminution of foreign exchange spending, because many process or assemble intermediate products, require imported fuel for power, and involve large foreign payments for licence fees and expatriated profits to foreign owners or participants. Once an initial range of 'simpler' industries is established, further growth will move into a more complex range, requiring heavier capital investment and larger scale; they may be unable to operate efficiently without access to larger markets. Many industries do not generate very large employment and their growth has failed significantly to check the rise in unemployment levels; effective demand in the internal economy is not sufficiently increased, and the agricultural sector is not greatly stimulated. Lack of adequate markets, and of the external economies of mass, has aggravated a trend toward inefficient operation; comparatively little new capital is therefore generated. Furthermore, the growth of highly-capitalized industry has often tended to eliminate labour-intensive manufacture in small plants and households. In Medellin, Colombia, to cite only one example, the net effect of 'modern' industrialization has been to *reduce* total industrial employment in the city (M. Santos 1974).

These considerations have led to the 'intermediate technology' thesis advanced in recent years, particularly forcibly expressed in the Cambridge volume by E. F. Schumacher (*in* R. Robinson 1971: 85–94). His argument has spatial implications, but it accords closely with Singer's (1970) view, discussed above, that the increasing unsuitability of modern technology for developing country conditions is creating a new and more deadly form of dualism. It is easy to say, as many do, that no intermediate technology exists, but this is simply to say that no expressed demand has brought it into existence. Yet the aim — as expressed by Schumacher — of an equipment cost of £70–£100 per average workplace is not un-realizable; it has been achieved to some degree in the rural industrialization programme of China (G. Dean 1972; S. Ishikawa 1972); surely no one is going to say that such achievements are beyond the technical capability of the efficient and innovative West?

The service sector

Until recent years, few writers on developing countries took much account of the third large group of occupations, in non-basic services; they were presumed to be of subsidiary importance in developing countries and to emerge as the major element only in the wealthy advanced economies. Nowadays, however, it is difficult to continue to ignore this sector, which is the most rapidly growing in terms of total employment in a great many poor countries, is absorbing far more of the workers leaving the agricultural sector than is industry, and employs more people than industry in a growing proportion of developing countries. The UN Economic Commission for Latin America, in its *Economic survey of Latin America for 1970*, pp. 42–8, has an interesting section on this phenomenon, pointing out that in a selection of 'advanced' countries there is fairly close and improving accordance between the structure of production and of employment, in terms of the share contributed by each of the three sectors. The situation in the less-developed countries of the region, on the other hand, is one of wide and growing divergence between the distribution of employment and of production.

There are few data available on this phenomenon, and it achieves inadequate notice in the development literature, but its seriousness is very evident. It would seem to be directly related, first to growing population, second to the near-static condition of agriculture, and third to the assimilation of modern technology into industry, which is enhancing production without enhancing employment in this sector. Furthermore, as Singer demonstrates, and as M. Santos and T. G. McGee both argue in books to appear in this series, it is through the expansion of this sector that job-splitting and fractionation is being carried from the countryside into the town. It is not too much to say that the rapid expansion of this sector, its localization in the burgeoning towns and cities, and the range within it through partial underemployment to virtually total unemployment, are coming to constitute the most serious 'development' problem of the late twentieth century. The inter-sectoral argument, and that of dualism, thus lead in precisely the same direction.

The comfortable myth of 'modernization'

The world of Dr Pangloss

During the later 1950s a sort of euphoria began to take hold of many social scientists, convinced that the development problem was at last being seriously tackled and that the efforts would surely succeed. The general feeling is rather well expressed by Clark Kerr (1960: 348):

The world is currently undergoing a great economic and social transformation. In essence, this transformation is the commitment of man to a new way of life. Throughout history most of mankind has been committed to a constant way of life .... The current period of history is distinguished from all others, however, by the immensity of the process of destroying old commitments, no matter how constant they may have been, and by the world-wide uniformity of the new commitment. Men everywhere are transferring themselves fully and finally into the industrial way of life . . . Viewed from the end result, the transformation is one great process of such overwhelming impact that the current and local variations are almost unimportant. Viewed from points in between, there are roads and alleys and even dead ends; some societies choose one of these and some choose another. The great questions are: why was one choice made rather than another, which choice is best, and how may the choice be influenced?

Viewed from the mid-1970s, such sublime confidence seems almost to belong to another planet, but it is important to remind ourselves constantly of the perceptions and conceptions of the time if we are to understand what was said and done. Confidence in the inevitability of progress rose steadily from 1945 to peak around 1960; its collapse since the late 1960s, in a welter of bitterness that is far from ended, makes it hard to see the former mood of assurance in proper perspective. We can, however, point to a fairly massive refusal to recognize contrary evidence, some of it ably digested and presented; we can also remark that the same monstrous lack of understanding continues to characterize a part of the literature.

Origins of modernization

The 'modernization' thesis was far more interdisciplinary in scope than the theories we have reviewed up to this point; its origins were also more diffuse. The 'acculturation' thesis of anthropology was an important element; others included Talcott Parsons's theories of 'action' and of social change, notions of the plural society originating with Furnivall, and theory in political science on the evolution of nationalism. In all cases, however, these strands were interpreted through a particular view of change which is essentially dualistic: tradition and modernity are seen as opposed forces, the latter growing at the expense of the former.

Dichotomous thinking thus underlies the whole argument of modernization, just as it does that of dualism and intersectoral analysis. The sort of dichotomies that were involved took shape in such conceptions as Sir Henry Maine's (1861) classical distinction between societies in which interaction is based on *status* and those in which it is based on *contract* — categories derived from Roman law. Closer to the essential theme of modernization is E. Durkheim's dichotomy between the 'mechanical' or 'segmental' solidarity of societies bound by consanguineity, and the 'organic' solidarity of more 'voluminous' societies in which individuals are grouped according to the nature of their activity, or role in society. There is an inevitable progression from one state to the other, for as the division of labour proceeds it finds the mould of the old, small-scale and segmental social organization incompatible with its needs. Therefore:

> The social material must enter into entirely new combinations in order to organize itself upon completely different foundations. But the old structure, so far as it persists, is opposed to this. This is why it must disappear. (E. Durkheim, 1893/1933T: 183)

There are shades of the Marxian dialectic in this, as also of Marx's scheme for the evolution of classes. Durkheim's dichotomy is, however, somewhat imprecise, and a more concrete form was provided by F. Tönnies (1935) who distinguished *within* societies between the institutions of *gemeinschaft*, based on intimate interpersonal contacts and common values, and of *gesellschaft*, in which relations are impersonal and individuals are strongly differentiated. The latter is seen as a development of civilization, and again it is presumed that the second overwhelms the first.

These ideas form the foundation of the theory of culture change, or acculturation, which became powerful in anthropology around the time of World War II. One presumed a basic, traditional society, such as had been carefully described by such pioneers as Malinowski, Firth, Fortune, Evans-Pritchard, Fortes, Lévi-Strauss, Redfield and others. It was not *necessarily* assumed that this society had been static and unchanging for a long period, and a slow measure of evolution was in principle presumed, but the analysis proceeded as though the 'traditional' state were given and static. Into this situation came external influences, which proceeded to introduce modifications through a process of 'acculturation' to new ways. R. Redfield (1947; 1953) erected the concept of a 'folk-urban continuum' between primitive, peasant and urban communities, using Mexican field data. The *gemeinschaft* characteristics of a 'folk society' became attenuated toward the urban end of the continuum, while *gesellschaft* characteristics are only weakly developed at the 'primitive' end. This relatively simple model of transition was displaced by J. Steward (1955) who proposed a theory of multilinear evolution, permitting an initial state to move in several possible directions according to the factors of change. From this point forward, the theory of culture change began to rub shoulders with the theory of economic growth, though it remained empirically based.

Alongside this stream there were others. Important as Talcott Parsons's turgid theory of 'social action' was as background, it was rarely applied in any direct way. A particularly significant aspect of Parsons's classificatory scheme (Parsons and Shils 1951) is the set of dichotomies called 'pattern variables' between which any actor in any situation must decide before the meaning of the situation becomes determinate to him, and hence before he can act. Each of these has to be evaluated within the actor's own personality system, his learned cultural system, and the social system within which he lives. The most important of the pattern variables, from the present point of view, are those concerning the scale of the context of a situation (particularism/universality), adoption of community orientation or self orientation, and whether to give priority to the normative aspects of a situation, according to its proper and accepted role, or to give priority to its actual or anticipated performance (ascription/achievement). It is to be assumed that the first of each pair will be chosen in a 'traditional' situation, while the 'modern' individual will choose the second. In other words, he behaves like a Rational Economic Man whereas the traditionalist does not.[15]

The ingredients are almost all assembled; only one major element remains. This is the concept of social mobilization, a force necessary for the creation of new social patterns and especially nationalism. It involves essentially the transformation of people from a local or tribal setting into a national setting. Thoroughly vague in even the best attempts by K. Deutsch to define the concept on which he depends so heavily, it is at once more political and more economic than acculturation; it involves the acceptance of a new social and political system, and the people who are 'socially mobilized' in developing countries are therefore the élites. Deutsch, who is a prime mover in the study of evolving nationalism and of the quantification of modernization processes, then describes his underlying view in these terms:

> The dynamic processes of social mobilization and cultural assimilation . . . are . . likely to be more powerful in uniting or destroying an emerging people or a newly-established state than are the mere static facts of the multiplicity of tribes or languages within its territory. (*In* Deutsch and Foltz, *eds.* 1963: 6)

This is the essential *credo*: the dynamic forces are external; the patterns of modernization are imposed from above; tradition must inevitably give way to modernity; the problem is to overcome

[15] One wonders why some critics of Boeke's classic dualism did not pay more attention to this massive body of supporting theory.

'stubborn resistance'; the people to be encouraged are the 'achieve-ment-orientated' élites.

The end-product is also fairly clearly expressed. Thus Eisenstadt (1966: 1):

> Historically, modernization is the process of change towards those types of social, economic and political systems that have developed in Western Europe and North America from the seventeenth century to the nineteenth and then have spread to other European countries and in the nineteenth and twentieth centuries to the South American, Asian and African continents.

More than this, by the consensus of many writers: 'Modernity is the social, cultural and psychological framework which facilitates the application of science to the processes of production' (M. Nash 1966: 123). It is a movement toward technocracy in a Western political framework.

There is a clear link between this 'Western' conception of modernization and the Marxist-Leninist view,[16] and the link is Marx himself. R. Bendix (1967/1970R) argues forcibly that the single-path evolutionism applied by the 'pure' modernizers owes an immense debt to Marx's interpretation of the historical sequence from medievalism to capitalism, and which was in turn based on the single-nation experience of Great Britain. In reviewing the work of modernizers such as D. Lerner (1958), Kerr *et al.* (1960) and Rostow (1960), he seeks to demonstrate that the whole sequence and processes which these writers propose have their roots in a 'social Darwinist' interpretation of history of which the prime originator was Marx. The difference between West and East there-fore concerns essentially the meaning of modernity and the present trend of events, whether it is toward an American-model capitalist democracy, or toward the replacement of capitalism by socialism. Equal ingenuity with the task of interpretation is demonstrated on both sides. Thus a recent Russian polemic seeks to demonstrate the convergence of African nationalism toward the Marxist model, and concludes (Y. Popov 1973: 144):

---

[16] Or views: there seems to be growing divergence between Russian and Chinese spokesmen on the next step in the evolution of world history.

Over one thousand million people have already shaken off the fetters of capitalism and are marching toward socialism and communism . . . The masses of whole continents, formerly doomed by colonialists to poverty and starvation, have taken the road of independent historical development.

Despite the variety and complexity of the developments in today's world, the basic content of our age is conveyed by these simple and clear words — the transition from capitalism to communism. The greatness of Marxist teaching lies in the fact that it predicted this transition a hundred years ago, that it not only explained the past, but also illuminates the future, lighting up the way to the morrow of all mankind.

It seems that everyone knows where the world is going.

Modernization: revisionism and dissent

Stage theories of history have always worried thoughtful men of historical bent; the stage elements in Marx's system are unacceptable to many who accept his analysis of process. Too often they lead to a 'game of pick-and-choose with the centuries according to the particular aspect of modernity emphasized' (Bernstein 1971: 152), or degenerate from being a means for the characterization of process into becoming a sort of comparative statics.[17] This becomes a particular source of weakness when the additional assumption is made that all societies began from a common baseline of traditional 'un-development' and have progressed according to a defined schema at different rates. Several attempts have been made to escape this trap, as for example by Bendix (1967/1970R) who treats the origin of modernization as located in the industrial revolution of Britain and the political revolution of France, both at the end of the eighteenth century. These societies then became 'advanced' while all others became 'followers', seeking substitutes for the factors which were the conditions of progress among the leaders. Government thus assumes an important role — as it did, historically, in the industrial-ization of Germany and Japan — and hence the most significant

[17] Geographers are familiar with this argument not only from old debates on stage v. process approaches to the study of historical geography, going back to the 1930s, but also from the unsatisfactory results obtained in attempts to convert static equilibrium models into dynamic models by the use of T_1, $T_2 \ldots T_n$ methods.

element in modernization is the formation and institutionalization of nation states.

Despite this attempt, however, and other efforts to escape the 'tradition/modernity' dichotomy by opening the possibility of multiple paths and selective adoption of innovations, the crux of any structured concept of modernization remains with the model of the two terminal conditions. These models affect all subsequent interpretation of progress along the continuum. If we assume the initial condition to be 'static' and 'passive' then all change is the consequence of innovation; if we assume it to be characterized by a particular class structure, a particular form of resource allocation, then we can interpret change in terms of a transformation of this system, which may be *sui generis* as well as the consequence of innovation from without; if we assume it to be already in a state of evolution which is then diverted into new paths as a consequence of external forces, then the problem becomes one of adaptation, and conflict.

Even more so, the 'model of the modern' affects interpretation of the contemporary condition in a most drastic manner. In a hard-hitting analysis of the context of American writing on modernization during the 1960s, Donal Cruise O'Brien (1972) argues that a major shift has taken place, leading to the transformation of this model from one of constitutional democracy to one of authoritarian control for the maintenance and defence of order. Linking this well-documented shift to American activity abroad and also to the reaction generated by protest and anarchical movements at home, he shows how the writings of a number of political scientists closely reflect changing official and majority opinions and practices.[18] In particular, he points to the growing warmth with

---

[18] Remarking on the growing alienation of American society and government from the 'ideal of constitutional democracy', Cruise O'Brien (1972: 372) observes presciently that:

> Established constitutional procedures may be disregarded as inadequate by those in power, with the support of the majority of the electorate, in the face of what they perceive as a fundamental threat to their authority.

This was written before the 'Watergate affair' demonstrated both the extent of such thinking, and also the willingness of a minority of 'constitutional democrats' to revolt, using both legal and quasi-legal means, in defence of their ideals.

which the work of Lenin and Stalin, in building up and entrenching a communist bureaucracy, is reviewed by right-wing American political scientists; such élitism accords well with the doctrines of modernization, given a prime emphasis on the nation state as a force for ordered change, and a downgrading of the emphasis on 'clusters of innovators' as its source.

Given this sort of analysis, it is not surprising that we can write of Western and Russian communist ideas about 'modernization' in parallel with one another, albeit that they use different terms and postulate different sequences. We are dealing here with what David Harvey (1969: 7) calls a philosophical position, from which a methodology follows. With him, it is important to stress that the converse is not also true: no philosophical position can be supported by methodological argument. The critics of modernization, therefore, waste their time in attacks on the details of a particular schema; to do so does no damage to the underlying philosophy, and the result is simply to replace one schema of modernization by another. The issue is more fundamental: it concerns the existence of a dichotomy between tradition and modernity, of another between lower and higher states, and of a predictable progression from one state to another. To deny these may seem to deny the possibility of scientific explanation, and to offer in its place only a chaotic empiricism. But this is not so; it is merely to say that the dichotomies are perceptual, ethnocentric and time-dependent, and that to pretend that we have yet understood the process of change so well as to be able to predict it — even to retro-dict it adequately — is the most arrogant conceit. The task remains before us, and what any of us has yet achieved is no more than a beginning.

The strongest critics of modernization theory are thus those who, while they may offer empirical generalizations based on Marxist or Marx-like analysis of historical experience, also deny the possibility of setting up any abstract schema on the basis of present knowledge and theory. One of the most effective of such is Henry Bernstein (1971) whose attack is directed especially at sociologists among the modernizers. Indirect, as well as direct critiques, also come from 'developing country' writers who appeal for an emphasis on the quality of life, deny that 'modernity' constitutes any demonstrably 'higher' state in this respect, and call for a fuller appreciation of the reasons for resistance to change. From this writing is also emerging a concept of continuous interaction rather than unilineal change. Nor need we suppose that the interaction takes place only among the 'receiving' societies, albeit that the flows are highly unequal. Opposition, interaction and symbiosis are all present, and all are obscured by dichotomous reasoning; replacement and revolution are not the only avenues of change and they may not even be the most important, even though both occur and will continue to occur. If we are to make progress we must eschew such simplistics as dual economy theory, intersectoral allocation and modernization, because they obscure the interaction that is fundamental to an advance in understanding. Fortunately, there is at the present time a strong trend toward such a new approach in the study of inequality and its causes.

4: Notions of inequality, space and polarized growth

Development economics today has a new and chastened mood. Attention has shifted away from the theory of growth and into areas that seem more mundane: employment generation and income distribution are the most obviously popular fields at the time of writing. Alongside these themes, and still only partially integrated with the central concerns of the field, is the emergence or resurgence of interest in the spatial aspects of development and planning. Regional development, as it is most commonly termed, had indeed a kind of abortive beginning during the years of depression and war, more than a generation ago. Though regional planning was never wholly neglected, in the developing countries, it was lost almost entirely from sight for much of a generation. Today, however, country after country is discovering that the regional dimension of its employment and income problems is of fundamental importance;[1] there may even be a tendency in some quarters to overemphasize regional inequalities at the cost of adequate notice of inequalities in other dimensions.

But the new awareness is still not paralleled by the emergence of a comprehensive system of theory. There are now numerous texts in

[1] In Fiji, for example, planning was concerned almost wholly with growth, and with intersectoral allocation, right through the 1960s; the regional aspect was scarcely mentioned. When I returned to Fiji in 1973 to plan and negotiate a UNESCO research project in the outer islands of Fiji, I found that far from my having to convince people of the importance of a regional approach to such a question, the government had already fitted the proposals firmly into their own large programme of regional development inquiry. What had taken place in the intervening years was an acceleration of the concentration of people and activities into the main towns and certain other growth industries (particularly tourism), so great that it was beginning to have very noticeable effects on the progress of rural development programmes. Large areas of the country, including many outlying islands, have lost almost all growth momentum. A similar story could be recounted of many other lands.

regional economics (e.g. H. W. Richardson 1969; H. Siebert 1969), and there is a body of literature which seeks to explain various aspects of the process. Writers who deal with empirical problems in which the spatial element looms large draw on this material, but for the most part they have to be content with informed descriptions of the process which lead them to suggest policy prescriptions in some cases; they are not able to find many such prescriptions in regional theory. Many of these empirical studies contain material which is of great value for the construction of theory,[2] but at present the theory that is available is only partial. A major inquiry, far beyond the scope of the present chapter, is needed in order to take this subject further, but my aim in this chapter does go a little way beyond mere recounting. I try to suggest that certain theoretical stands have been inadequately emphasized, and organize the presentation to support this contention. I thus begin with a gloss on some ideas that emerged in contexts other than regional development, and only then turn to regional theory. Also in this chapter I bring in the work of geographers for the only time as a major theme, and give emphasis also to the role that geographical theory has played in the work of others. I do not discuss industrial location theory, even though it is relevant and underlies some of the argument; also I take central place theory and innovation diffusion theory as given, and make no attempt to review their content.

Some antecedents

Joseph Schumpeter

Writing in the early years of this century, from diametrically opposed philosophical viewpoints, J. A. Hobson and Rosa Luxemburg on one hand, and Joseph Schumpeter on the other, had insights which are fundamental to much of the subsequent dis-

[2] Four studies might be cited from a large number. In the European context C. Clark, F. Wilson and J. Bradley (1969) provide a valuable basic study of economic potential in relation to industrial location, and their maps accord rather remarkably with the estimates of regional GNP in Europe mapped from time to time in *The Economist* in 1972 and 1973. In southern Africa, the pioneer regional development survey of L. P. Green and T. J. D. Fair (1962) was given a more quantitative basis by C. Board, R. J. Davies and T. J. D. Fair (1970), and most recently has appeared the very thoughtful study of P. Selwyn (1973), in which he draws widely on theoretical strands from the dual economy to industrial location in a discussion of the problem of industrial development in peripheral Lesotho.

cussion about the inequalities that arise between people and places in the course of development. Neither fully realized that they were doing this, and Schumpeter was not concerned with variation over geographical space at all. Hobson's and Luxemburg's views have already been discussed in outline. Here I begin with a presentation of part of Schumpeter's argument, so as to isolate in its proper context an idea which has been very influential with some, but ignored by others, and will then try to trace this idea through the involved web of thought that is becoming the 'theory of regional development'.

Schumpeter wrote the first book in which a theory of economic development as such was presented. Published in German before World War I, and in English, with some modifications, more than twenty years later (Schumpeter 1911/1934T), this book theorizes out of Western historical experience. Its central concern shifts toward the phenomenon of the business cycle, on which he later wrote specifically. Part of the subsequent neglect of Schumpeter stems from the speed with which his ideas on this subject were overwhelmed by those of Keynes. But the book also constitutes a true theory of development, and contains much that is of continuing value.

Schumpeter was a lifelong believer in capitalism, and his recognition of changes in the structure of capitalism through the growth of large firms did not diminish his faith. His process of development, however, is only partly specific to capitalism; some elements have universal validity. He opens with a presentation of an equilibrium that is not stable; in his 'circular flow' economy the leader is the consumer, and the level of production and its management are governed by demand, or by needs. Such an equilibrium is not necessarily static: it may be dynamic as population changes and as small innovations are absorbed into the system without generating any major disturbance. The flow remains essentially circular, change is slow and in no sense revolutionary.

His second chapter then presents the most critical elements in his argument. He begins by stating certain general propositions. He eschews all notions of unilineal development or social-Darwinism. Treating economic development as a part of economic history — as it then was — he notes (p. 58) that 'it is not possible to explain *economic* change by previous *economic* conditions alone. For the economic state of a people emerges from the preceding total situation' (italics in original). He then observes that the equilibrium situation is simply an adaptation to the 'data' existing at any time. Growth of population and of capital are no more than increases in the quantity of certain 'data-elements' — continuous changes which fall within the ambit of 'static' analysis.[3] Hence growth, whether of population or of wealth or both, is not development. Nor does development arise from response to external change:

> By 'development', therefore, we shall understand only such changes in economic life as are not forced upon it from without but arise by its own initiative, from within. Should it turn out that there are no changes arising in the economic sphere itself, and that the phenomenon which we call economic development is in practice simply founded upon the fact that the data change and that the economy continuously adapts to them, then we should say that there is *no* economic development. By this we should mean that economic development is not a phenomenon to be explained economically, but that the economy, in itself without development, is dragged along by the changes in the surrounding world. (1934: 63)

The essence is therefore the emergence of qualitatively new phenomena within the economy, and such are normally generated by the producers; development thus entails a qualitative shift away from the demand-based equilibrium state. This shift is achieved by the 'carrying out of new combinations of production'. These may include (p. 66):

> (1) The introduction of a new good ... or a new quality of a good. (2) The introduction of a new method of production ... which need by no means be founded upon a discovery scientifically new, and can also exist in a new way of handling a commodity commercially. (3) The opening of a new market ... whether or not this market has existed before. (4) The conquest of a new source of supply of raw materials or half-manufactured goods ... (5) The carrying out of the new organization of any industry, like the creation of a monopoly position ... or the breaking up of a monopoly position.

The essence of development is therefore a volume of innovations,

---

[3] Later, at p. 116, he expresses the view (wholly italicized in the original) that: 'Capital is nothing but the lever by which the entrepreneur subjects to his control goods which he needs, nothing but a means of diverting the factors of production to new uses, or of dictating a new direction to production.'

spread over a wide range, and sufficient to bring about qualitative differences in society through the replacement of old 'combinations' and firms by new. Such an innovation surge is achieved by 'entrepreneurs' — risk-takers and leaders who emerge solely in the carrying out of new combinations'; once this is done the entrepreneur settles down to running his business within the new 'data' set, and becomes simply a manager. Entrepreneurship is not therefore a lasting condition, and entrepreneurs do not form a class; while they may be 'captains of industry', may grow wealthy and powerful, they are quite distinct from capitalists or from bureaucrats, who may simply be managers. Schumpeter's entrepreneurs are the innovators while and where they are innovating, and this only.[4] They do not become an élite.

The vital point then follows. Entrepreneurs respond to opportunity, and this tends to occur in waves after one surge of

---

[4] Schumpeterian entrepreneurship is therefore not a phenomenon specific to the competitive capitalist system, nor to the capitalist system at all. Schumpeter himself notes that the effect of massive growth in firm size is to internalize innovation so that the 'entrepreneur' is most readily identified among the rising general executives, as Galbraith (1967) later remarked. Kari Levitt (1970) also provides a valuable discussion of this topic, directly linked to Schumpeter's formulation.

Equally, it is possible to identify Schumpeterian entrepreneurs in socialist societies, though not among the *apparatchikii* — the time-serving bureaucrats. We may also find them among the leaders of the peasantry and among tribal chiefs, though here their role is less specialized. I knew a Schumpeterian entrepreneur very well in Chimbu, New Guinea; he introduced innovations over a wide range, but few of them were lasting because he was isolated and lacked the institutional framework within which to inspire others or link up with other innovators. A different situation is described fictionally by Liu Ching, whose novel *The builders* (Peking, 1964) is the most sensitive and profound study of peasantry under change that I have seen. Entrepreneurship in this case emerges in the aftermath of the Chinese land reform of the early 1950s. It is not found among the adequately-provided middle peasants, nor in the person of the unimaginative local party leader, but in the son of a poor peasant who introduces a new strain of rice and sees the possibility of organizing the poorer peasantry through mutual aid teams to develop supplementary sources of income and so gain the shared capital to invest in other improvements. Unlike my New Guinean, he is supported in his enterprise by the wider system, and his efforts link up with the efforts of others. In all this true Schumpeterian entrepreneurship he steers a difficult path through the task of manipulating people whose willingness corresponds with their immediate interests, and has only one signal failure: he loses his girl friend, on whom he lavishes quite insufficient attention.

innovation has been absorbed or as new demands are created by some new situation. Entrepreneurs then appear in clusters, the appearance of one facilitating the emergence of others; hence development is jerky, entrepreneurship and the adoption of inno- vations occurring in 'swarms' at points in time when profit opportunities are greatest and risks least — that is when demand for new men is greatest after a period of stability or downturn, and when the 'social climate' is right. This 'social climate' is a vague element in the theory, and hence a weakness, but its expansion would be fundamental to any projection of the argument into the present-day problems of 'developing' countries.

François Perroux

There is nothing spatial in any part of Schumpeter's writings except in the sense that the time dimension is space. But the emphasis on irregularities and on the emergence of 'swarms' and 'clusters' of individual entrepreneurs and innovations should prompt questions of a spatial order. It was the particular contribution of François Perroux to open up these questions, in two contrasted papers which form a sequence of ideas, but which also lead in divergent directions (Perroux 1950/1964R; 1955/1971R).

The common background of Perroux's two papers — and of his empirical studies which fed them — was discontent with economic reasoning within the confines of national boundaries, including the basic assumption of international trade theory that capital and labour are immobile between countries. The effect of this assump- tion, even where not explicit, is to be seen in an immense range of the economic literature, and it seems primarily responsible for continuity of the fiction that national economies are individual and autonomous units capable of independent management. To Perroux (1950/1964R: 22):

> A banal sense of space location creates the illusion of the coincidence of political space with economic and human space . . . we go on depicting to ourselves the relations between different nations as consisting exclusively of men and things in *one* space, conceiving them as *material* objects contained in a *container.* (Italics in original)

Perroux therefore argued the notion of an abstract space in economic reasoning, and showed that for economics there can be as many spaces as there are constituent structures of abstract relations. Thus for example the 'national income' and the 'income of the nationals' draw on two quite different spaces, the one geographically contained, the other not bounded. For a firm, the 'banal space' is that in which its material and manpower are situated, but its economic space is far more extensive and is geographically discontinuous; it should be viewed in topological terms.

Perroux went on to define three forms of abstract economic space for a firm. Its 'plan space' is the set of relations between the firm, its suppliers and buyers, and hence is determined by means of an input-output analysis. Its 'space defined as a field of forces' is essentially its field of influence, both centripetal in attracting men and objects, and centrifugal in repelling other activities or preventing their development. Its 'space as a homogeneous aggregate' concerns its cost-plus-distance relationship with other similar firms with whom it must compete at a comparable price; two firms whose different production costs are equalized at the market by their contrasted distance costs are in the same 'homogenous' economic space. In a much later paper reviewing and examining Perroux's ideas and their contribution, J. R. Lasuén (1969/1972R) proposed the addition of 'organizational space', being the map of linkages within the firm and with its affiliates and subsidiaries: we shall find echoes of this concept in later chapters.

In his more influential 1955 paper Perroux extended his argument against national space as an economic concept, and both developed its potential further and also paved the way for a limitation which has had most unfortunate consequences. He shifted the analysis back to geographical space, but to a geographical space not composed of national compartments. Developing the concept of 'space defined as a field of forces' he observed that (1955/1971R: 279):

> growth does not appear everywhere at the same time; it manifests itself in points or 'poles' of growth, with variable intensities; it spreads by different channels and with variable terminal effects for the economy as a whole.

For a process he turned to Schumpeter, though with some modifications, and:

> took Schumpeter's tool-box of concepts and hypotheses from its original sectoral-temporal setting and applied it to a sectoral-temporal-geographical universe. He was able to do it, thanks to

his concept of topological space. He viewed the changes in a system of industries as transformations in sectoral space and asked what form they would take in geographical space. The geographical pole is the geographical image of the newly innovated industry and its linked activities. (Lasuén 1969/1972R: 23)

For this purpose Perroux distinguished between 'propellent industries' (*industries motrices*) and 'impelled industries'. When the former expand their output they increase the sales and purchases of several other industries which are linked to them as buyer or seller. A propellent industry will then induce an aggregate increase in the sales of a whole group of industries which is very much larger than the increase in its own sales.[5] Such a whole group of industries is equivalent to the 'industrial complex' of interrelated activities studied and described by Walter Isard (1956; 1960). In this identification Perroux parts company with Schumpeter — though perhaps less so than he maintains — by remarking on the fundamentally non-competitive relationship of the industries forming such a complex, where supporting self-interest leads to a condition of oligopoly. Finally, he notes in contradistinction to the argument of his earlier paper that such complexes most readily emerge in geographical concentration. However, their economic space is not defined by national borders, and he identifies a dialectic between 'growth regions produced by poles of growth and politically organized territories' which seek to derive exclusive benefit from the growth poles contained in their own national space.

Before he wrote his 1955 paper Perroux had already used the concept in a study of the Ruhr, and he was greatly influenced by this experience. The notion of economic space as distinct from 'banal' space was substantially weakened by the too-ready emphasis on geographical concentration, and this was the origin of an immense confusion that is by no means ended. The argument also became heavily involved with manufacturing industry and related

[5] In this argument he relies heavily on T. Scitovsky's (1954: 1963R) study of external economies, showing how the growth of one industry can induce profits in customer industries, in industries with complementary products, in industries producing goods demanded by firms and households whose incomes are increased in the above ways.

urban activities, and thus contributed to the 'urban-industrial bias' that we have already noted. Most serious, however, was the consequence of losing the distinction between the physical notion of 'space defined by a field of forces', which is the origin of the 'pole' concept, with the 'plan space' by means of which his growth-poles are identified and analysed. This led to a dependence on inter-industry analysis which, in Lasuén's words (1969/1972R: 25):

> shifted the school's attention away from Perroux's original translation of Schumpeterian development. They have failed to develop the point that the activity creating a growth pole was essentially a sectoral and a geographical disturbance not because of its larger than average size, nor because of its higher multiplier, but because it was an *innovation.*

It also led to the heavy use of input-output matrices and hence should have led toward the other elements of theory relating to inter-activity linkages. These contain elements not adequately exploited because of the confused directions taken by later growth-pole research, and must also be introduced before we can go further.

Some lessons from history

A rather loose bundle of theory, originating from different sources, is concerned with the interrelation of economic activities. On the one hand is the input-output analysis developed by W. W. Leontief (1951), and both utilized and described in detail by W. Isard (1960).[6] This method has been used to show interregional flows classified by industry, and has also been used to analyse the interrelationships of a single firm. It has led to the concept of 'inter-industry linkages' developed by A. O. Hirschman (1958: 98–119) and used by him to examine the effects of a particular industry on other activities. Leaving aside industries catering only to

[6] The production of each industry is classified by its sales to all other industries, including 'final demand' sectors – principally households. The resultant matrix shows the whole of inter-industry transactions in a national or regional economy; the principal diagonal represents sales and purchases within each industry; in the total gross outputs of all industries match gross inputs. Data can be treated in several ways to show, for example, the direct input, per unit of output in each industry, from all other industries, thus providing a matrix of production coefficients. The assumptions, and the data problems involved, are of a massive order.

'final demand', Hirschman distinguishes between 'backward linkage effects' and 'forward linkage effects'. The former arise from the inputs needed to supply production in the industry in question: for a farming economy, they include the production of farm tools and machinery, fertilizers, buildings and other fixed investments, as well as transport systems needed to market the produce. The latter, the 'forward linkage effects', arise from the utilization of the output of the industry as inputs in new activities; in the farming case these include food processing and preparation, and the treatment of industrial farm products such as cotton and wool, edible oils, or rubber. The forward linkages of one industry thus become the backward linkages of another, which in turn has its own forward linkages.

This concept is capable of obvious dynamic uses. Hirschman utilized it in a discussion of capitalization and industralization. But it also has historical uses, as M. H. Watkins (1963) was the first to point out in a paper which made a major advance in the export-base theory of economic development.

This latter body of theory arose in the search for a model of North American economic history alternative to the stage theories based on European experience.[7] The 'staple-product' approach used by Harold Innis (1930; 1940) was particularly influential. Dealing with the economic history of Canada, Innis traced the manner in which commercial relations with the metropole influenced the country's development, and in particular the manner in which the fur trade and the western North Atlantic fisheries influenced the formation of Canada and the structure of its economy and society. During the 1950s a group of American economic historians and economists undertook a somewhat parallel reinterpretation for the United States,[8] in which they made economic growth dependent on resource endowment, location, initial regional exports and the differing capability of such exports to generate diversification. North (1955/1964R) distinguishes sharply between export industries and

[7] The problem was not unrelated to that faced by J. E. Vance (1970) in his later attempt to find a model alternative to the European-based central-place model, in order to explain the evolution of urbanism in the United States.

[8] Relevant papers by H. Perloff and L. Wingo, D. C. North, C. M. Tiebout, R. E. Baldwin and R. K. Pfister are all reprinted in J. Friedmann and W. Alonso (1964) at pp. 209–302.

'residentiary industries' serving the local market. The importance of the former rests on their primary role in determining the regional income level, and hence the amount of residentiary production that will be generated. Tiebout regarded this as an oversimplification, but North insisted that:

> Since residentiary industry depends on income within the region, the expansion of such activity must have been induced by the increased income of the region's inhabitants. Therefore, increased investment in residentiary activity is primarily induced investment as a result of expanded income received from outside the region, and, correspondingly, expanded employment in locally oriented industry, trade, and services primarily reflects long-run changes in income received from the export base. (1964R: 262)

Baldwin's contribution (1956/1964R) was distinctive, and to a large degree anticipated his later (1966) analysis of the Zambian economy, which we reviewed in the dual economy context in chapter 3. Employing Leontief's input–output data, together with some data on labour coefficients in modern plantation economies, he pointed out that the production functions of plantation economies would lead to a much more unequal distribution of income than those of family farming. The skewed income distribution of a plantation economy diminishes the possibilities for development of residentiary industries because of the low effective demand of the mass of the population.[9] A region of family farms, on the other hand, is much more likely to be able to break out of an export orientation, since effective demand quickly becomes sufficiently strong and widespread to attract investment for domestic production. The nature of the natural resource base, and the institutional form of its development, thus interact to produce radically different conditions for evolution away from an initial export orientation. The spatial implications of this argument are ably reviewed by J. M. Gilmour (1972: 14–20); the export-base theory

[9] More recent work by quantitative economic historians has, however, thrown considerable doubt on the validity of these arguments, at least in relation to the American southeast which was the area Baldwin had in mind. S. L. Engerman (1967/1973R) has suggested that the slave economy was consistent with both growth and reinvestment, and that demand 'on behalf of' the slaves is ignored in the earlier argument.

is then tested and exemplified by him in a study of the spatial evolution of manufacturing in nineteenth-century Ontario.

For these reasons it was quickly recognized that an explanation of regional economic growth and diversification based on the multiplier effect of export incomes could not become a general theory, but was limited in its domain to the quite special case of lands of new settlement, relatively sparse in population, and of capitalist economy. This is not to say that it should not form an element of total explanation in other situations, but its successful use has, in effect, been confined to North America. It was in this context that Watkins (1963) clarified the process at work by introducing Hirschman's classification of inter-industrial linkages.

Watkins first added to Hirschman's 'backward' and 'forward' linkages a definition of 'final demand linkage' as a measure of the inducement to invest in domestic industries producing consumer goods for factors in the export sector. This then becomes the key to his whole discussion, and it is the effectiveness of final demand linkage which measures the success of an economy in developing away from its initial and dependent export orientation. Much of his paper is concerned with the obstacles to such an evolution — partly in relation to Canadian economic history, partly in general — and he sees such in the resource base itself, in an inability to shift resources at the dictates of the market, in an excess of foreign ownership and consequent want of perception of local opportunities, and in an inhibiting 'export mentality' which he strongly identifies with Canada's contemporary economic difficulties.

A great deal, however, depends on a single consideration: entrepreneurship, the ability to perceive and exploit market opportunities (Watkins 1963: 146). Whereas the emphasis on inter-industry linkages connects his argument with the 'plan space' of Perroux, the emphasis on entrepreneurship as the dynamic force leads straight back to Schumpeter. The core of the matter is innovation: 'resource flexibility and innovation sufficient to permit shifts into new export lines or into production for the domestic market' (*ibid.* 149). If this is so, a 'growth pole' in the abstract sense of an export industry with large backward and forward linkage, or 'multiplier' effects, will not generate economic transformation if it remains wholly related to a national or regional export; it is only if the stimulus to final demand linkage is present, is not shut off by institutional barriers, and is acted on by entrepreneurs that 'development' in the Schumpeterian sense is likely to become self-sustaining and independent of forces which might simply drag the economy along in accordance with changes taking place in the outside world.

It seems to me that these strands of theory, all present in the literature a decade or more ago, might constitute part of the basis of a dynamic theory of regional development even more applicable to the open, regional economies of subnational areas than to the relatively closed economies of whole nations. The variables which they emphasize: entrepreneurship, interactivity linkage, natural resource endowment, contrasted production functions, institutional and perceptual inhibitions to flexibility, dependence and the effects of income distribution; all these are the variables with which real world regional development problems are concerned. The role of capital as a means to the ends of entrepreneurship is also made clear. Perhaps most valuable of all contributions were the abstract concepts of economic space which Perroux introduced in 1950 and so quickly lost in 1955. Here were means of discussing primary production, manufacturing and the tertiary or service activities as interrelated parts of a single whole, divorced from the 'container' of national statistics, the compartments of sectors, or the physical distinction between town and country. But this was not to be; at least, not yet. The theory of regional development and of polarized growth has in fact moved in different directions, in which the methods of aggregation and ideal type continued to be used long after they ceased to be of service. We shall now follow the theorists — economists and latterly also geographers — down this dismal path that led from initial insight toward ultimate futility.

Spread and backwash: centre and periphery

Albert Hirschman and Gunnar Myrdal

The 'take-off' of the theory of regional development occurred through two books published toward the end of the 1950s. Hirschman's (1958) book was a general polemic on the means of getting economic development under way, and particular a statement of dissent with the 'balanced growth' views of Nurkse (1953/1967R) and others. Following an argument of Scitovsky (1954: 1963R) that rapid development in one economic sector will create a demand for the products of another, Hirschman advocated development through a 'chain of disequilibria'; the expansion of industry A will create external economies[10] for industry B wherever the two industries are in a complementary relationship of any kind. New investment will thus be induced as a result of increases in output of existing industries, so that something like a multiplier effect will operate through backward and forward linkages, and through stimulation of additional production in other parts of the economy. He therefore favoured an approach through 'unbalanced growth' and cited Perroux's growth poles in support. In the final chapter of his book he introduced a spatial dimension into the argument. Geographically, growth is necessarily unbalanced. Development takes place through 'master industries'[11] which must be located somewhere; new plants will then gain by being located close to the 'master industry'. A 'growing point' will therefore be established.

Entrepreneurs — here equated much more closely with the notion of capitalists than in Schumpeter's reasoning — will thus concentrate at the growing points; they will overestimate the economies of agglomeration and will underestimate or simply ignore opportunities elsewhere. Space preferences will therefore become distorted, and growth in the developing region — 'North' in Hirschman's

[10] Scitovsky's 'external economies' are briefly summarized in a footnote at p. 92 above. The point should be emphasized that in growth theory, as here, external economies arise principally from the effect of one investment on the profitability of another, actual or potential. No agglomeration or even propinquity is necessary. In static, Marshallian, analysis, on the other hand, external economies arise from possession of a pool of common services, common skilled labour, and common infrastructure. Hence they spring of necessity from agglomeration. In practice, Hirschman is using the concept of external economies in both senses. The static sense operates to induce agglomeration in the spatial part of his argument, while the dynamic sense is used to justify the doctrine of 'unbalanced growth' and, as we shall see below, also operates in ensuring the 'trickling-down' effects of the spatial argument. The question of differing definitions of external economies is discussed very helpfully by M. D. Thomas (in N. M. Hansen, ed. 1972: 60–2).

[11] The operation of his process depended on the 'importance' of linkages, measured by the potential net output of industries that might be induced by investments in one master industry, multiplied by the probability that the requisite plants will be established.

terms — will be paralleled by retardation elsewhere — in the 'South' — as skilled labour is withdrawn, savings are re-invested in the growing North, and terms of trade will set against the Southern producer of goods experiencing low income-elasticity of demand.

These polarization effects are, however, offset by an increase of Northern purchases in the South, and by an increase of Northern investments in the South that is 'sure to take place' if the economies are at all complementary, following the argument summarized above. The North may also abstract sufficient labour from the South to increase the marginal productivity of labour there, and raise *per capita* consumption levels, as in some versions of the dual economy model. The important consideration that will ensure that these 'trickling-down' effects take place is that the North has to rely on the products of the South to some important degree for its own expansion. Seen in this light, the regional development problem is simply a spatial case of unbalanced growth. And, as in the case of the wider theory, it is also presumed that the State will intervene to influence the correction of imbalances whenever the normal market mechanism proves inadequate. However, the temptation to 'scatter investment far and wide' must be resisted.[12]

The Swedish economist and generalist Gunnar Myrdal (1957) published a little before Hirschman, and though he identified closely similar processes his approach was both more humane and more direct; it has, in consequence, had far more influence. Concentrating almost wholly on the problem of inequality rather than treating it in the context of a general theory of development, he also reached far more pessimistic conclusions. His starting point was the unpalatable fact of growing differentiation between rich and poor countries, and rich and poor people — a subject little touched at that time in

[12] Grossly over-optimistic as he may be, Hirschman's proposed investment strategy contains elements of inevitability. Where resources are scarce they cannot be invested everywhere at once, and certain projects within certain sectors must obviously be selected for their growth potential. Efforts to obtain 'uniform development' over a whole country are doomed to inevitable failure, as I have earlier tried to show in the specific case of New Guinea (Brookfield with Hart 1971: 287–313). However, arguments such as Hirschman's have unfortunately provided a major justification for the 'urban-industrial bias' of which I have already complained, and which has led to some frightful consequences. As in so much reasoning of this type, the social miseries are ignored, the rationalization being that 'in time' the end will justify the means.

development writing. He then turns to discuss the 'vicious circle' of poverty and disadvantage, drawing on his own earlier (1944) study of the status of American negroes. From this he induced a theory of 'cumulative change': white prejudice and negro standards mutually 'cause' each other in a circular manner, but if either factor changes it forces the other up or down, so leading to 'cumulative change'.

Myrdal then suggests that the principle of 'interlocking, circular inter-dependence within a process of cumulative causation' has wide validity, and should be the main hypothesis in studying under-development. The play of free market forces works toward in-equality between regions, and such inequality is reinforced by the movements of capital, goods and services. All these forces, which are virtually identical with those perceived by Hirschman, he calls 'backwash effects'. Contrary to these are the 'spread effects' of expansionary momentum, which he does not elaborate in much detail. At this point, however, he departs from Hirschman, for:

> In no circumstances, however, do the spread effects establish the assumptions for an equilibrium analysis. In the marginal case the two kinds of effects will balance each other and a region will be 'stagnating'. But this balance is not a stable equilibrium, for any change in the forces will start a cumulative movement upwards or downwards. (1957: 32)

Backwash is stronger in depression than in boom, so that business cycles affect poorer areas more seriously than the growth centres.

Myrdal goes on to elaborate his thesis into areas of public policy, and leads on to a comprehensive and intellectually agile attack on equilibrium notions in economic theory; he concludes with the view that no adequate theory of economic development and under-development exists. But the basic idea which has attracted such attention in fact contains not much more than the gloss presented above. He recognizes no explicit debt to any of his predecessors, and his treatment is impressionistic. Process is not analysed in any detail, except in a later chapter concerned specifically with international trade and the inequality problem. His contribution was simply the presentation, in simple language, of the obvious that so many had ignored. And while it is hard to see why Myrdal's simplistics, or Hirschman's spatial aside to a text on growth, should have been regarded as a starting point rather than the more elaborate theorizing that we reviewed earlier, there is no doubt that this was so. For it was only after Hirschman and Myrdal that the fact of disequalization in the development process became firmly established among *explicanda* demanding close examination.

Disequalization as transition: John Friedmann

Perhaps because, like Myrdal's, his specific contribution to regional development theory has been insightful more than theoretically elaborate, John Friedmann's name is outstanding among those who have created this new sub-discipline during the 1960s. It is also outstanding because he has had the courage to shift his position quite noticeably over time, as reality has confronted theoretical expectation. Friedmann was involved early in the growth of regional science in the United States. In one of his statements on regional development, jointly with William Alonso, he set out a theoretical position which sums up much of the wisdom of the time, translated into a spatial dimension (Friedmann and Alonso 1964: 2):

> Spatial patterns will change with shifts in the structure of demand and of production, in the level of technology, and in the social and political organization of the nation. The economic and social development of the nation is reflected in its patterns of settlement; its patterns of commuting and migration; and its reticulation of areas of urban influence. And if there is a spatial pattern corresponding to each 'stage' of economic development, it may be further suggested that there is an optimal strategy for spatial transformation from one stage to the next. In the early period of development, marginal returns to the factors of production differ greatly between regions. With economic advancement, economic functions become more differentiated in space, and the relevant scale of many functions will increase. At an advanced stage of development, the national economy will appear as a fully integrated hierarchy of functional areas, with most of the population and activities polarized in metropolitan areas and, in effect, with national markets for labor, capital and commodities.

Hirschman and Rostow are the most obvious pregenitors here, but the ideas were further elaborated. The famous 'centre-periphery' model[13] was then set out in these terms:

[13] The 'centre-periphery' concept was first advanced by R. Prebisch (1949/1950T/1962R) and in ECLA REPORT for 1949 (1951). The context was that of international trade, and the distinction drawn was between the industrial economies of the world 'centre' and the primary-producing economies

centers not only grow so rapidly as to create problems of an entirely new order, but they also act as suction pumps, pulling in the more dynamic elements from the more static regions. The remainder of the country is thus relegated to a second-class, peripheral position. It is placed in a quasi-colonial relationship to the center, experiencing net outflows of people, capital, and resources, most of which redound to the advantage of the center where economic growth will tend to be rapid, sustained, and cumulative. (*ibid.*: 3)

This was the regionally aggregated model, elaborated in greater detail, which Friedmann then took to Venezuela. He worked there during the early 1960s on the planning experiment centred around the supposed 'growth pole' at Ciudad Guayana, a new city built on the basis of mineral resources and structured around an iron and steel industry. Venezuela was then supposed to be in a 'take-off' stage of a Rostovian development path, and very ample resources were poured into the Guayana scheme, which was to establish a pole of counter-attraction in the south of the country and reduce the excessive centralization of the economy into Caracas. It was Friedmann's task to integrate the Guayana programme into spatial planning for Venezuela as a whole.

The book which emerged from this work (Friedmann 1966) sustains the theoretical position of ultimate convergence, but gives greater weight to the empirical evidence of persistent dis-equalization:

The indisputable fact is that regional convergence will not automatically occur in the course of a nation's development history. Impressive evidence has been collected to show why the equilibrium mechanism that has been posited in theory will, in fact, break down. Even with a century and a half of sustained industrialization, the advanced economies of the United States and western Europe continue to be preoccupied with problems of

---

of the world 'periphery'. The concept was further developed, and adopted, in the international context during the 1950s and early 1960s: Friedmann, however, gave it the usage that has become more firmly entrenched in recent years.

depressed and backward regions inside their own national territories ... It may be that, in the very long run, when the society has advanced into an era of prosperity and mass consumption, interregional inequalities can be made to dwindle into insignificance ... Although the government can make use of technological possibilities and changing demand structures in order to promote the development of peripheral economies, this is clearly a matter of deliberate planning. On the whole, unrestrained forces of a dynamic market economy appear to be working against a convergence of the center and the periphery. (Friedmann 1966: 14–18)

This is now Myrdal rather than Hirschman, but Friedmann is much more precise in his posited mechanism. He identifies: failure of diminishing returns to set in at the centre; failure to perceive peripheral investment opportunities; export demand for goods produced at the centre; the coincidence of the centre with the national market for goods produced in the 'modern sector'; the concentration of high-order services at the centre; the intensity of culture contact at the centre; inability of the periphery to make adjustments appropriate to constant change at the centre, because of high replacement rates due to population growth, the disruptive effects of emigration, a lack of capital, and a general national inability to see the regional problem for a nationwide perspective.

He treats regional economies as 'open'. It follows that the initiative to exploit investment opportunities may be drawn from outside, and hence tends to be concentrated heavily in the more developed parts of a country. Growth may begin with an export sector, as in export-base theory, but the successful translation of this beginning into a viable residentiary economic complex depends on the socio-political structure. Many subregions, and whole countries, fail to make this translation, and become locked into a pattern of 'economic colonialism' toward national or overseas metropoles. The pattern of income distribution is also important — following Baldwin — for a highly skewed distribution will generate little multiplier effect from new investments.

Except for its integrated form of statement, this much contains little that was then new. But at this point Friedmann shifts the 'urban–industrial' emphasis of his argument into more concrete terms, first treating the regional growth problem as, in part, a problem in the location of industry, and following on from this with these propositions:

> Economic growth tends to occur in the matrix of urban regions. It is through this matrix that the evolving space economy is organized. (p. 28)

> The population of an urban field will be proportional to the population of the central city ... The spatial incidence of economic growth is a function of distance from a central city ... The growth potential of an area situated along an axis between two cities is a function of the density of interaction between them ... Impulses of economic change are transmitted in order from higher to lower centres in the hierarchy. (p. 31)

A direct link with central place theory, and an implied link with the theory of innovation diffusion, are thus established. It follows that:

> since regional policy must fit into this normative framework [a high rate of growth plus structural change and modernization], I shall posit as its major goal the achievement of that spatial structure of the economy which, at any point in time, is judged to be satisfactory for promoting and sustaining an efficient process of economic growth ... Subsidiary objectives are consequently two in number: 1. The gradual elimination of the periphery on a national scale by substituting for it a single, interdependent system of urban regions. 2. The progressive integration of the space economy by the extension, on a national scale, of the sytem of efficient commodity and factor markets. (p. 54)

The means of achieving these goals is then elaborated, and applied to Venezuela.

Friedmann was not, however, satisfied with his work and with its emphasis on economic forces. Within a year or two he was already developing a 'general theory of polarized development' of much wider span and very different direction. But before we examine this revision of ideas, and attempt to evaluate it, we should first look around to see what was happening elsewhere.

Growth poles and central places

Growth poles after Perroux

We have seen how Perroux himself initiated the translation of growth pole theory into a theory of industrial complexes and of cities as centres of growth. This trend was carried much further by some of his successors in France, outstandingly J.-R. Boudeville (1966) whose concern was with regional planning in Western Europe, and who observed that (1966: 10):

> The polarization concept would be of no practical value unless the interdependencies and hierarchy which it discovers were the expression of stable relations . . . The concept of the polarized region is the offspring of observations of the structure of cities . . . A polarized region has been defined as a set of neighbouring towns exchanging more with the regional metropolis than with other cities of the same order in the nation.

In other words, growth pole theory has become the process wherewith to explain central place systems, which is a long remove from the original concept. Boudeville was concerned first with the identification and delimitation of such polarized systems, and second with the development of regional operational models utilizing this structure. Lasuén (1969/1972R) tested the proposition of stability, and found that in Spain the hierarchical order of cities has become increasingly stable. He notes that 'this is obviously one manifestation of regional convergence in income levels and economic structure' (1972R: 48fn.). The abstract sense of growth poles has been almost totally lost.[14]

But so was clarity also lost. A few writers sought to retain a

[14] It should, however, be emphasized that Lasuén's concern was to rescue the concept. Commenting on Lasuén's article, N. M. Hansen (1969a) suggested that the emphasis on business organization may in fact lead to a contrary conclusion to that drawn by Lasuén. He thought that the change in organization might make large firms more free in respect to location within a country, but less free in respect to the size of community: the increasing inflexibility of the urban hierarchy might therefore simply reflect this change. Taking up this point in a later paper (1969b), he suggested that both Perroux and Lasuén have diverted attention away from the increasing importance of external economies in their effect on spatial polarization.

definition of an areally sited growth pole which retained something of the original concept; such included N. M. Hansen (1967), R. F. Darwent (1968/1969R) and H. Siebert (1969). The last-named, for example defined a 'regional growth pole' as (1969: 191–2):

> a set of interdependent expanding industries of an area. The complex of industries is viewed as consisting of a key industry and a set of activities which are linked to the key sector. The key industry is by definition expanding at a high rate, has a high level of output, and has strong linkages with the other activities of the region. The backward or forward linkages refer to the input and output side of an input-output matrix. The direct diffusion effects of an expansion in the key industry on the input side can be calculated by using the input-output coefficients in the column of the key sector . . . One of the basic reasons for a growth pole to arise is the immobility of at least one growth determinant . . . Only these immobilities can explain the location of the key industry and its development. Also, the growth pole will only persist if the immobilities are upheld or if additional immobilities – such as immobile external economies and immobile new technical knowledge – arise.[15]

Though Siebert has donned the industrial blinkers proffered by Perroux in 1955 he retains a clear notion of process. This is not true of many others. It does the real course of events no great violence to parody the devaluation of the growth pole notion through a progressive modification of Boudeville's (1966: 11) definition, itself essentially a simplification of Perroux's 1955 statement:

> A regional growth-pole is a set of expanding industries located in an urban area and inducing further development of economic activity throughout its zone of influence.

We might say that this became, in successive hands, first:

> A growth pole is an urban centre containing a set of expanding activities which induce further economic development throughout its hinterland,

[15] Some might be tempted to hear in this last sentence echoes of the principle of 'changing geographical values' enunciated by some historical geographers about the end of the 1920s.

And then:

> A growth pole is an urban growth centre from which growth diffuses through its hinterland,

and finally, at least in some hands:

> A growth pole is an urban growth centre.

Some may feel that this is a *reductio ad absurdum*, and that what has really happened is that a separate concept of a 'growth centre' has emerged from the original 'growth pole' notion; if so, however, a great want of clarification still remains. Thus three geographers (Semple, Gauthier and Youngman 1972) can be found not only interpreting a growth pole as 'an urban growth center that transmits growth impulses to a surrounding hinterland', but then concluding a computer-taxonomic exercise in the identification of such places with these words (p. 598):

> the identification of growth poles in geographic space can only be a first step in attempting to understand economic growth and its diffusion in a regional context. Clearly, there is need for research aimed at understanding the exact mechanism whereby a potential growth centre is propelled into one of self-sustaining growth.

Comment on this latter would be superfluous. However this is by no means the furthest remove from the original insights. Growth points, poles and centres have now been recognized in both descriptive studies and planning analyses among towns ranging in population down to only a few thousand people. Methods of identification have varied from the purely intuitive to the use of multivariate techniques on huge data matrices, but containing data of very different types. One suspects, with M. J. Moseley (1973), that a great many growth centres identified in such work exist as such only in the eye of the beholder. Not only the original insights, but also the structure of theory built on or assembled around these insights have been almost completely lost from sight. In the absence of some principles of selection and organization, that is of some 'vision of theory' (Myrdal 1957: 163) which constitutes at least the outline of a paradigm for research, it is high time that such enquiries were discontinued, or at least stored for possible future use in the ragbag of formless empiricism to which — notwithstanding their pretensions — they truly belong.

Central place theory, central places and diffusion
Fortunately, there has also been some more constructive thinking, especially on the interrelationship of economic with geographical theory; the astonishing rider to this statement is that the thinking has been contributed almost entirely by economists. One important contributor, however, was not an economist, but an economic historian. E. A. J. Johnson (1965) was so struck by the paucity of towns in northern India, and by the effect of this paucity in isolating the villager from markets, supplies, incentives and information alike, that he probed deeply into the literature on urban systems, and in a general book (Johnson 1970) argued that the main thrust of regional policy designed to offset polarization should be to bring into existence 'a complete spatial system of urban centers arranged in a hierarchy from agro-urban towns through several intermediate types to the metropolis' (1970: 377). He concludes (ibid.: 418–19) with a strong plea for the applicability in planning of Lösch's general theory:

> The ideal goals are patently evident from Lösch's analysis. Every rural producer should be within convenient travel time of some adequately competitive selling place for his produce, some equally competitive source of consumers' and producers' goods, and some adequately diversified service center. But these market centers are only the basic building blocks of a much more complex hierarchy of central places, capable of knitting the entire spatial economic structure together in a truly functional sense. For, unless there is a graduated, interlinked, and functionally integrated market system which covers all of a nation's space, serious handicaps inevitably result. Geographers and economists have devised tools by which the potentials of any portion of terrestrial space can be quite adequately measured. Not only can the resources, both physical and human, be evaluated but, within a given compass of space, particularly promising 'growth points' can be located . . . These estimates can become the directing guidelines for policy, serving not as absolute and rigid parameters but as proximate goals of 'indicative planning'.

He rejects the 'trickling-down' myth, along with the myth of grassroots development at the village level, and calls for a strategy based on the appreciation of a whole urban system as the foundation of widely spreading development.

This is one approach. Others called on central place theory viewed from the top down, rather than from the bottom up. The clearest expression of this approach is by Tormod Hermansen (1969: 1972R), who seeks to interrelate the fundamentals of growth pole theory, central place theory and innovation diffusion theory. Like Lasuén and M. D. Thomas (1972), he focuses attention back to the central point which Perroux received from Schumpeter — the significance of innovations in development — and remarks that both Schumpeter and Perroux recognized that most innovative activities take place in large firms that are able to exert domination over others.[16] His paper, which is possibly the best single review of growth pole theory and its linkages with other theoretical streams in the literature, then goes on to discuss the significance of the central-place theories of Christaller and Lösch, and to suggest that (Hermansen 1972: 180):

> central place theory may be viewed, not as some sort of static version of the dynamic development pole theory in which all movement has come to an end, but as the mechanisms through which development occurring in functional space can be projected into geographical space. (italics omitted)

But this requires a dynamization of central place theory that it does not possess, or alternatively a supplementation of central place theory by theories dealing specifically with the spatial transmission of development: after a search for such in the work of Hirschman and Myrdal, he finds what he is seeking in the enquiries of Torsten Hägerstrand (1953/1971T; 1965). After a review of innovation diffusion theory as developed by Hägerstrand and other geographers, he concentrates especially on the hierarchical network of mean social communication fields suggested in Hägerstrand's later work, permitting innovations to 'jump space' between larger centres, and

---

[16] That is, in the firms of the 'center economy' of Averitt (1969). See footnote at p. 70 above. We accept this point for the purposes of the present argument.

from higher order to lower order centres. Having thus found the linking process that he seeks between the theory of localized development poles and central place theory, he concludes with a tabular presentation of the whole complex body of theory, both static and dynamic, distinguishing abstract functional or industrial space, geographical space, and their 'combined super space in which the interplay between the factors pertaining to the two spaces takes place'.

Enter certain geographers, deep in conversation: stage right

Brian Berry is an incoherent wanker.

We have seen that the stage of regional development theory is becoming well-peopled with geographical concepts and theories; what of the geographers themselves? One geographer is quite frequently quoted in the economic literature. This is Brian J. L. Berry, whose work in India was critical in the development of Johnson's views, and whose expositions of central place theory have had wide influence on several other writers cited. However, when joining a collection with Hermansen, Lasuén, Thomas, Friedmann and others (Hansen, *ed.* 1972), Berry disappointingly confines himself to a highly mathematical paper on hierarchical diffusion employing his well-known, but doubtfully relevant data on the diffusion of TV in the United States. His justification is a somewhat bald statement that the 'role played by growth centers in regional development is a particular case of the general process of innovation diffusion' — a statement which goes far beyond Hermansen's, and which is only somewhat unconvincingly justified.[17] One feels, as a geographer, that an opportunity was not used to best advantage. But then, perhaps Berry has been listening to some of his colleagues.

[17] His argument is that innovations are filtered down the urban hierarchy, and then spread from urban centres. 'Regional inequities arise in this scheme because the income effect of a given innovation is a declining function of time and also subject to a threshold limitation — a minimum size of region — beyond which the diffusion will not proceed. As a consequence, the lowest levels of welfare are found in areas peripheral to small urban centres in outlying hinterland regions' (Berry 1972: 108–9). This might be true if 'welfare' is equated with access to TV, but W. Bunge, and others who have worked with him in the slums of Detroit, might have some persuasive arguments against the general proposition!

The 'geography of modernization'

By contrast, a group of geographers who have worked very directly in the area of regional development through time in developing countries had achieved almost no mention at all in the general literature up to the early 1970s. The founder of this group is Peter Gould who, first among the Young Turks of the 'new geography' at the end of the 1950s, took his ideas and methods into the Third World, and there applied them both empirically and in the generation of some very seminal new thinking.

Gould began with studies of the evolution of the urban and transportation system in Ghana; this work led to a paper (Taafe, Morrill and Gould 1963) setting up an 'ideal-typical' sequence of town and transport growth in developing countries which, notwithstanding its unfortunate acceptance of a stage-theory approach, remains the basic document on the topic to this day. About this time Gould became keenly aware of the modernization school among political scientists, and at once realized that temporal advance and spatial diffusion are different dimensions of the same process, while nation-building through the growth of social mobilization constitutes a theme amenable to spatial analysis (Gould 1964; 1967). His work in Tanzania (Gould 1970) appeared after that of some of his students, but is a most elegant essay on the diffusion of change, glossing over both the highly innovative methods used to treat intractable data and also the conceptual and technical problems involved in generating the 'modernization surfaces' which should now supersede all intuitive attempts to map centre-periphery patterns (e.g. Friedmann 1966). His theoretical conclusions parallel those of Hermansen: what we need to understand modernization — or any related process — is a deeper, dynamic theory of central place systems.

Two of Gould's former students have by now raised the banner of the 'geography of modernization' higher than Gould did himself. Barry Riddell's (1970) work in Sierra Leone, using trend-surface analysis, initiated the term 'modernization surface' and perhaps went furthest in the diffusionist approach to development:

Modernization is a spatial-diffusion process, assuming patterns of varying intensity and rate. Its origins are localized to specific regions or zones, indexing a contact situation, and the patterns of change move like waves across the map, and cascade down the urban hierarchy as they are funneled along the transportation system. . . While the growth of the transportation system is part of the modernization process, it is also much more. The spreading network of rail and roads continually redefines the spatial fabric of the country in which health services are located, schools are opened, communications are structured, ideas spread, and new ways of life emerge. (1970: 45, 47–8)

Riddell leads on to a study of migration into Freetown, finding that levels of urbanization and distance from the city are key elements for understanding. The hierarchy and the network structure the entire system, both process and response. Finally, even the nature of geography itself is redefined in a neatly recursive argument (ibid.: 131):

Thus the human geography of the country provides the framework for change. Cultural and ethnic patterns within the population are very real and do influence alterations, but the over-all pattern of change in the country is a function of its geography – the spatial organization of the countryside by network and hierarchy. The spatial dimension affords the key focus toward understanding the phenomenon of modernization.

Edward Soja has gone much further than Riddell or Gould in developing and redeveloping the 'geography of modernization'. The term is his creation (Soja 1968), and he has written much more than his colleagues on the underlying theoretical problems of the diffusionist approach (Soja 1970; 1973; Soja and Tobin 1972). He makes it clear that the geography of modernization evolved initially from the methodology of the 'new geography' infused with ideas drawn mainly from political science; the potential relationship to regional economics and to wider and more contentious aspects of development theory did not emerge until after the first enquiries were already published. This was the product of an initial enthusiasm that we have also seen in other writing. Now, a more deeply theoretical geography of modernization is beginning to emerge, but the printed contribution up to now still bears the stamp of its narrow initial base. There is heavy emphasis on quantitative method, basically principal components analysis but by now including a very much wider range of techniques. The main element of geographical theory that is introduced is central place theory, but essentially in the role of explanation for the observed patterns. These patterns, in turn, are based on the analysis of variables that have a heavy urban bias. This bias follows reasonably enough from the underlying theory of modernization that inspired the work, but it leads to a circularity which has hitherto inhibited the geographical modernizers from leading their work away from description, and away from reliance on the weak explanatory power of central place theory, into more innovative directions.

Some enigmas of the geographers' contribution

The geography of modernization has come in for some severe onslaughts from fellow geographers. In mounting order of criticism, M. I. Logan (1972), Brookfield (1973a) and P. W. Porter and A. de Souza (1974) have attacked the indices employed to describe modernization, the appropriateness of the methodology and of the conclusions drawn from its results, the circularity of the argument internal to the studies, the failure to link up with wider development discussions, and — above all, perhaps — the attachment to the value-loaded and Americo-centric modernization school in the social sciences. The criticism has been unusually severe, doubtless in response to the inflated claims for the new approach made by some of its innovators. Rather than review these criticisms, it would perhaps be more useful here to seek the positive contributions made by the geography of modernization to the wider discussion, and to ask why geographers as a whole have been so extraordinarily ineffective in this area.

The geographers of modernization are unanimous in concluding that the core urban system, together with the 'mobilized periphery' (Soja and Tobin 1972) around it, constitute the focus of dynamic change in the developing countries they have studied. The maps of the modernization surfaces — like a few volcanic cones on a plain of low relief — carry several lessons if we can assume that they accurately reflect societal differences. First, they emphasize transition and so provide a corrective to the simple duality of centre and periphery; second, they emphasize not only primate cities but also other centres and certain of the corridors between them. Third, the studies through time show something highly suggestive. Peter Gould's method in Tanzania, also employed in a very similar analysis by Soja and Tobin on Sierra Leone data, was to obtain for each hexagonal unit a relative value from zero to 1000 showing the relative weight assigned to the first dimension score in a principal components analysis. Repeating this for successive dates shows that not only is the incidence of modernization variables diffused through time, but also that the relative standing of places varies very greatly through time. This is especially true of inland centres, some of which show up very much more sharply on the modernization maps at early and intermediate dates than at the most recent date. The potential relationship of this finding to Perroux's original Schumpeterian notion of shifting foci of growth has not yet been explored.

In connection with this last observation is a clear statement of hypothesis — though presented as a conclusion — first put forward by Soja (1968) and repeated by him and others in different territorial contexts. This is the hypothesis that since the spatial patterns of modernization reflect the objectives and perceptions of the former colonial power they are therefore dysfunctional in the context of independent nationality, and hence that a major planning objective must be the restructuring of spatial systems to correspond with new national needs. The view has already been challenged, for example by N. S. Ginsburg (1973) who maintains that these spatial systems are a valuable legacy to the newly independent countries. It should properly be presented in hypothetical form and in a wider context. The idea that spatial systems which are functional for one purpose may be dysfunctional for another is, after all, implicit in Christaller's three distinct principles of central place formation. To link the hypothesis with an area of theory discussed earlier in this chapter, logical reasoning would suggest that the spatial system of a country undergoing economic transformation from an initial export base would show a continual lag in adaptation, and hence remain always dysfunctional until a stable economic configuration is evolved. This would correspond entirely with Perroux's original notion, with the Schumpeterian addition that transformations would be expected to occur in surges, as 'swarms of entre-preneurs' — or government innovators — perceive new opportunities.

My criticisms of the geography of modernization (Brookfield 1973a) are not lessened by this discussion: indeed, they are sharpened in a new direction. But the positive side which I also noted now emerges much more clearly in the context of theory about spatial inequalities as a whole. Given much greater care in its interpretation, the modernization surface, invented by Riddell and developed by Gould and Soja into a sensitive device for the analysis of shifting spatial patterns, has an important role to play.[18] Closer study of the shifting emphasis between growth points, of the stresses of dysfunctionality and the consequent adjustments, and the identification of what the 'mobilized periphery' really means in terms of the linkage effects of both production and social overhead investments, are avenues toward a more profound understanding of change in spatial systems. They might well take us further even than Hermansen's insightful union between growth pole theory and central place theory through diffusion — a union which lacks the flexibility of true dynamism. Even in its present primitive stage of evolution, the geography of 'modernization' has this much to offer. But the contribution is only potential: it emerges in the context of theoretical systems which the authors seem yet to have hardly penetrated at all.

The reasons for the failure of this creditable initiative to 'light a prairie fire' are perhaps not far to seek, though a full examination demands a separate and very different essay. In the terminology we have been using, the linkages have not been perceived by the entrepreneurs, and in any case the resource base utilized is too slender to permit the necessary transformation. These geographers, outstandingly Gould, have been primarily intent on the reconstruction of their own discipline, and on demonstrating the superiority of

---

[18] It will be objected that the problems inherent in the use of principal components analysis are too great to permit this optimistic statement. There is heavy dependence on the data, which are weak; the strong first dimension may be illusory; the interpreted factors are not independent, and so on (see the contribution of Jan Lundqvist on this subject *in* Porter and de Souza 1974). However, Lasuén (1969/1972R) based some very weighty conclusions about the growing stability of spatial patterns on nothing more than an analysis of Spanish urban population data. These too are a surrogate, and only a single one, for the variables he is really discussing. No one doubts that there is a great deal more work to be done before satisfactory indices of changing spatial patterns are evolved, but the interesting contribution of the 'modernization surface' is that it describes fluctuating variability in these patterns, rather than convergence or divergence, in a manner which opens up a new set of questions, and corresponds with an idea that has been left virtually unexploited for twenty years.

the new paradigm over the descriptive empiricism of the past. To this end they, and most especially Gould himself, have at times seemed concerned more with method than with the empirical problems to which the methods have been applied.[19] Thus Gould's idea of the well-trained geographer is of a man versed in computer expertise, linear programming and 'theory' (Gould 1973: 258), but not subjected to the dis-inspiration of either factual or systematic training — in short a superb craftsman ignorant of the material with which he is working. The folly of such an approach was never better demonstrated than in the prolonged failure of his group to make its real contribution in an area where the direct participation of geographers is increasingly wanting.

General theory?

Horst Siebert

There is a considerable number of surveys of theory in the literature. Most find any sort of integration wanting.[20] However, two significant attempts at synthesis appeared at the end of the 1960s. They are very different in nature and emphasis. Horst Siebert's (1969) synthesis adopts the basic strategy of dichotomy, dividing his 'country' into two regions; his analysis therefore harks back to dual economy theory at several points. His method is a rigorous use of economic calculus, based on assumptions clearly stated at the outset, and as such differs somewhat sharply from many other contributions we have noted. He is concerned only with growth, but growth of welfare, output and the availability of final commodities; he sidesteps the wider definition of development, but regards certain non-economic changes as fundamental to the achievement of growth. His main concern is with interregional movements of production factors, and

[19] Gould's major statement from the modernization work to his professional colleagues was in a paper 'On the geographical interpretation of eigenvalues' (Gould 1967). The empirical base was somewhat insensitively termed 'the space called Tanzania' (Gould 1970: 169). This is rather less true of the others: Soja points the main thrust of his work toward his own less enlightened colleagues in one paper (Soja 1970), but his more recent work demonstrates far greater social and interdisciplinary awareness.

[20] A good example is the survey by M. J. Hilhorst (1969), who concludes that regional development theory is an 'underdeveloped' sector of the theory of development as a whole.

he assumes that the supply side is the limiting factor, while the demand side can be neglected.[21] For his point of origin he takes Schumpeter's emphasis on invention and innovation and, after a survey of growth within a single region, begins his two-region analysis with the theorem that growth differences will be greater the stronger the difference in the rate of inventions, and the lower the mobility – or diffusion rate – of technical knowledge. This statement is followed by a second, that regional growth is simply correlated with the rate of growth of capital and labour supply.

After these initial theorems, Siebert then postulates that 'the greater the weight of a factor in the production function, the higher the growth rate of that region with an increase in that specific factor'. From this follows a discussion of the mobility of growth determinants and production factors. Differentiation cannot exist without differences in factor mobility – otherwise there would soon be equalization. Given one scarce factor and one abundant factor, differentiation will be greater in direct proportion to the mobility of the scarce factor, and in inverse proportion to the mobility of the abundant factor: different factor combinations will then emerge in the two regions. If external economies are highly mobile interregionally, this will operate to reduce differentiation, and *vice versa*. Also if social institutions are uniform throughout the country, labour will be mobile in all directions and some other factors will also move more readily; these conditions also operate against differentiation. But conversely, sharp differences in institutions, social structures, attitudes and behaviour will reinforce differentiation by reducing factor mobility; the conditions of 'classic dualism' are thus a force for regional difference. Improvements in transportation reinforce factor mobility and hence diminish differentiation. The degree to which the forces of differentiation are reinforced through the operation of the model thus depends fundamentally on factor mobility. However, the strongest

[21] This is in contradistinction to export-base theory, and also to Friedmann's (1966) analysis, in which it is assumed that rising external demand is the decisive motive force for growth. Siebert seeks to demonstrate that regional income need not necessarily increase in harmony with export growth, because variations in the interregional terms of trade are a necessary consequence of internal expansion; 'export-base theory neglects changes in the terms of trade. This procedure is due to the assumption of a high production elasticity with respect to an increase of demand' (p. 98).

reinforcement effect of all is the introduction of technical change adapted to the factor endowment of only one region; this introduction will increase the movement of other factors to that region, and reinforce differentiation.

Most of this is demonstrated mathematically as well as verbally. Siebert then turns to the effect of variation in the prices of commodities and of factors. Price differences for commodities are caused by the immobility of factors; the terms of trade will therefore vary. But this may have more than one effect on differentiation, because the allocation of gains from trade may be unequal, and because a high mobility of commodities may encourage wide markets, larger plant sizes and external economies — all forces which call differentially on the factor endowment, and may reinforce differentiation. Hence he maintains that no conclusive single proposition concerning the effect of trade can be developed.

Moreover, the relative pricing of factors and commodities has complex effects. For example, an increase in the price of immobile factors — principally land — will encourage substitution of mobile factors, and hence induce levelling. It follows that the easier it is to substitute factors in production, the more effective will such price variations be in the levelling process. All this is summed up in the view that rising factor prices, together with increased demand, in an expanding region will move the terms of trade against that region, and so lead to a reduction in differentiation. This, of course, is the classical view of a process which will lead to the ultimate triumph of 'spread' over 'backwash'.

Siebert is aware of non-economic forces, and he introduces them at several points. However, his model relies principally on the concept of factor substitution, and on the elasticities of supply and demand. It is a major aid to comprehension by virtue of its solid stiffening of a great deal that has been imprecise in other hands. But it is an aggregated model, it is concerned only with growth, and it specifically neglects changes in the social system. It is therefore incomplete, and Siebert does not face the fact of widespread failure of economies to 'level' in spite of the presence of many of the necessary conditions.

The later John Friedmann

In his profound rethinking of regional development theory after the Venezuelan experience (Friedmann 1966), Friedmann moved in quite the opposite direction from Siebert, away from purely economic argument and toward a linkage between regional interaction theory and the theory of social change. For the latter, Friedmann (1967/1972) relies on a modification of R. Dahrendorf's (1959) analysis of change through conflict in an authority-dependency situation, but his use of this model reflects his own empirical observation.

Like Siebert, he begins with innovation, but treats development as taking place through constant innovative forces arising from or injected into an existing 'traditional' system.[22] Innovation is the successful introduction of new ideas, artifacts or combinations, and requires an innovating agent — that is, a Schumpeterian entrepreneur. The probability of successful innovation within a spatially organized social system varies according to the 'effective demand' for innovations, the capacity of the system to absorb innovations without major structural change, the frequency of innovative personality traits, the ability to marshal human and material resources and the social rewards offered to innovative activity: these conditions, which are elaborated, make some progress toward the definition of Schumpeter's 'social climate'. Large cities or urban regions normally offer the best combination of these conditions.

He then introduces the 'authority/dependency' model. Successful innovation increases the potential power of innovators, and when the exercise of this power is socially legitimated it becomes authority.[23] This may be achieved smoothly, or only through conflict, a process which may be one of progressive replacement, or which may take place through violent shocks of varying outcome. The 'development' of a system, however, requires the modification of its structure to facilitate constant integration of innovations. This is pure Schumpeter.

The points of 'highest potential interaction within a communication field' tend to be the centres of such change; innovations tend to spread downward and outward from such points. This concept

[22] Friedmann's use of the term 'traditional' varies from that of the modernizers: he defines it (1972: 87) as 'simply that which, at any given moment, is established and with respect to which an innovation is defined'.

[23] This is, of course, a departure from Schumpeter: at this point the innovators are transformed into something else. There is a jump in argument here, which should be closed. Friedmann is speaking of entrepreneurs at one point and of a power oligarchy at the next. They are not at all the same.

then leads Friedmann (1972: 93) to redefine the centre-periphery system in the following terms:

> Major centers of innovative change will be called *core regions*: all other areas within a given spatial system will be defined as *peripheral*. More precisely, core regions are territorially organized subsystems of society that have a high capacity for innovative change; peripheral regions are subsystems whose development path is determined chiefly by core region institutions with respect to which they stand in a relation of substantial dependency. Peripheral regions can be defined by their relations of dependency to a core area.[24]

The next stage of Friedmann's theory involves the conditions by which core regions consolidate their dominance over the periphery. He identifies six self-reinforcing, feedback effects. The first is the *dominance effect*, the steady weakening of the peripheral economy by net transfers of natural, human and capital resources to the core, essentially through the mechanisms identified by Siebert, Hirschman and the earlier Friedmann. These are accompanied by the *information effect* of an increase of potential interaction within the growing core and the *psychological effect* of innovation success, facilitating more innovation. The *modernization effect* is then the transformation of social values and behaviour, again at the core, to conform with the needs of innovation, and this is accompanied by the *linkage effect*, or the tendency of innovations to breed new innovations, and the *production effect*, or the creation of an attractive reward structure for innovation. The last includes the growing economies of scale and specialization.

Conflict then arises in a spatial sense from attempts within the periphery to gain access to the benefits of innovation and the means wherewith to accept and encourage innovation. This is encouraged by information flow from core to periphery and leads to demands

---

[24] Although Friedmann does not make the point, it should be noted that this relationship can also be applied in abstract social or economic space within any chosen universe, and has no *necessary* expression in terms of a clear geographical dichotomy. It might, indeed, make his analysis more meaningful to view it in terms of such abstract Perrouxian space.

for peripheral autonomy, which may encourage core élites to adopt decentralization policies or may lead to direct conflict. One possible consequence may be the successful replacement of core élites by peripheral élites in the national system, and subsequent events depend on the behaviour of the new power group.

Core-periphery systems occur in nested hierarchies, from the world level down to the very local scale of a single city region. The core regions organize the dependence of their peripheries through market and supply systems, and patterns of administrative control. Within the hierarchical system, smaller core-periphery regions form part of the periphery of larger cores. Innovation is greatest in core regions forming part of high-order systems, so that the process of progressive asymmetry is self-reinforcing. Therefore (1967: 98):

> Up to a certain point in time, the self-reinforcing character of core region growth will tend to have positive results for the development process of the relevant spatial system; eventually, however, it will become dysfunctional, unless the spread effects of core region development to the periphery can be accelerated and the periphery's dependence on the core region reduced. The approach of this critical turning point will be registered in growing political and social tensions between core and periphery that are likely to drain core region strength and reduce its capacity for further development.

> The probability of innovation will increase over the surface of a given spatial system with increases in the probability of information exchange over that system. This tendency — the result of a successful challenge of core region autonomy by their peripheries — will induce the physical spread of existing core regions, a weakening of their hierarchical order, the emergence of new core regions on the periphery, and the gradual incorporation of large parts of the periphery into one or more system cores.

This structure of theory thus leads back to the non-spatial identification of 'centre-periphery' systems among populations by sociologists in the 1950s. It constitutes a theory of revolutions as much as a theory of spatial development, and as such seems to have greater verisimilitude at the international level, or at the level of national politics in federal or other plurally constituted nations, than at the subnational level to which it is alleged to apply.[25] It leads Friedmann finally to the conclusion that (1972: 100–1):

> In the context of the General Theory, contemporary regional growth theory may therefore be treated as a special case, applicable only to situations where the dualism of core and periphery is of relatively little consequence, such as the reasonably advanced and integrated spatial systems of the United States, West Germany, or Sweden. It is applicable neither to the industrializing countries nor to multinational regions where core-periphery dependency relations are still predominant influences. In their case, the transformation of authority-dependency patterns in spatial systems is a fundamental condition of development and, consequently, also of sustained economic growth.

Discussion

It is rather surprising that Friedmann (1972: 83) should describe Siebert's formulation as close to his own. It might be more accurate to say that, together, they form the closest approach to a single general theory thus far achieved. However, one inescapable conclusion arising from the discussion in this chapter is that a considerable number of theoretical strands of great value have not yet been incorporated into any synthesis. It is also obvious that the conditions governing development and weakening of regional inequalities — or of inequalities in any dimension — vary greatly

[25] Thus it is a plausible interpretation of the Russian challenge to the progressive domination of its economy from western Europe which was taking place in the decades before 1917, or of the rejection by western Canadian voters in 1972 of a government with a power base in the dominant Windsor-Québec 'corridor', which had consequences in the form of modified federal economic policies toward the west. It forms at least a partial explanation of Scottish, Welsh and Breton nationalism, and of the recent attempts of such peripheral populations in western Europe to form a united political action group. Similarly, it helps explain the separation of Bangla Desh from Pakistan. It has obvious links, whether realized or not, with the Marxian dialectic, and seems at some points to be simply a spatial interpretation of the 'class struggle' and of the doctrine that oppression will always generate resistance, leading to the replacement of the rule of the oppressors by that of the oppressed. As we shall see, this view projects regional development theory into the altogether different area of 'internal colonialism'.

from place to place, have varied greatly through historical time, but include forces that are present in all places and at all times. Even in the simplest, most egalitarian societies there are inequalities between persons, and between groups on the basis of the resources they command and can use, and the locations that they occupy. And although the reduction or elimination of inequalities is perhaps the most fundamental of social goals, it is also opposed to the self-interest and group self-interest of those with power, ambition and wealth. Possibly this is the basic dialectic which underlies all others, and should first be viewed at this most fundamental level, taking note of the fact that unequal advantage is an inevitable concomitant of any system of organization, viewed in whatever dimension; the dimension of geographical space is merely one in which unequal advantage is most obvious. If these fundamentals are first isolated, then theory based on any particular form of socioeconomic organization, on the conflict of different forms of socioeconomic organization, and on any particular scale of wider-than-local socioeconomic organization can be isolated as alternative paths containing common elements. Common elements are certainly present, and a great number have already been identified, but not properly separated from elements that are of limited-domain. We are as yet a very long way from any true general theory, but the knowledge and understanding wherewith to lay its foundations are present. A small part of this fund has been set out in this chapter, but the task of bringing it into even partial integration is beyond the scope of the present work.

5: Voices from the periphery X Whalecly.

The 'centre-periphery' model of John Friedmann, and its reformulation in terms of a theory of conflict, offers a link between Western regional development theory and some of the central issues of Marxist thought. Not only does the exploitation of the periphery correspond with notions of the expropriation of the surplus but we are also brought face to face with the conflict between revolutionary and reformist strategies of change.

The contrast in approaches is expressed most obviously in the several versions of communist thought on development questions, and we begin with a brief gloss on Russian and Chinese experience. However, it is in Latin America and the Caribbean that some of the most interesting and innovative revisions of both Marxist and Western thought, in opposition and in conjunction, have emerged. The particular interest of the Latin American school from this point of view is its base in empirical reality, for the new thinking has not arisen through the slavish adoption of external models, but rather through questioning the relevance of these models to the historical and actual experience of the region. For reasons that will emerge as we go forward, I describe the writers of this school as constituting a 'neo-Marxist' group; the Marxism of their views is 'new', and is not simply derivative.

Original and orthodox Marxism

The revolution did not take place where Marx predicted

To Marx himself, the developing countries — indeed, the whole integument of the capitalist heartland — was little more than a space to be filled by the expansion of the capitalist system in its last, 'imperialist', phase. A little thought about the area of the world actually occupied by 'high capitalism' in the middle of the nineteenth century will show that his was a very Eurocentric view of things, and relegated the rest of the world to a passive and insignificant role. To Marx the central fact was the triumphant revolution of a capitalist, individualist, exploitationist European bourgeoisie, which had made the country dependent on the town, the backward on the advanced, the East on the West. His theory sought to show that the triumph of this bourgeoisie contained the seeds of its own destruction through unrestrained competition and exploitation, the treadmill of the capitalist struggle, the concentration of capital and the creation of such intolerable conditions for the proletariat that this class would ultimately rise and establish its own dictatorship. All this would obviously take place in the countries most advanced through capitalist industrial exploitation — those of Western Europe.

The shift of the focus of Marxist thought to Russia, and the successive bourgeois and communist revolutions in that country in 1917, therefore demanded some reinterpretation. And the reinterpretation was in terms of imperialism. The Russian revolution was a first stage leading the way to a greater revolution in the capitalist heartland; the revolutionaries were the 'advance guard of the international proletarian army' which would arise in the death struggle of the imperialist powers then in progress. This emerges in Lenin's speech at the Finland Station in Petrograd (E. Wilson 1940/1960R: 473–4), more clearly in the textbook on communism published by N. Bukharin and E. Preobrazhensky (1920/1969T), most clearly in Stalin's essay on the 'foundations of Leninism', first published in 1924, and subsequently in the official history authorized by Stalin (CC of the CPSU(B) 1943). Since the 1870s Russia had been industrializing rapidly, but remained at the stage where the new industrial economy stood out sharply, even dualistically, from the peasant mass. Much of Russian manufacturing capacity and infrastructure was foreign-owned or at least penetrated; the concentration of ownership was much higher than in the West. Tsarist Russia had thus become a 'major reserve of Western Imperialism', and in this situation were found the starkest forms of 'capitalist, colonial and militarist' oppression.[1]

---

[1] One is reminded of Boeke and Furnivall on Indonesia. In an essentially pluralistic colonial economy, lacking any homogenous social will, we find oppression and extortion by a:

> capitalist structure, with the business concern as subject, far more typical of capitalism than one can imagine in the so-called 'capitalist' countries which have grown slowly out of the past and are still bound to it by a hundred roots. (Boeke 1930: 781, cited in translation by Furnivall 1939: 452)

The revolution thus took place in the periphery, in a 'backward', semi-capitalist country. The 'chain of imperialism' was broken 'at its weakest link' where the 'contradictions of capitalism' were more sharply defined than in the heartland. But this is Lenin, not Marx. And it was in part because of the pre-revolutionary condition of Russia and its deviation from the Marxist ideal-type, that a policy of rapid industrialization incorporated not only considerations of national security, but also the creation of a stronger proletarian base which necessitated the proletarianization of the peasantry. Its effect, in the view of some writers — such as Milovan Djilas (1957T) and E. Wilson (1940) — was to create not a proletarian but a bourgeois revolution, albeit under new rules. Lenin's emphasis, which has been sustained, on the need for both revolutionary enthusiasm *and* material incentive in order to achieve the development of socialism, has had the effect of taking Russia decisively out of the ranks of the 'underdeveloped' nations.

China: the 'village' and the 'city'
The initial attempt of Chinese communism to mount an urban-based revolution was a disastrous failure, and the party then turned to a reliance on the rural base which ultimately brought it success. In this circumstance lies the origin of several of the very fundamental ideological differences that have come to separate the Russian and Chinese parties. From the early 1930s, the strategy of revolution began in the countryside, and moved thence into the towns — the smaller towns first, and last of all the big cities.[2] Generalized, this experience forms the basis for the postulated conflict between the 'world village' and the 'world city', the former comprising the 'developing' countries and the latter the 'advanced', with its core composed of the two great powers, 'imperialist America' and 'social-imperialist Russia'. Revolutionary victory requires the successful encirclement of the latter by the former — including nations of whatever political complexion, even sometimes the West European capitalist democracies so long as their efforts contribute to independence from great-power domination (Shih Chun 1973).

Internally, China has found limited use for the model of socialist

[2] Resolution of the Central Committee of the Chinese Communist Party, April 1932, cited in Anon., *ed.* 1972: 228. The 'diffusion process' of the geographical modernizers is thus neatly reversed!

reconstruction 'led by the working class and its *avant-garde*, the communist *cadres*', when the former comprises hardly 2 per cent of the population. The class conflict of classical Marxism is of little relevance to a country where:

> society is small at both ends and big in the middle, that is, the proletariat at one end and the landlord class and big bourgeoisie at the other each constitute only a small minority, while the great majority of the people consists of the peasants, the urban petty bourgeoisie and other intermediate classes. (Mao Tse-tung 1941, cited in C. P. Fitzgerald, *ed.* 1969: 54)

Initial attempts to apply the Russian model of development were reversed in stages through the 'Great Leap Forward', the commune movement, and the Cultural Revolution, each successively enhancing the rural bias, and reducing the intermediate role of urban (proletarian) structures between the village and the central power. This progressive change is reflected in development policy as a whole, especially in relation to industry (S. Ishikawa 1972; Dean 1972). For the first few years a 'Russian model' of centralized, technologically advanced, large-scale industry financed and equipped from the Soviet Union was followed. In the period of the 'Great Leap Forward' after 1958 the policy of 'walking on two legs' was enunciated, involving a deliberate technological dualism with a modern large-scale sector supplemented by a great number of small-scale local enterprises with largely indigenous technology. This scheme at first failed, but in the Cultural Revolution and its aftermath there was a renewed emphasis on small-scale, widely dispersed industry supported now by a much stronger system of research and development, and supplemented by a more gradual introduction of foreign technology — from more widely dispersed sources — in a core large-scale sector. A growing measure of success has latterly been reported.

The emphasis given to rural development, with which is included the progressive capitalization of village agriculture, involves a major departure from the Russian and Western models of development, but is in line with the peasant-based philosophy of the Chinese revolution. The ideological basis has been variously interpreted. Ishikawa (1972) sees the goal of maximum growth sustained throughout, though with growing emphasis given to the principle of equalization in the later phases even at the cost of growth in output. The successive Chinese plans consistently call for increases in output and in real income, but with weight given to the ideal of a uniform basic sufficiency, the task of reconstructing society and nation itself constituting the incentive (L. Veilleux 1973). This is viewed differently by critics, including particularly Russian students of China. For example, A. Arzamastsev (*in* Anon., *ed.* 1972: 174–96) places emphasis on the 'cult of poverty', alleging that the Chinese leaders are relying wholly on the transformation of man through revolutionary zeal, and disregarding the material incentives advocated by Lenin. The Russians see nothing but disaster, and progressive compromise with the still-strong petty bourgeoisie of the Chinese countryside, as following from a course which deviates so much from the essential proletarian path of socialist revolution.

But such a 'cult of poverty', if properly interpreted, may not be mere utopian idealism of a bourgeois-socialist sort as the Russian observers suppose, but an accurate reflection of developing country realities. Though it may be rationalized through insistence on the permanency of opposites in Chinese Marxist philosophy, and leads to a uniformism which Russians describe as a 'barracks egalitarianism', it perhaps reflects a clear choice between gradual and disciplined uplift of the whole, and the more immediately spectacular gains available from encouragement of an élite in a poor country. That is to say, it is in direct opposition to Western strategies as well as those of Russia. The essential philosophy is summed up in the still-new policy of eliminating the 'three big differentials' — between mental and manual workers, industry and agriculture, and town and country (Ishikawa 1972: 172). The first aim is therefore to reduce the risk and uncertainty of peasant production, by strategies which make agriculture the leading sector and set up an 'investment-inducement' mechanism which leads to forward- and final-demand linkages from agriculture. The call on social discipline is great, and perhaps unrealistic in the eyes of many, but the alternative is a dominance-dependence relationship in which the peasantry is — in Latin American terminology — marginalized.

Up to the present time, the Chinese internal policies have made little impact abroad, except perhaps in Vietnam, Tanzania and Cuba, where some policies of similar construction have been adopted. This is partly for want of information, but partly also because the scale of

China makes possible an independence that is not feasible elsewhere. There has until lately been much greater interest in Chinese external policies, though it is possible that the fuller significance of these — at least in regard to the Soviet Union — has not been fully appreciated.

The international socialist division of labour

In the ideal international socialist system there is equality of welfare, the factors of production are freely mobile, and there is a perfect fit of production to natural resources (J. Novodamsky, *in* Kaser, *ed.* 1964: 148). There is no exploitation, and mutual aid is freely given in the spirit of socialist brotherhood. In the early days of the Russian revolution, for example, Bukharin and Preobazhensky (1920/1969T: 208) looked forward with enthusiasm to the role of Russia in supplying raw materials to the industry of a communist Western Europe. And more recently it has been noted, also with enthusiasm by Latin American writers longing for some alternative to their own dependence, that the 'central' Russian power in COMECON supplies a net surplus of raw materials and receives a net surplus of manufactures from other members — which, however, include nowadays Czechoslovakia and East Germany (A. Pinto and K. Kñakal 1971/1973T). In any case the gradual equalization of economic development levels in the socialist community is an 'objective historical process' (CMEA 1971: 18); the deepening international division of labour is believed to be conducive to this end.

Since alternative consequences of international specialization form an important element in the theory of 'dependent development' that we shall shortly examine, it is important to pursue this matter a little more closely. There has, unquestionably, been considerable export of technology and equipment from Russia to the less industrialized members of COMECON, and also to China before 1960; indeed, Russian observers (e.g. Y. Vladimirov, *in* Anon., *ed.* 1972: 305-43) hold that a major part of the Chinese core of heavy industry owes its existence to aid which Russia could ill afford during the 1950s. This is not denied by the Chinese. Under a consistent state monopoly of all international transactions, the essential lines of policy involving industrialization coupled with international integration based on deepening specialization have been followed undeviatingly in the COMECON countries. In the early post-war years, many developing countries looked to the socialist block for an expansion of their own trade under more favourable conditions than with their traditional trading partners in the West; this has not occurred except in a few isolated instances — most importantly Cuba.

In 1964, an interesting East-West discussion among economists took place at a conference in Bulgaria (M. Kaser, *ed.* 1968: 125–59). It was revealed that international specialization was still encountering severe difficulties, and that the 'evening out of differentials' was not proceeding as rapidly as was hoped. Certain of the less-developed countries in the socialist group had expressed the wish to 'close' their economies to some degree, in order to establish a wider economic base before re-entering full-scale international specialization. However, both Eastern and Western economists were agreed that international specialization of production was preferable to such autarkic policies. The Chinese experience was not raised at this conference, but since the avoidance of economic dependency was a major Chinese objective in their abrupt reduction of economic relations with Russia after 1959, this experience is relevant.[3]

China consistently declined to enter into any long-term trading agreement with the Soviet Union' and its partners. There were complaints about relative pricing, about exchange rates, about credit arrangements, about the quality of Russian manufactured imports and machinery, and about the practice of accepting loan repayments in the form of basic raw materials. Pricing was particularly significant, for the basis of agreements was the ruling world price for the commodities concerned, or their equivalents, as determined on the 'free' capitalist market but subject to a greater measure of stabilization. After the end of the Korean War, and the general decline of raw material prices on the world market, the terms of trade thus set

[3] Chinese trade with Russia was less than 5 per cent of the total Chinese foreign commerce before 1949. It then expanded to 23 per cent in 1950 and 50 per cent in 1958, but declined to 15 per cent in 1965 and only 2 per cent in 1967. Imports from Russia exceeded exports until 1956, and consisted mainly of machinery and manufactures, metals and petroleum products. Chinese exports to Russia consisted mainly of agricultural raw materials, forming 90 per cent in 1950 and 72 per cent in 1957; later mineral concentrates and textile manufactures formed an important part (Vladimirov, in Anon., *ed.* 1972).

against China just as against all other primary exporters, and the repayment of loans became more onerous. The real objection, however, was the growing dependency on Russian manufacturing industry, Russian technology, and Russian research and development, which evolved during the 1950s, and which was capable of being used to put pressure on China. Chinese policies of the 1960s, both internal and external, have been in large measure geared to the search for greater economic independence, even at high cost in productivity and in the rate of economic growth. Russians feel aggrieved that their substantial aid was rejected in this way, but the fundamental problem is one that transcends political ideology — a dislike of dependency, in whatever form it is presented.

The problem continues. Cuba has received massive aid from its East European trading partners, but its dependent condition is not yet relieved, or in sight of relief. The Mongolian Peoples' Republic, the least developed member of the 'Council for Mutual Economic Assistance', is recognized as a specific challenge to the policy of 'levelling up'. But the remedy is a policy of completely 'open' economic development, based on large-scale mineral exploitation, agricultural betterment, infrastructure building and massive technical aid, together with the establishment of 'joint enterprises' (CMEA 1971). Pricing in international trade continues to be based on the world market. Thus while many leftist groups in developing countries continue wistfully to hope for economic support from the socialist countries in relieving their trade dependency on the West, not many of their economic thinkers — even of Marxist persuasion — now espouse this course. As N. Girvan (1973: 25–6) puts it in a review paper that we shall mention again:

it is worth asking whether the alternative presented of international socialist integration does not solve the problem of deriving a strategy for internalizing the growth process, by avoiding it entirely. The true 'dependence' of this option is that it makes the development strategy of the country in question dependent on the foreign economic policy of socialist states, and by derivation on the *domestic* economic strategies of these states. How feasible in fact is a development strategy which relies on the assumption of the *automatic* support, of the nature, quality and quantity required, from a given set of foreign countries?

This is perhaps the most fundamental lesson of the Chinese example: China was able to gain the freedom to experiment politically and economically at the cost of external support and guaranteed trading arrangements. But how many of the world's developing countries are willing, or able, to adopt this alternative?

Historical necessity or choice?

There is a further aspect of the Marxist models that needs to be considered before we pass to a review of the Latin American school. In Russia, and to some degree also in China, there has been a very strong tendency toward the establishment of rigid orthodoxy based on an interpretation of the classic writings in the light of national history. In no area is this more evident than in the role given to the bourgeoisie in international orthodox Marxism based on Russia. The bourgeoisie are the allies and servants of monopoly capitalism; it is the rise to power of this class which brings the proletariat into massive existence, and thus creates the conditions for revolution. In dependent economies, the bourgeoisie has a dual role. On the one hand its members constitute the lubricant of international capitalist exploitation: this *comprador* or consular bourgeoisie comes to be identified with foreign interests, and with the foreign exploitation of its own people. But there may also arise a 'national bourgeoisie' which seeks to gain control of the economy for its own benefit, and which may thus provide the leadership in the first struggle against imperialism. It may even support the existence of a large and active state sector in the economy, as its best defence against the international monopolies (Popov 1973).

Orthodox Marxists may thus require the emergence of a strong bourgeoisie as a precondition of their own revolution. The point is well expressed by an orthodox informant cited by Régis Debray (1965/1969T: 521-2):

> At this moment, then, it is necessary to wait for the national bourgeoisie to mature, since they clearly cannot appear overnight. The growth of a national bourgeoisie means the simultaneous growth of *two* contradictions: the first with imperialism, which no longer exercises its exploitation as it once did, and the second with the nascent proletariat, which it is beginning to exploit. With a strong bourgeoisie, there is a strong proletariat. It is necessary

for us to count on this double contradiction. Since national industries are still too weak, there are not the necessary conditions for a revolution.

There is a large body of Marxist thinkers who hold that this remains true of the developing countries as a whole, and that the experiences of both China and Cuba do not vitiate the 'historical law', being based on special and non-replicable conditions in each case. They thus pin their hopes on national revolution before proletarian revolution; to the Chinese, national revolution is the *only* pattern for developing countries. But these views imply a rigidity and determinism which is anathema to many who otherwise accept large parts of the Marxist analysis. Most of the writers whom we review below are in this class: they accept the essential historical analysis, but reject the predictive element of orthodox Marxism. Furthermore, they ground their theories on empirical reality as observed and analysed with the aid of Marxism, but base their prescriptions on the principle of choice. This is why they are, perhaps, best classed as neo-Marxists — the intellectual descendants of the pre-1917 Marxist analysts, but not of the post-revolutionary teachers.

The Latin American structuralists: 'neo-Marxism'

Latin American origins
The 'development' history of the Latin American and Caribbean region is both quantitatively and qualitatively different from any other. Its beginning was marked by far greater destruction, deprivation and enslavement of the resident population than elsewhere; its colonial period saw the high development of both the plantation system and the *hacienda* system. Its political revolution came soon after the North American, but the sequel was quite different, being a period of renewed and even reinforced economic colonialism (or imperialism) from without; its modern phase of reform and revolution is encountering intensified resistance of many forms from both local ruling groups and external forces. No other major region has this sort of colonial history; it is therefore no cause for surprise that this region has been in the forefront of a whole school of new thinking on the processes operating in so-called 'development'.

Throughout the nineteenth century the emphasis in Latin American thought seems to have been almost wholly political.

National leaders such as Cuba's José Marti, who declared that Cuba must be independent both of Spain and the United States, may have understood the economic dimension, but it was not dominant with them. Insightful leaders, such as Lucas Alamán in early nineteenth-century Mexico, who attempted to establish the bases for industrialization, found their efforts thwarted by political instability and foreign intervention. Later in the century the scale of foreign intervention and investment increased. The *haciendas* greatly extended their control over land: various 'liberal' measures eliminated the privileged position of the church and also the colonial safeguards — such as they were — for Indian lands. The *hacienda* system spread over wide areas in which its progress had hitherto been restrained.[4]

[4] The *hacienda* system, and its wider meaning, is basic to an understanding of the Latin American situation. It is described in detail in many of the sources listed here. The meaning of the word is simply 'an estate', and there are in fact many small estates which are excluded from the discussion that follows. The '*hacienda* system' is a means of establishing minority control over the factors of production among a settled, indigenous population. It replaced the *encomienda* system of early colonization, in which rights to the labour of a specific population were ceded in return for certain duties. The *hacienda* is a unit of land, but the *hacendero* acquires control over the population residing on the land. In return for the right to reside and to cultivate a portion, a *peon* is obligated to provide a portion of his labour time. This labour is a commodity, which the *hacendero* may sell to other employers. But the *peon* may also expect the protection of the *hacendero*, even from the law.

In order to obtain labour in this way, it is necessary to control large areas of land and to constrain or absorb the lands of Indian villages, or *communidades*. The dispossessed or inadequately endowed are then obliged to accept *peonage*, while others offer as 'free' labour to supplement an inadequate living on their own land. The *peon* is also commonly bound to the *hacendero* by debt: and the *hacendero* also achieves control over distribution and marketing on his land in order to deny alternative channels to the population. The system has therefore constrained urban growth.

This is the 'pure' *hacienda* system. Its actual impact has varied greatly through time and space. Originating in pastoral exploitation in most areas, *haciendas* are commonly low-intensity occupiers of land; in time of economic depression they can retreat to a near-subsistence economy, but in periods of boom can become highly commercial, restricting the land available to their own *peons* and engrossing more land from villages by a variety of legal and quasi-legal means in order to obtain a larger and more proletarian labour force. This latter aspect has become more important in modern times: earlier, intensive exploitation (e.g. for sugar) was more usually achieved with the use of slaves, thus converting the *haciendas* into plantations. After the abolition of slavery, *haciendas* could only increase their labour force, or the amount of

This was the period which Marxists term the 'imperialist era', when the dynamic forces of European capitalism became worldwide in their impact and territorial aggrandisement accelerated. Major technological changes made possible whole new systems of production and the commercial use of new areas — such as the Amazon basin. In settled areas, large tracts of land now came under intensive

---

time obtained from labour, by an intensification of the methods described. In such periods, large *haciendas* have also absorbed the smaller. Such a process of concentration is described in the Chicama valley of Peru (CIDA 1966: 19–30), where 65 estates have been concentrated into 4 in the present century, while community land has also been reduced. Around the Cerro de Pasco copper mine large tracts were ruined by the smelter fumes and acquired, after which fumes were controlled and the land developed. A major extension of sugar lands in the Morelos valley of Mexico after 1900 triggered the peasant revolution described below, and a more modern uprising in eastern Peru was triggered in the same way (J. Womack 1968; H. Blanco 1972T). Different methods have been used in different areas, but the basic system whose origin is most fully traced — for Mexico — by F. Chevalier (1952/1963T) has been able to survive from the sixteenth century to the present in most parts of Latin America.

Though the *hacienda* as a developed institution is purely Latin American, the '*hacienda* system' as a means of appropriation and control has many parallels. Furtado (1970T: 71–8) points out that it is predicated on conditions in which land is abundant but labour the scarce factor. The 'total institution' plantation, using imported labour, is therefore a special case of the system. Where the control over land has been removed commercial output has usually declined, but middlemen have come to acquire a comparable social and economic role: this has been the case in Haiti.

Outside Latin America, the system has parallels in the form of control applied by the sugar factories in Java, to secure supply, which is described by Geertz (1963a; 1965). In highland Scotland, a change in the economic base to sheep production in the early nineteenth century led to action by the lairds, to reduce population on clan lands to the levels required, by means of massive evictions (Hobsbawm, 1968). In their use and abuse of the 'free selection' laws, the Australian 'squatters' were similarly able to acquire legal title to large areas with just sufficient population to sustain a pastoral economy. There is even modern establishment of true *haciendas*; in the Solomon Islands Tikopian migrants have been offered part of the land of a large plantation group, a sufficient area to supply basic needs but not to permit cash cropping: the migrants then provide the estate labour. In this case, as often in Latin America also, definite advantages are offered to the *peons*, given their acceptance of a client status. The system needs to be understood in the wider context of all methods designed to achieve monopoly control of the factors of production necessary for a commercial economy.

production for such crops as sugar, coffee, sisal, tobacco and bananas, just as elsewhere in the world for rubber, copra, palm oil and cotton. In certain areas most favourably endowed for this form of capitalist development — for example Cuba, parts of Mexico and coastal Peru — pressure on land and labour resources became extremely onerous.

These conditions sharpened the will to real independence, but leadership belonged to élites whose interest in gaining freedom for their own expansion rarely coincided with those of the oppressed peasants, *peons* and the tiny proletarian class. Like intellectual activity generally, the political movements were élitist and even racist. But these élites also became increasingly Latin Americanist, particularly in opposition to the swashbuckling new American imperialism that burst into the region in the 1890s. They were strongly influenced by new European ideas, and at least idealistically with notions of democracy.

The first major shock was the Mexican revolution of 1910. Initially this was an élitist movement concerned only with political democracy, but it had need of peasant support and found this among the oppressed peasants of the pastoral north and especially of the sugar region of Morelos, south of Mexico City. At first the new leaders did not even slow down the process of land engrossment by the *hacenderos* (J. W. Wilkie 1970: 41–9), and they quickly alienated the peasants who resumed the revolution with new determination. Especially in Morelos, a truly revolutionary movement organized and held together by Emiliano Zapata adopted land restitution as its main plank (J. Womack 1968; G. Huizer 1970), and though the bourgeois constitutionalists ultimately gained complete control, the new constitution incorporated land reform, as well as improved conditions for the working class. But there was no guiding ideology. Though the power of the *hacendados* was greatly reduced and wholly eliminated from certain areas, and the advance of foreign ownership and control was decisively checked, the urban bourgeoisie were the real victors. Many of the benefits gained by the peasantry were on the way to being lost by 1930. The most outstanding result of the Mexican revolution was the forging of a new nationalism in which the Indians had a firm place; this new mood was most dramatically expressed in a flowering of the arts, and Mexico's revolutionary painters, muralists and writers provide its most striking testimony.

The Marxist infusion

Writers and artists were prominent in the nascent communist movements which appeared in Mexico as elsewhere in Latin America in the 1920s. The main source of inspiration came through France (J. Franco 1967/1970R), but the Marxist movement contributed a philosophy and a theory which matched the new nationalism; its influence has been lasting. In Peru, early in the 1920s, a group of writers, journalists and academics began to hammer out such a new philosophy. One of them, W. R. Haya de la Torre, was exiled in 1924 and went to Mexico; another, J. C. Mariátegui, spent three years of exile in Paris. Haya de la Torre founded an international (but basically Peruvian) movement called the *Alianza Popular Revolucionaria Americana* (APRA), with an anti-imperialist programme calling for the rejection of foreign models and based fundamentally on Latin American revolutionary experience. Not initially intended to become a political party, but rather a broad-based union of workers and bourgeois intellectuals, APRA was also concerned with land reform, industrialization, the unity of Latin America and action against American interventionism and commercial imperialism. It became in time a powerful political party in Peru, but grew increasingly gradualist and pro-capitalist; more revolutionary elements split off from APRA in the 1960s.

Mariátegui followed a different path, one which led him to break quickly with APRA. Fundamentally an analyst, he was quickly attracted by Marxist dialectical method and the force of its interpretations, which he applied to Peruvian experience. Much more than this, however, he was also a most penetrating thinker who saw that the core of a nation's — or a society's — ills is to be found in its most fundamental injustices: this led him to argue for the incorporation of the Indian into Peruvian society, economy and literature, and to stress that the root of the Indian problem lay in the land tenure system of the country, which denied the Indians access to the means of production. After his break with APRA he founded a socialist party, but one seeking a middle-class as well as a proletarian base; immediately after Mariátegui's early death (1928) this was, under foreign pressure, reconstituted as a communist party.

The importance of Mariátegui lies in his collection of essays (Mariátegui 1928/1971T), since translated into many languages, and influential far outside Peru. Brilliantly written, they offer a Marxist, nationalist and humane interpretation of Peruvian history, economy, society and literature, penetrating to the bone of the *hacienda* system and the problem of foreign investment and control, drawing wide comparisons intelligently and effectively, and anticipating by many years some of the conclusions of post-1945 Latin American thinkers. He had, moreover, a keen spatial sense. One of his essays is specifically concerned with the problem of regionalism, with the dominance of Lima and the spatial structure of the Peruvian economy; elsewhere he noted the effect of land engrossment by the *haciendas* in stifling the emergence of an urban system based on full exercise of urban functions. His prediction of the future spatial system of Peru — one based on a shift of power away from the capital to the indigenous centres — may have been erroneous, but the analysis is none the less intriguing.

Mariátegui was perhaps the prototype 'neo-Marxist'. He employed Marxist doctrine and analysis, but his frame of reference was national and Latin American; where this base in reality led him away from orthodox Marxism, he was unhesitatingly led. Some others of like mind arose to positions of power; the most important was Lázaro Cárdenas, president of Mexico from 1934 until 1940. By his own later self-identification, Cárdenas was a Marxist (Wilkie 1967: 73), but he kept the orthodox communists in his administration under firm control. He revived the Mexican revolutionary spirit, carried out the land reform that his predecessors had deemed unnecessary, inaugurated a policy of major government intervention in economic matters, introduced a 'cooperative system' and set up state corporations, expanded welfare, and finally expropriated the foreign-owned oil industry in 1938. His successors turned back to a more individualist and capitalist approach to development, but the initiative of Cárdenas has endured. The modern ideology of balanced revolution, and the contemporary rapid transformation of large sectors of Mexican economy and society[5] are its long-term product.

[5] To say this is not to fall into the error that the spectacular modern economic growth of Mexico, the rapid structural transformation, industrialization and urbanization imply a successful 'take-off' without serious continuing problems (cf. Higgins 1968: 635–53). Urban poverty and contrasts of wealth remain severe; land redistribution has failed to create a large viable peasantry, and through a series of devices much land has fallen back under the control or management of large holders and companies: the smaller holdings, and the *ejido* (village-collective) lands are far less productive and profitable than the larger farms. More than half the population employed in agriculture is without

National Marxism was not the only new force emerging in Latin America in the 1920s and 1930s; politicians and other thinkers were also greatly influenced by the Italian Fascist model, and in the 1930s this became dominant in several countries. This form of 'benign Fascism' corresponded with the interests of the bourgeoisie without offending the oligarchy, and its innovations brought some benefits to the poor. The world depression polarized the advocates of change between such corporative-nationalist and communist models, so that except in Mexico the neo-Marxist movement was weakened. It was also weakened by the adherence of the communist parties to the Comintern line, an adherence that has continued so that when right-wing movements became increasingly authoritarian and tied to international capitalism after World War II, the communist parties did not offer a widely acceptable alternative. What became necessary was a new surge of neo-Marxist thinking, building on the foundations of the inter-war period.

Towards a new paradigm: Prebisch, ECLA and industrialization

After World War II, a new and distinctive pattern of development thinking began to evolve among academics and practising economists in Latin America, and was no longer confined to political circles. As N. Girvan (1973) suggests, in his excellent review article on the new movement in both Latin America and the Caribbean, there was a common reason in the failure since 1930 of the old economic model based on international specialization of production and trade. The focus of new thinking was the UN Economic Commission for Latin America (ECLA which began to operate in the late 1940s, and quickly presented a distinctive statement of position (R. Prebisch 1949/1950T/1962R); ECLA Report 1949, Part I). The central argument was an attack on traditional theories of international trade

---

land, and the proportion is rising despite massive emigration to the towns. Thirty-one per cent of holdings occupied only one per cent of the land in 1960; there are new movements of peasant unrest. But the reform has had other consequences, including, indirectly, the creation of a rural bourgeoisie mostly located in the smaller towns (R. Stavenhagen 1973: 129–71). Though contrasts remain striking in Mexico, above all in the regions south of the capital, no observer can doubt that the 'continuing revolution' of Mexican life and economy is leading to major transformations whose end result is not yet in sight.

(cf. Viner 1937), in which specialization is assumed to convey equal benefits to its participants, the primary producer no less than the industrial. This led in three main directions: first, an analysis of trade relations among countries on the basis of 'centre-periphery' imbalance, most specifically in regard to the 'terms of trade'; second, a strong emphasis on industrialization with the objective of rectifying this imbalance; third, and somewhat later, a concentration on the social and structural problems of underdevelopment. Other lines of argument included the financial problems of external financing and inflation, and the advantages of economic integration among the countries of the region in order to enlarge markets for industrial produce.[6]

The basis of the 'centre-periphery' argument, in this context, was that technical progress has been concentrated at the 'centre' and has had the effect there of diminishing the share of primary inputs in the value of end products. This has led to a progressive deterioration in the 'terms of trade' experienced by the primary producers, so that for the latter a given unit of manufactured imports has come to cost larger and larger measures of primary exports. The gain from increased primary production has therefore been appropriated in the economies of the world 'centre', and this situation has even been augmented by the tariff policies of the advanced nations and by the differentially strong bargaining power of workers in the industrial countries, whose income gains are paid for by the importers of industrial produce. Balance-of-payments difficulties are created for the primary producers, and these have inflationary effects.

These views have been hotly disputed, both on grounds of the data themselves — for the meaning of 'terms-of-trade' is not as easy to specify in practice as in theory — and also on grounds of the weight given to this factor in interpretation of underdevelopment.[7] The debate has been highly inconclusive.

[6] An excellent summary statement, together with partial reprints of some of the more important studies, is to be found in ECLA and C. Quintana (1970). An analysis of the international centre-periphery system, carrying forward Prebisch's work to the present, is contained in A. Pinto and J. Kñakal (1971/1973T).

[7] For a general, but hostile, review see Higgins (1968: 277–95). Important papers in the argument that developed around 1960 — when the issue gained force in the depression of the primary produce market which followed the end of the Korean war boom — include W. Baer (1962) and M. June Flanders

But the golden remedy was industrialization. These were the days when industrialization was the main hope of poor countries everywhere, as we recall from chapter 3. It was through industrialization that the concentration of technical advantage in the 'centres' could best be combated. Industrialization would also overcome the severe unemployment problems supposedly created by the collapse of the export base. It would reduce balance-of-payments problems by replacing imports, and would provide goods made unobtainable by limitations on the capacity to import. Industrialization was already government policy in a large number of countries, not only in Latin America: ECLA's contribution was to provide the theoretical justification (ECLA 1951/1970R). In particular, it was sought to justify the production of goods at a cost higher than that of the imported equivalent, on the grounds that for the economy as a whole it was more advantageous to use production factors in this way rather than leave them idle, or use them for an expansion of primary exports which would lead only to a fall in received price. The problem of shortage of capital, and its best application in conditions of surplus labour (cf. Lewis 1954), was seen as central, and this in turn led to an encouragement of foreign financing and direct investment, and hence to what has been called 'industrialization by invitation'.

Policies developed along these lines have led to substantial growth, and to the spectacular rise of major industrial centres — most especially in the two largest countries of Latin America, Brazil and Mexico. But while São Paulo and Mexico City have become industry-and-service-based metropolitan centres of world order, dominating the whole economic and financial structure of their countries, the industrialization strategy has had unsought consequences that have made themselves felt in new thinking. Some of these consequences were noted in chapter 3. ECLA (1967/1970R) focuses on the rising importation of intermediate products and

---

(1964), in which a large area of Prebisch-ECLA economics is scrutinized. By this time both Hirschman's 'unbalanced growth' and Myrdal's 'backwash effect' had also been injected into the argument. A recent study of international trade and development, concerned with present problems rather than with historical trends, remains noncommittal but broadly hostile to the Prebisch thesis (G. K. Helleiner 1972: 18–23). He points out that the whole discussion 'has demonstrated, above all else, the difficulty of making historical generalizations with imperfect data'.

spares which, together with the capital cost of industrial plant itself, has raised the volume of imports above the original import-substitution output. The external imbalance, and the balance-of-payments problem, have therefore been aggravated rather than eased. This condition has been worsened by rather indiscriminate import-substitution carried out within the confines of national markets restricted not only by size — and this is hardly a true limitation in the cases of Brazil and Mexico, at least — but also by the low purchasing power of the population.[8] The 'capacity to import' has thus continued to be a limitation, with the effect that dependence on exports has in fact increased: the example of Mexico, which has been able to increase its foreign exchange earnings sufficiently to keep pace with the rising demand for imports, and hence avoid the relative stagnation that has affected other countries, is often cited. Given the continued reluctance of the 'centre' economies to reduce tariff barriers on industrial imports, and the fact that the export capability of many new industries is in any case constrained by their high cost structures, ECLA has now shifted its emphasis toward regional common market arrangements. Meanwhile, however, the drive to export primary products has, willy-nilly, returned to centre stage of Latin American economic policies.

It will be seen that ECLA economics is revisionist, but offers little fundamental departure from standard approaches: in particular, there has been very strong emphasis on national aggregates, only partly breached by a greater concern for internal structural problems which has mainly originated in other quarters. Contributions to this area, several originating from economists who worked for a time with ECLA, must now be examined.

Underdevelopment as autonomous process: Celso Furtado

Deterioration of the terms of trade, the unsought consequences of import-substitution industrialization, the inroads of the TRANCOS

---

[8] It is pointed out that blanket protection has offered conditions of widespread *de facto* monopoly, thus permitting much inefficient operation with high costs, and a large import quotient. This is true also of industrialization in many other regions, though structures such as the Australian Tariff Board, which conducts detailed industry-by-industry inquiries on the basis of which a discriminatory protection is offered, have restricted the impact of this problem.

— transnational companies and conglomerates[9] — and the growing volume of debt repayment and repatriated profits that were coming to exceed the volume of capital inflow and aid, all led to a growing emphasis on the disabilities of Latin American economies as 'dependent' rather than merely 'peripheral'. Given this shift of meaning, it was easier for the new approach to ally itself with other streams of thought, including the strong Marxist streams whose evolution we have already traced.

Though the real flowering of 'dependency economics' took place only in the later 1960s, the germ of the new integrated approach, stressing both the internal and external structures of dependency, can be traced back more than a decade earlier. The bulk of this literature is in Spanish or Portuguese, and has not been translated into English.[10] By the late 1950s, however, and much more substantially in the 1960s, a selected group of authors were increasingly translated, while a small number of Anglophone or Francophone writers also entered the field. One of the most influential of Latin American writers in this period has been the Brazilian, Celso Furtado, and even in his translated writings the changing ideas of the Latin American school can be traced out. At the beginning, Furtado was a revisionist. In an early paper he took issue with certain aspects of Nurkse's (1953/1967R) ideas on the problems of capital formation in poorer countries — initially

[9] Henceforth I use the term TRANCO suggested in some of the Latin American literature, rather than the more usual 'multinational corporation', or MNC. The point is that such enterprises may or may not be truly multi-national; they may have only minor operations outside their country of 'residence', or they may be so independent as to be able to move their headquarters from one country to another in accordance with their best interests in such matters as taxation and legislation. Also they may not be corporations; there are also, as I point out in a later place, many small companies with transnational operation. The term TRANCO originally means 'transnational conglomerate': I use it here more widely as simply 'trans-national company'.

[10] Many of the references can be found in such English-language studies as A. G. Frank (1967, revised 1969), K. Griffin (1969), C. Furtado (1970), R. Stavenhagen, *ed.* (1970) and I. L. Horowitz, J. de Castro and J. Gerassi, *eds.* (1969). Perhaps the most comprehensive bibliographies at the national level, however, can be located in the reports of the Comité Interamericano de Desarrollo Agricola (CIDA) listed at p. 153 (*fn.*), below.

presented in lectures in Brazil in 1951 — where the limited size of the market restricts capital formation, where rising consumption levels make it hard to achieve savings, and where measures to induce entrepreneurial savings are required. Broadly, he agreed with Nurkse on the problem of savings but linked this with the need for import substitution, greater incentives to save and even compulsory savings. He places emphasis on external factors in combating the deficiency of capital. But in querying Nurkse's reliance on Schumpeterian entrepreneurship, he also asks a question of some significance for his later work (Furtado 1952/1954T/1958R: 315):

> And what factors make for the existence of such an [entrepreneurial] class in our society? . . . the problem of economic development is but one aspect of the general problem of social change in our society, and cannot be fully understood unless we give it a historical context.

During the next few years, as an ECLA economist, Furtado remained strongly in favour of industrialization and means to achieve this goal. At one stage, indeed, he seems to have considered a self-sustaining industrial dynamism to have been achieved, at least in Brazil. But a series of collected essays published in the early 1960s (Furtado 1961/1964T) exhibits at once a growing concern with the historical analysis of underdevelopment as a discrete process, and also his problems in isolating the structural insights of Marxism from its unacceptable teleology, on the one hand, and of the value of Keynesian economics in opening up new vistas of the role of the state, while concealing the necessary structural transformations on the other. It was in this collection that he presented a 'theory of underdevelopment' which relies on the manner in which the capitalist system has achieved only partial penetration, with resulting disequilibriation of the dependent economy, but without transformation. A point from his 1952 paper recurs:

> If underdeveloped countries had the chance of investing with an eye to the external market, there would be no problem. The fundamental question, therefore, is the absence of an expanding external market . . . [also] . . . A market is small only in relation to something. And, in the case in question, the market of underdeveloped countries is small in relation to the type of

equipment used by developed countries. (1952/1954T/1958R: 312)

That is to say, the expanding market of the capitalist economies in their own development process is a condition without parallel in modern 'underdeveloped' economies. In the latter, the industrial sector develops in a condition of permanent competition with imports, and the technologies adopted inhibit faster transformation of the economic structure through absorption of the subsistence sector. The industrial sector can grow even while the primary-product export sector declines, for the latter process causes exchange devaluation which spurs the demand for domestically produced manufactures. But this process is self-annihilating. Arguments of this order are expanded further, in an historical context, in his study of the economic growth of Brazil (1959/1963T).

Close involvement in the problems of the northeast of Brazil in a period of revolutionary ferment, and under the shadow of events that led to the 1964 *coup d'état,* then produced a critical theoretical statement (1964/1965T). He begins with a definition of development that departs significantly from his earlier emphasis on increasing the physical productivity of labour (1964/1965T: 47):

Economic development, being fundamentally a process of incorporating and diffusing new techniques, implies changes of a structural nature in both the systems of production and distribution of income. The way in which these changes take place depends, to a large extent, on the degree of flexibility of the institutional framework within which the economy operates.

Dealing then with the 'dialectic of capitalist development', he argues that the dynamic forces are the twin drives to accumulate and to improve living standards. These belong to the 'rising' class, initially the bourgeoisie but in the later stages of capitalist evolution the working class.[11] This can lead to the evolution of the modern

---

[11] This book, written largely in Marxist language and employing a dialectical form of analysis, none the less departs substantially from Marxist conclusions. It seems to represent a high point in the struggle between Marxist and liberal approaches that is evident throughout Furtado's writing, and which makes his work of particular interest.

capitalist democracies, where the interaction of forces creates limitations to capitalist power, and hence institutional flexibility, ideological polyvalency and integration of the several interest groups into the body politic. But in underdeveloped societies where the preceding economy was of colonial type, the structures have great inflexibility. Technical innovations take place in terms of the price structure of the importing sector, and not in terms of the whole economy, as we saw above. In the Brazilian case, the colonial economy was a projection of expanding capitalism based on international specialization of production;[12] it broke down in consequence of the 1930s depression. However, the government then took action to sustain the system by buying and destroying surplus coffee, thus defending the level of employment while capacity to import was declining. This created conditions for accumulation, and incentives for import-substitution industrialization. But the failure to transform the land management system led to continued agricultural inefficiency, continued constraints on the capacity to import, and hence early saturation of industrial possibilities. The export sector financed early industrialization, but in turn siphoned off the benefits, as the inflation resulting from rising but unsatisfied demand benefited those in command of internal supply — who continued to be the established oligarchy. The possible emergence of a new industrial class was further weakened by dependence on foreign technology, and by foreign investment; inflation enabled foreign lenders and investors to appropriate national savings at negative rates of interest, thus adding external strangulation to internal constraints.

Furtado, and others (e.g. A. Bianchi 1973, and the later ECLA Reports) have expanded and modified this view in later writing. Equally important with the inelastic supply of agricultural produce in the home market is the continued reliance of the economy on the

[12] This touches on a matter of interpretation of some consequence in the Latin American literature. The *hacienda* system, and the economic system of which it forms part, are often described as feudal, especially in Marxist literature where a feudal stage precedes the bourgeois revolution, which in turn precedes the proletarian revolution. While most observers agree that the forms of the *hacienda* system are feudal, most modern writers — including some Marxists — insist that its formation and purpose are entirely capitalist, i.e. that its origin is in capitalist expansion, that its purposes are capitalist, and that while it employs a set of feudal devices, its appropriation takes a purely capitalist form.

old range of primary exports, mostly of slow growth on the world market, in order to finance the rising and increasingly essential import bill for capital goods, intermediate goods for established industries, and imported produce for the urban markets. Neither external dependence, nor dependence on primary exports, have in reality been reduced at all. This fact has been made abundantly clear by the manner in which starvation of foreign credits and capital, coupled with external action to restrict ability to sell the produce of nationalized primary industries, had such a devastating effect on the partly industrialized economy of Chile between 1970 and 1973, leading to catastrophic inflation and facilitating the growth of anti-government interests among the salaried workers and petty bourgeoisie in support of the 'national' bourgeoisie.

The Cuban case is relevant. Initial industrialization policies failed because of rising import demand and failure of traditional exports; this was followed, as elsewhere, by a new drive to increase exports of primary produce, pressed so hard as to constrain the growth of other parts of the economy by starving them of production factors. When this in turn produced new checks, a third and more balanced policy was adopted, but still with a primary emphasis on exports. A principal difference, however, is the drive to mechanize the export industries to free labour for other sectors. But there has been no reduction in external dependence (A. M. Ritter 1972; J. le Riverend 1965/1967T).

Furtado's disenchantment with the ECLA industrialization policies became in time complete. In place of his lyrical approval in earlier years, he now saw a vicious interaction between a wedge of industrial economy linked both in interests and behaviour to its external patrons, and an untransformed internal structure whose existence enabled both local and foreign capitalists to maintain high profit levels by relying on a 'reserve army of the unemployed', so that their interests became inimical to internal dynamism. The capitalist sector is not moved to resolve its own internal contradictions, and the state sustains this situation, protecting capitalists supported by the internal market from competition, upholding the position of the landowners, and providing infrastructure and a suitable 'climate' to aid the group allied to external interests. He sums up (p. 68):

In short, the social structure . . . can be outlined as follows: at the top is a ruling class composed of various groups of interests, in many respects antagonistic to each other, therefore unable to form a plan for national developments, and holding the monopoly of power unchallenged; lower down we have a great mass of salaried urban workers employed in services, which forms a social strata (*sic*) rather than a proper class; beneath this is a class of industrial workers, which hardly represents one tenth of the active population of the country but constitutes its most homogenous sector; and finally the peasant masses.

Emphasis on the social structure, thus attained, has become a dominant characteristic of the school. As we shall see, in this chapter and also in the next, it forms the basis of a gradually widening set of interpretations. In the empirical portion of the same book — which has strong geographical relevance — Furtado goes on to show the manner in which events operated in an anti-developmental manner in each of the ecological regions of the northeast. In the sugar region, an improved market led landowners to drive workers off their plots; the workers reacted, very successfully, through the 'peasant leagues', but their gains increased the cost structure of the industry without improving its efficiency and increased its reliance on the protected internal market. In the interior, where the basic problem is rising population on drought-stricken land, improvements have all gone to the benefit of the ranchers rather than the sharecroppers, and have consolidated the position of the oligarchy whose production is of low intensity. Growth has merely aggravated the structural problems.

After the *coup d'état* of 1964, Furtado left Brazil, and has since worked mainly in Paris. In numerous subsequent writings he has consolidated and enlarged his position of 1963, but a certain continuing ambivalence both over industrialization and in political outlook are evident, as in the work of a number of his Spanish-American contemporaries.[13] Two books, the one historical

---

[13] In the 1963/64 book most references are to Marxist works, with special emphasis on the writing of Lenin concerning the role of revolutionary cadres acting in the interests of the working class — i.e. the Peasant League of the northeast acting on behalf of the Brazilian peasantry. This aspect swiftly vanishes from his writing after the mid-1960s, and we find him instead concluding that the political problems of dependent countries 'reflect historical situations essentially different from those through which the currently advanced countries have passed in the earlier phases of their development, [so

and the other contemporary (Furtado 1969/1970T; 1968, 1969/1970T), extend the analysis to Latin America as a whole, emphasizing the principle of development based on the assimilation of technological progress rather than its generation, giving rise in the context of existing institutional structures to (1969/1970T: 251):

> a new type of dualism between highly capitalised productive units employing modern technical processes and productive sectors employing traditional techniques and having a low level of capital investment, a dualism superimposed on the former polarization between market-economy sector and subsistence-economy sector.

Along with the ECLA economists, he now sees the main channel of advance in a conjunction of national planning with expansion of international trade within the region; in this way the disarticulation of national economies might be reversed. But he is not optimistic. In a more recent study of Brazil (Furtado 1973) he is more concerned to emphasize the consequences of dependence in a global context. What is happening is 'modernization' rather than development,[14] based on the adoption of new patterns of consumption by a minority. Consumption patterns now become critical, as in other contemporary writing. The mass of low-income consumers support industries with weak linkages and small-scale organization; the main raw materials are drawn from agriculture. The high-income minority has a far more diversified consumption pattern, based either on imports or a complex domestic industrial structure. The latter cannot emerge with only a limited market. The manufacturing sector

---

that] the outlining of the different conditions is beyond the ideological rationales derived from the experiences of classical capitalism' (1967, 1968/1970T: xxv). This need for an indigenous political ideology is perceived by many, and the search for such an ideology is an important element in the work of the structural school.

[14] In this redefinition of 'modernization' it is taken to mean a process of adoption of new patterns of consumption corresponding to higher levels of income; 'development' requires access of more people to the use of known products, and is based on capital accumulation, and the diffusion of more efficient production processes. It will be seen that his definition of 'moderniz-ation' corresponds to some degree with the reality actually measured by the 'modernizers' whom we studied in earlier chapters.

is capable of most rapid change, but its spontaneous growth possibilities are limited. Being capital-intensive, its benefits are sharply confined; for the mass of the population, the price inflation produced by its expansion against limited capacity to import may lead to a reduction in real income. This much is a reinterpretation of what we have already seen.

How, then, has the rapid industrial growth of Brazil and some other countries been resumed since the mid-1960s, and what is the meaning of the concomitant gain in GDP? This has been done by attracting TRANCO operations, from the USA and, increasingly, Japan, and by creating a demand profile most attractive to such companies. Technical transmission is maximized, and the flow of foreign resources increased, by policies aimed at increasing the purchasing power of the wealthy minority and encouraging reinvestment by this minority, while widening the income gap between the minority and the majority. A reduction in real wages is ameliorated for the proletariat by creation of additional jobs, and enforced on the mass of the population by the suppression of opposition. The position of the oligarchy and of the service-based middle class is entrenched within a type of capitalism dependent on the state to ensure 'appropriation and utilization of profits to generate a certain type of consumption expenditure' (1973: 130). The mass of the population is excluded from the benefits of accumulation and technical progress.

Furtado has travelled a long road, in the course of which he has more than once swung from the side of optimism and participation to that of pessimism and revulsion. Many others have walked with him, and among them one of the most effective spokesmen for the philosophy of dependent development has been the Chilean economist Osvaldo Sunkel. During an optimistic phase in the later 1960s he wrote and revised a paper (Sunkel 1969) which expresses very clearly the dynamic interaction between internal structures and foreign dependence; a later, more pessimistic elaboration of this topic (Sunkel 1973) is deferred to chapter 6. Emphasizing the point that Latin American development has entailed the addition of new structures rather than the internal transformation and evolution of original social forms, he emphasizes the role of the middle classes which, instead of becoming leaders in the mobilization of national life, have resisted change and its danger to their privileged position.[15] He then analyses the critical vulnerability of the Latin American economies to the vicissitudes of foreign trade and capital flows, and the manner in which industrialization has merely increased this vulnerability, and hence reliance on an un-reconstructed traditional export sector. It is as though (1969: 37):

> The structure of manufacturing production is now organized basically to produce for the consumer and the traditional export sector has been left to 'produce' the investment goods. This seems to me the fundamental reason why our economies have become more dependent, more vulnerable and more unstable. (Original italicized)

The central state, though very active in income redistribution, as a financial intermediary for industrial development and as provider of economic infrastructure, has been unable to lift the export sector from its stagnation, partly for external reasons (the technical changes which are reflected in Prebisch's 'terms of trade') and partly for want of ability to develop any truly national development policies, an inability which rests on the nature of its power base. This is a worsening situation, because the power base is increasingly linked with foreign and specifically TRANCO interests, while financing of the necessary support for this dynamic sector rests on appropriation from the export base. Sunkel concludes optimistically that a liberalization of the external forces will present greater opportunity for the creation of truly national development policies; he has not sustained this optimism in more recent writing.

Erroneous theses and other dissents

A somewhat distinctive stream of writing has converged on similar conclusions to the above. This has come from studies of the agrarian base, stemming from a concern that has been consistent from the

---

[15] It may be remarked that Hobsbawm (1968), like other observers, has said as much about the English middle classes; their inability to preserve their position (in contrast to the upper income groups, who have preserved theirs very well) reflects the comparative lack of differentiation, greater proletarianization, greater vertical mobility and — most importantly — the greater bargaining power and purchasing power of the English working class. But the point should be made, in anticipation of the next chapter, that shifting interest-groupings of this order are in no sense peculiar to the Latin American scene.

time of Mariátegui and the Mexican land reforms, but which achieved the serious notice of ruling groups only under the shock of the rural-based Cuban revolution. The resulting anxiety, which led to the inclusion of a strong agrarian reform plank in the programme of the 'Alliance for Progress', was sustained through several years by localized peasant uprisings especially in Peru (Béjar 1969/1970T; Blanco 1972T), Guatemala (Galeano 1967/1969T) and northeast Brazil (F. Julião 1972T), by massive land invasions[16] in several parts of the continent, and by Ché Guevara's unsuccessful revolt in Bolivia. Substantial land reform movements were put in hand by the governments of Peru, Bolivia and Chile, but the force of the wave was almost completely spent by 1970.

Under the 'Alliance for Progress' a series of inquiries into the problems of land tenure and agrarian reform, coupled with other surveys of land resources, were initiated in the early 1960s. These inquiries provided an immensely valuable body of data on the scale of the agrarian problem. Among 8.7 million rural families in 6 countries, 48.4 per cent were rural workers with only precarious tenancy or without land, 20 per cent operated farms too small to support an average family without additional sources of income, and 17.3 per cent operated adequate family farms. Among 7 countries with reasonably comparable data, the distribution of numbers of farms and the area they occupied was as follows:

Type of exploitation	Per cent of farms	Per cent of area
Sub-family farms	51.7	2.5
Family farms	30.1	21.0
Medium, multi-family farms	15.6	31.0
Large multi-family farms	2.6	45.5

The range of farm sizes differed greatly from country to country: farms in Argentina were both larger and with less unequal distribution than in the other countries, but the situation in Chile was almost as extreme as that in Guatemala: 77 and 98 per cent of

[16] These are spontaneous movements by peasants, almost always the members of *communidades* adjacent to *haciendas* rather than the *peons* themselves, onto the land of *haciendas*. Some have been successful.

farms respectively, in these 2 countries, occupied only 7.4 and 27.8 per cent of the land.[17]

Data of this order have obvious implications for the study of income distribution necessary to provide a foundation for the theorizing of ECLA and their former associates. Some points on income distribution are made by the CIDA reporters, especially in CIDA (1971); recent data garnered by ECLA (1971) and even the *Consejo Interamericano Economico y Social* of the Organization of American States (CIES 1973) have converged on similar conclusions. The ECLA study provided the following data for an aggregate of Latin American countries (ECLA 1971: 34–5):

Income group	Percentage share in total income: weighted average	Average per capita income about 1965, in 1960 dollars
Lowest 20 per cent	4.0	60
30 per cent below median	12.4	130
30 per cent above median	24.5	310
15 per cent below top 5 per cent	24.9	750
Top 5 per cent	34.2	2600

[17] Values are aggregated from country data given in the final report on the studies of the Comité Interamericano de Desarrollo Agricola (CIDA 1971). The countries concerned include Argentina, Brazil, Chile, Colombia, Ecuador, Guatemala, and, in the 7-country context above only, also Peru. The farm-size categories were developed in order to overcome the comparability problem posed by ecological variation, and are defined in summary as follows:

Sub-family farms: insufficient to satisfy the minimum needs of a family, or to allow the utilization of their work throughout the year.

Family farms: sufficient land to support a family at a satisfactory living standard, and employ their labour throughout the year.

Medium multi-family farms: sufficient land to employ a number of workers outside the family, but not sufficient to justify appointment of a manager or overseer (i.e. a small *hacienda*).

Large multi-family farms: sufficient land to give permanent employment to a group of workers, much larger than the family of the owner, requiring division of labour and an administrative hierarchy (i.e. a large *hacienda*, otherwise a '*latifundia*').

This somewhat subjective classification does not eliminate all problems, as the CIDA reporters themselves recount, especially in the case of Argentina (CIDA 1965).

There is every indication that these disparities are increasing. It may be noted that the *per capita* income of the top 5 per cent corresponds almost exactly with the US *per capita* income for 1960, or that of Canada for 1965; that of the 15 per cent below this corresponds with values for Spain or Ireland within the same period. Even the CIES study (1973: 134) points out that a more equitable distribution might, on conservative assumptions, increase the volume of savings and of growth.

It is often argued (e.g. Griffin 1969: 276) that an agrarian reform would, in addition to increasing food supply and the size of the domestic market, be the most conducive of all measures designed to reduce income inequalities. On the basis of a rather doubtful calculation, Feder (1971: 47–51) maintains that land supply is no limitation. Indeed, on the basis of the crude CIDA data used above, there were over 50 hectares of farm land available per family in agriculture in the 1950s: however, the range is from 227 hectares in Argentina to only 9 hectares in Guatemala. Such calculations ignore ecological variations, but the potential for a solid measure of equalization through land reform is not in question. It has been held back through other considerations. Engels's 'law' that the consumption of food takes up a major share of low incomes, but decreases as a percentage of income with growth, may be widened to suggest that the income-elasticity of demand for consumer goods diminishes as income increases. Thus enlarged, it has obvious empirical relevance. In the short run, at least, production does not increase in proportion with capacity to produce; as A. V. Chayanov (1925/1966T) demonstrated, the calculus of peasant production is a trade-off between needs and the drudgery of self-exploitation. Needs depend on their perception, and this depends on opportunity, and hence on the expansion of the consumer-goods supply system into

---

The country reports of this inquiry constitute an immensely valuable body of data. That on Peru (CIDA 1966) is particularly valuable. Not many, unfortunately, are still in print, and the inquiry has been run down and terminated. Good general summaries are, however, to be found in S. Barraclough and A. Domike (1966/1970R), and the results of the survey are summarized, ably and with fierce partisanship, by E. Feder (1971). Material collected for the CIDA inquiry, but not used in view of its contraction and closure, sometimes appears in separate places. One example is material on Mexico, briefly discussed by R. Stavenhagen (1970/1973R: 127–72).

new regions. This cannot happen at once, and given the constraints on consumer-goods supply in Latin American countries which we have discussed, the necessary expansion requires the production that only expansion of consumer-goods supply can produce. Thus while modest results in terms of enlargement of a market system have been reported from land reform areas in Peru and especially Bolivia (D. A. Preston 1969), any country embarking on a massive land reform that breaks up the integrated structures of capitalist agriculture must expect a short-run diminution of rural supply: the lethal effects of such diminution in Chile have now passed into the lessons of history.

There are alternatives. In Mexico the land-reform peasants found themselves short of capital and exposed to the risks of the market: capitalists were therefore able to lease land, or obtain a lien on its production, in return for guaranteed — if small — returns (R. Stavenhagen 1973: 129–71). Faced with the threat of expropriation in the name of improved efficiency, *hacenderos* have been able to obtain loans to capitalize their estates in many parts of Latin America, and thus have been able to provide the increased production that land reform cannot match in the short term (Petras and Laporte 1970). The success of this alternative, coupled with the lack of real success in the half-hearted efforts at cooperative agriculture, as so strongly advocated by E. H. Jacoby (1971: 169–252),[18] have combined with the mastery over rural insurrection achieved by 'security' forces since the mid-1960s to take all the steam out of the land reform movement.

But the land reform surge at least had the effect of drawing some very useful minds into an area hitherto dominated by ECLA economists, with their industrialization biases. While this may seem a small gain, the widening of the structuralist movement that has resulted might have important consequences for the future of Latin America. The contribution of political scientists and sociologists, such as A. Quijano and J. Cotler to cite only two Peruvian contributors, has already been of major importance in expanding the

---

[18] The substantial failure of the Mexican *ejidos* is a case in point, though some of these cooperative ventures continue to operate with some success (Stavenhagen 1973). Womack (1968) has some pungent comments on the support given to the *ejidos* from central government sources. New experiments in this field have been undertaken in Peru since the 'Nasserist' military *junta* took over in 1967, but their fate has not been adequately reported.

empirical base of the school. The study of the role of social classes has been greatly widened,[19] and this has facilitated the incorporation into the structural stream of other non-economists, such as P. G. Casanova (1965/1970T), the originator of the valuable concept of 'internal colonialism' which presents an opposing view to the internal 'centre-periphery' model of Friedmann. The concept of 'marginalization' of dependent groups, a process by which they are deprived of the opportunity to envisage higher goals or to participate effectively in decision-making (S. Barraclough, *in* CIDA 1971: 5–6), arises out of studies of the unequal division of land, income and power, and has been elaborated by a number of writers; it is now being found valuable well outside Latin America. New thinking, based firmly in empirical reality, has increasingly been set against the 'modernization' theories diffused from North America, and the contradictions have generated a rising anger that has been productive of some very fertile writing.

One particularly influential product of this anger is an article by the Mexican sociologist Rodolfo Stavenhagen (1966),[20] entitled 'Seven erroneous theses about Latin America'; this is an attack on accepted ideas, constantly repeated and taken almost as dogma at the time, which had survived intact despite the rising onslaught of evidence. Stavenhagen begins by denying that Latin American countries are 'dual societies', maintaining that both poles arise from a single historical process. He prefers to describe the situation as 'internal colonialism' or the sway held over the rest of society by

---

[19] This is made particularly clear by the contents of a volume on élites, based on a seminar at Montevideo in 1965 (S. M. Lipset and A. Solari, *eds.* 1967).

[20] This article, one of the best known pieces of the Latin American literature, was a product of frustration written initially in 1965 for the Mexico City newspaper *El Dia* (which shares with the *Washington Post* and the Montreal *Le Devoir* a very distinctive role, emergent from the massive non-intelligence of North American newspaper journalism). It was several times reprinted and translated. The first English version appeared in 1966, in the place cited here; however, the subsequent reprinting in the volume edited by L. Horowitz, J. de Castro and L. Gerassi (1969: 102–17) is more usually cited in the literature. A French translation, printed together with several other of Stavenhagen's articles (Stavenhagen 1973) is also given in the list of references of this book. There are several variations of content, and even title, between different versions of the article.

'poles of growth'.[21] He goes on to attack the 'trickle-down' or 'modernization' thesis that progress will come about by the 'spread of industrial products into the backward, archaic and traditional areas', maintaining that progress has taken place at the expense of these areas. This leads him to dispute the view that national capitalism is interested in reform and development in the periphery, and that 'backwardness' is an obstacle; the national bourgeoisie is concerned with its own development, and has no interest in breaking the power of the landed oligarchy, for this oligarchy aids in the policy of internal colonialism which itself contributes to the wealth and status of the bourgeoisie. Nor is there any identity of interest between urban workers and peasants, for the former gain their higher real incomes at the expense of the latter.[22] The middle class, so far from being progressive, enterprising and expanding, is tied to foreign consumption patterns; policies designed to strengthen the middle class reinforce the ruling class, and do not lead to any 'diffusion' of development.

The convergence with the economists is obvious. In a later article, Stavenhagen (1972/1973R) has concluded that all polarizations in Latin America — social, spatial and economic — are increasing.

[21] This concept is fully developed by Casanova, cited above, who maintains that the several concepts of marginality, dualism and pluralism are inter-related, and form elements of a deeper problem — the dominance of certain groups by others. This is persistent, despite revolution, reform, industrialization and development; it defines many of the characteristics of society and internal polity in Mexico and, by extension, in other lands. Surprisingly, this approach seems to have had little effect on the essentially static theory of plural society, as developed by modern anthropologists in the West Indies and Africa.

[22] This is, of course, the phenomenon of the 'bourgeois proletariat' or 'labour aristocracy' of the Marxists (cf. Lenin 1917/1926T/1970R). A very parallel situation is described for central Africa by G. Arrighi (1968; 1970), albeit in a less 'developed' region: the fully proletarianized workers benefit from the policies of income concentration which marginalize the semi-proletarianized 'circular migrants'. This process replaces a former condition akin to that described by W. A. Lewis (1954) when all labour was marginal to the capitalist economy; the intervention of the TRANCOs is primarily responsible for the change, which attaches a proportion of the proletariat to policies opposed to any spreading of income to benefit the mass of the population. Arrighi is also concerned, as Stavenhagen is, with the importance of an historical and socio-logical perspective in development study: all theory must be 'located in time'.

Partial land reform has failed, mainly because of the success of the production efficiency school,[23] but this success is achieved at the cost of eliminating a growing number of small farmers from the market, leading to further marginalization, proletarianization, and exodus to the cities. The large-scale sector is also gaining strength in industry and commerce. But it is wrong to regard the marginalized population as excluded from the system; they form part of it, but in its lowest, least rewarding and most dependent niche. Marginalization is an inescapable accompaniment of 'dependent development', facilitated by international aid in its present form, the TRANCOs, and a growing number of right-wing governments. All ruling interests are increasingly opposed to structural change. Though he still hoped to see an autonomous national capitalism on the lines sought by Sunkel a few years earlier, he found the strongest hope in an indigenous revolutionary socialism — one which would not, however, lead to the adoption of yet more foreign models.

The Caribbean version: plantation economy and branch plant
In almost complete detachment from the Latin American school, parallel but more restricted trends of thinking have been in progress in the Anglophone Caribbean. There is a similar prehistory among politicians and writers: one of the most trenchant was the Trotskyist historian of the Haitian revolution, C. L. R. James (1938/1963R), who in many writings linked the 'yes men' of the colonial system together with the plantocracy. The industrialization model was taken up after World War II, just as in Latin America; W. A. Lewis (1950) was its initial and most consistent advocate. After independence a national bourgeoisie took control, and this group retained and even enlarged the economic and cultural ties with the metropole. Dependence on foreign trade increased, and income differentials widened to levels perhaps exceeding even those of Latin America. The problem of unemployment, on the other hand, grew steadily worse, even in countries with the greatest growth in GDP.[24]

---

[23] Feder (1971) analyses this question in much greater detail than Stavenhagen.

[24] There is a very large literature on the Caribbean, setting out various interpretations of problems and prospects. Perhaps the most penetrating single source, though from a Marxist viewpoint and by an expatriate-resident scholar,

A new wave of thinking began a little later than in Latin America, in the 1960s. It was greatly influenced in its early stages by the work of the English economist Dudley Seers (1963; 1964) on the effects of large-scale business, and mineral development, in small, open economies. There was a preoccupation with small size of national economy, natural in this region, and it led to a quick rejection of the 'closed economy' assumptions of growth theory and its offshoots. The first major theoretical statement was that of W. G. Demas (1965), constituting a thorough analysis of the policy options open to small countries. He saw structural transformation[25] as the essential ingredient of self-sustained economic growth, and this is hard to achieve in a small economy because of skewed resource distribution, the need to specialize in order to take advantage of economies of scale, the corresponding dependence on international trade and the small size of the internal market. He advocated integration of the region in a 'common market' system as the most hopeful escape from this trap, and has since worked consistently toward this end.[26]

---

is the historical survey by G. K. Lewis (1968). Foreign dependence is more specifically examined by E. de Kadt, *ed.* (1972), and more deeply in articles and monographs by Norman Girvan, published by the Institute for Social and Economic Research. The Institute's journal, *Social and Economic Studies,* has become a major vehicle for the publication of modern Caribbean thinking on development questions.

[25] Demas (1965: 19–20) defines 'structural transformation' as including (a) reduction of dualism between the productivity of different sectors and regions, (b) elimination of surplus labour through its absorption into high productivity employment, (c) elimination of subsistence production and the establishment of a national market, (d) a rising share of manufacturing and services in GDP, responding to a changing composition of demand, (e) growing volume of inter-industry transactions *within* the economy, (f) a long-term fall in the ratio of imports to GDP, mainly achieved by reduction of consumer-goods imports, (f) greater adaptability and flexibility, arising from political, social and institutional changes.

[26] The Caribbean Free Trade Association (CARIFTA) has not worked out wholly as planned: intra-regional trade remains only a very small part of total trade, and even within this system the benefit has accrued mainly to the more developed countries. Trinidad, especially, has assumed the role of regional growth centre within this partial economy. The new Common Market which replaces CARIFTA will still have to solve these problems, which smack of 'internal colonialism'.

The hoped-for coordination of external economic policies among the Caribbean countries has proved very hard to achieve in the face of dependency, and several writers have suggested that the contrast in structure between the integrated TRANCOs and the fragmented local economy is a major deterrent to such trends. The separate linkages of each island with the metropole are seen as conducive to disunity. Thinking along these lines has led to an historical approach toward explanation which emphasizes the institutional and structural disadvantages of dependent economies, and their continuity through time.

The leader in this new approach, shifting away from considerations of size toward those of structure and historical process, has been the Trinidadian economist Lloyd Best, both independently (Best 1968) and jointly with Kari Levitt (Best and Levitt 1968) who brought from Canada the model of export-based growth to ally with dependency economies. The model of 'plantation economy' is evolved as a special case of export-led growth under expansive capitalism. Initially, all decision-making, organization, capital, supplies and transport are provided by the metropole; labour is supplied by slaves (fixed capital), and the site of production supplies only the land. The 'rules of the game' permit no significant product elaboration, allow trade only through the merchants of the metropole, and provide a wholly dependent monetary system. There is no structural interdependence between units within the region, and all linkages run back to the metropole. This is a situation of total dependency.

In a somewhat gimmicky manner, this model is elaborated in stages generalizing experience from the sixteenth to the nineteenth centuries. After emancipation of the slaves, adaptation permits a peasant sector to emerge alongside the plantation, but the oligarchy retains control, and dependence is not eased. New staples arise in the modern period, import-substitution industries are established, and a large public sector emerges. But the new TRANCOs replicate many features of the old plantation joint-stock companies, combining organization, capital and entrepreneurship in a single unit with a high degree of vertical integration. Linkages still run mainly back to the metropole in this 'new mercantilism', factor- and product-markets remain segmented, and dependency even regains force.

George Beckford (1972), in a wider examination of plantation economies, treats the nature of the agricultural institution as a critical consideration. He admits substantial contributions to income growth, but finds these benefits offset by structural rigidities which retard transformation and induce a 'dynamic process of under-development'. Resources are diverted away from domestic production, and this is not compensated by rising earnings because most plantation products have low income elasticity of demand, while imports have higher income elasticity. Linkage and spread effects are relinquished because linkages 'jump space' and their multiplier effect is located in the metropolitan economies. This consequence — the loss of forward and final-demand linkage to the metropole — leads to a radical departure from the export-growth sequence as elaborated for North America. Social consequences include persistence of unequal income distribution, because of the low level of skills required in plantation work, a lack of incentive to improvement generated by the loss of decision-making, a weak community structure, rigid social stratification and a general absence of social responsibility. He also remarks on the high propensity to consume imported goods and services, but departs from the Latin Americans in spreading this over the whole population, in proportion to their income.

The 'development of underdevelopment'

Beckford remarks (1972: 235) that the most intractable problem of dependent societies is the 'colonized condition of the minds of the people'. To a great degree this is a comment on all these writers, even himself — as he probably would admit. A preoccupation with past process and a sense of dependency encourage a 'cult of uniqueness'[27] which limits the generality of almost the whole of the work of this school. Writers such as Furtado, Sunkel, Stavenhagen and Beckford have achieved insights which, collectively with those of some others, constitute a major contradiction to established paradigms which development study now has to resolve — as I try to suggest in the next chapter. But their close link with the empirical

[27] It is most strikingly a feature of the West Indies, where an obsession with the slave past seems at times to inhibit positive thinking. But a similar cult can also be identified in Australia, based on a colonial past and isolation. It has contributed powerfully to compartmentalized thinking, even if it is also expressed at times in national brashness or xenophobia.

base has prevented them, even until now, from extending their analysis outside a limited domain. The political involvement of several of these writers has also been a constraint to wider thinking: the ideas to which they give form and theory are also reflected in national politics, and numbers of 'structuralist' scholars have run foul of their governments; several have been forced into exile.

Yet these ideas find many echoes. In the next chapter I suggest that there may be links with an older tradition which remain to be exploited, while in the contemporary field similar ideas are arising in Africa (e.g. S. Amin 1967; 1970) and also in Asia. Even in the Pacific, my own independent interpretation (Brookfield 1972) was reaching toward parallel conclusions, but without benefit of similar rigour. More local interpretations in the Pacific (e.g. I. Q. Lasaqa 1972; B. R. Finney 1973; D. Howlett 1973) call on parallel structural limitations, while a combination of internal with external structural constraints to development is most interestingly analysed by Scarlett Epstein (1970). There is also a 'grass-roots' thinking, even at the most primitive level; cargo-cult theorists, if the term may be used, in New Guinea identify very similar forces.

The unification of a theoretical system alternative to the established paradigm, of which the core must lie in the Latin American and Caribbean work, remains for the future. But meanwhile a number of foreign scholars who have worked in these areas have projected these 'contradictions' into the central arena of development thinking with a higher order of generality than has yet been attained by the regional scholars. A. O. Hirschman (1971) has done this to some degree, but with a measure of resistance which has blunted rather than sharpened the new thrust. Kari Levitt (1970) has carried the 'dependency economics' thesis subtly and indirectly, but effectively, into Canadian thinking. A series of articles in the *Journal of Development Studies* has done much to project the structuralist approach, and the Jamaican, Norman Girvan (1973), in the course of introducing a special number of translated articles to Caribbean readers, has made a major contribution toward synthesis. The most effective interpreter up to now, however, has been K. Griffin (1969) who has not only presented structuralism and its opposing views forcibly in an excellent survey, but has also shown how many conclusions of the reigning paradigm can be reversed, or modified, by using 'standard' logical devices with new assumptions. Though it is specific to Spanish America, without much reference even to Brazil, Griffin's book is the most useful single source on the structuralist approach presently available in the English-language literature.

But it remains true that by far the best known expositor of the thesis that underdevelopment is 'caused' by the development process itself is Andre Gunder Frank, an extraordinarily prolific writer who began as a 'revisionist' economist in the early 1960s but underwent a most rapid conversion to radical ideologies in the Latin American setting. Using to the full a highly developed ability to glean effectively from the literature, and coupling this with his own inquiries in Mexico, Chile and Brazil, he reached the following statement of position within a very few years (Frank 1967; revised 1969: 9):

> Economic development and underdevelopment are the opposite faces of the same coin. Both are the necessary result and contemporary manifestation of internal contradictions in the world capitalist system. Economic development and under-development are not just relative and quantitative, in that one represents more economic development than the other; economic development and underdevelopment are relational and qualita-tive, in that each is structurally different from, yet caused by its relation with, the other. Yet development and underdevelopment are the same in that they are the product of a single, but dialectically contradictory, economic structure and process of capitalism ... One and the same historical process of the expansion of capitalism throughout the world has simultaneously generated — and continues to generate — both economic development and structural underdevelopment.

This process operates both internationally and internally within countries. Frank asserts, as Mariátegui pointed out in the 1920s, that the backwardness of the Indian populations does not arise from their separation from the capitalist system, but rather from their integration at the bottom of an hierarchy of dependence. He argues elsewhere (1966/1970R) that development is limited by satellite status, and hence that satellite economies experience their greatest development, and especially their 'most classically capitalist industrial development' during periods when their ties with the metropolis are weakest.[28] He goes on to argue that those regions which are most underdeveloped today are those most closely tied to the metropolis in the past, where the structures assumed a rigidity that prohibited all possibility of internal transformation: he cites the West Indies and northeast Brazil as examples.

In one sense, Frank elaborates 'dependency economies' into a worldwide interdependent system, much as I am seeking to do in this book. But he does so on the basis of a very simple dialectic; his approach is, in fact, far closer to orthodox Marxism than any of the work he is interpreting. His own ideological position thus becomes rigid, and though his argument is penetrating, he is sometimes guilty of misinterpreting the views of other writers. In a 1968 paper revised for inclusion in J. D. Cockroft, A. G. Frank and D. L. Johnson (1971) — a review and representation of the whole 'dependent underdevelopment' argument in strongly Marxist terms — he specifically denies the possibility that the bourgeoisie in a dependent economy can become a national bourgeoisie, pursuing national interests; it can only remain a '*comprador* bourgeoisie'. The views of those orthodox Marxists who require a bourgeois revolution to precede a national revolution are rejected on this ground, but so also are the writings of such 'nationalist bourgeois' thinkers as Prebisch, Furtado, Sunkel, Pinto, Casanova and the ECLA group as a whole: the latter do not 'recognize imperialism and its colonial structure' and they divert 'all attention from the class structure'. This is hardly fair comment. Reformism is eschewed, and new revolutionary ideas are required. Hence (1971: 425):

> Tactically, the immediate enemy of national liberation in Latin America is the native bourgeoisie in Brazil, Bolivia, Mexico, etc., and the local bourgeoisie in the Latin American countryside. This is so — in Asia and Africa included — notwithstanding that strategically the principal enemy undoubtedly is imperialism.

---

[28] Griffin (1969: 134–5) develops this into a 'growth model' which is essentially a structural modification of Rostovianism. He supports his view elsewhere in the book (pp. 121–4) by demonstrating a negative correlation between domestic savings as a percentage of GDP on the one hand, and capital imports as a percentage of GDP on the other. But Griffin's sequence, unlike Frank's, ends with the return of capitalism after a period of 'independence' in cooperation with a now-strengthened economy which has achieved 'take-off'.

It is a pity that the Latin American school has come to be known in the English-speaking world most widely through the interpretations of this writer. While his use of a rigid Marxist dialectic strengthens certain weak sections of the argument, and clears away many of its complex nuances and uncertainties, it also comes close to destroying the principal quality of this work, which is its constant search for relevance to changing reality. Imposition of a derived framework has advantages for exposition, but it may obscure the search for truth. There is no doubt that political trends in Latin America since 1970 have caused many neo-Marxist writers to move much closer to Frank's essential position, but this is again in relation to changing reality: the growing force of the external capitalist presence, and its deeper and deeper penetration of economy and society, has reduced the options for reformism. But the search for an indigenous ideology has not ceased, even among many who describe themselves simply as 'Marxists': it has been the essence of the Latin American approach from the outset, and remains its strength to this day.

6: Interdependent development: approaches towards synthesis

It is time to cast back a little over the history of ideas. The discipline of economics arose from the search for laws producing order in an economy without centralized control. It achieved this mainly through deductive reasoning from a limited set of premises about the real world, but a set of premises based on the conditions of a specific period in time. It follows (Heimann 1945: 10):

> that economic theory is the doctrine of the system of free enterprise, and originally of nothing else. It is a historical discipline, in the specific sense of the word, emerging at a certain moment and bound to be reabsorbed into a more comprehensive and complex structure of social science as the system of free enterprise is itself transformed and absorbed into a more centralized structure of economic society, with central and local controls in complicated combination.

The aim of economics was both vast and restricted: vast, in that it sought to 'divine the nature of the economic forces in the world, [and hence] foretell the future' (R. Heilbroner 1972: 311); restricted, in that its premises were those of *laissez-faire* capitalism, and in the view of some its analysis is therefore appropriate only to a comparatively small proportion of humanity, within which the capitalist system flourishes or has flourished. Others maintain that, being concerned with 'decentralized controls', it has far wider span, and that the laws of economic life can be dissociated from exclusive reference to any one system of society, the difference being in their application.

This debate tacitly underlies the argument of the present chapter, which is concerned with a search for generalities about development theory, within a framework of world interdependence. Heimann's statement would seem to be supported by the sort of arguments we have reviewed in the last two chapters, in which considerations drawn from history, sociology and sometimes geography have been prominent. But we face the fact that the dominant role of economic theory has not become merged into a 'more comprehensive and complex structure of social science' as Heimann expected. This is especially true of development studies where:

> To be brutal, economists are forced by the realities to seek to impose their own quantitative and testable hypotheses on interdisciplinary studies work in less developed countries, so long as other single-discipline specialisms do not put such hypotheses forward. (M. Lipton 1970; 12, abbreviations spelled out according to stated definition)

What happened was a change which Heimann failed to foresee. The effect of the Keynesian revolution was to recreate the discipline of macroeconomics, and to give rise to the new subfield of growth economics which dominated the development area from the outset, after World War II. Other disciplines, particularly sociology and political science, and a little later even the 'new economic history', became absorbed in the study of growth and its analysis (e.g. J. D. Gould 1972; P. Temin, *ed.* 1973). In the words of the latter's introductory essay, the new economic history is seen as (p. 8):

> a form of applied neo-classical economics. Examples of this kind of analysis typically start with a formal model of some aspect of economic behaviour, assemble data for use in the model, and draw conclusions by joining the data and the model.

The whole theory of modernization proceeded by a comparable, if less rigorous, form of analysis. Furthermore, economics itself changed within the new framework by ceasing to regard state interference with the market process as peripheral to its theoretical concerns, and by incorporating a highly applicable theory concerning state interference into the heart of the new development economics.

The effect of all this has been to open a twenty-year break in the continuity of evolution of other approaches to development study. The new wave swept all before it and has continued to do so even up to the present time: we have seen its effect in geography. Not only did other social sciences become subordinate to the ideas emanating from the 'master discipline', but the methods of the latter led to an aggregation of phenomena into spatial units which has had profound effects. The whole massive structure of national income data, national fiscal policies and sectoral development plans, international aid, organizations and conferences in which the 'country' is always the unit, has meshed with the growth of state regulation and state-owned sectors in national economies to give the national unit an overriding significance, in conceptual work as well as in data use. Furthermore, the same principle of 'spatial aggregation' has been applied at the subnational level. In regional analysis, the central thrust has often concerned the interrelations and flows between spatial aggregates — regions, centre and periphery, town and country. In another range of analysis, towns have become points and their interconnections lines, while 'modernization' has been diffused over a space composed of statistical-collection areas, or hexagons.

There has been a sound and healthy reaction to both the subordination of the empirical base and to spatial aggregation, and sometimes the reaction against one of these forms has come from participants of the other. Michael Lipton, who is unrepentant about the dominance of economics, writes of 'irrelevant macrocosms called "countries"', and calls for the comparative use of data at a village level. Others have departed from both approaches, but have reserved their fire for one or the other. Thus G. Arrighi (1970a: 227), on the question of a-historicism:

> . . . in economics assumptions need not be historically relevant. In fact, they are often plainly untrue and recognized as such. Historical processes fall into the background and are summarized by statistical series of *ex-post* data, the 'stylized facts' as they are sometimes called, which by themselves reveal nothing about causation . . . Causal relations, on the other hand, are not derived from historical analysis, but are imposed from without, that is, through *a priori* analysis: and a set of assumptions which yields the stylized facts is held to have explanatory value, irrespective of its historical relevance. But since there will normally be many such sets, this methodology leaves room for considerable arbitrariness of choice and therefore for mystification of all kinds. In view of this, the low scientific standards attained by modern 'development economics' and, for that matter, by economics in general should surprise nobody.

Two intersecting oppositions are delineated, and it will be helpful to employ them in an attempt to clarify the combined meaning of the several contributions that we have briefly reviewed. We shall not get far in this small book, written from the edges of development theory and dipping in here and there to sample the contents, but the attempt may be useful. On the one hand, we seem to have a dialectic between model-based and empirically based approaches; focused around the question of the use of history; on the other, there is an evident distinction to be drawn between spatially aggregative approaches and analysis through individual units, structures and institutions — which we may call the macro/micro dialectic.[1] Clearly, the two planes of differentiation intersect, but between them they seem to sum up the basis for a comparative review and synthesis of the ideas that we have discussed. In the course of analysis on these lines, I hope also to find an integrative principle in the concept of 'interdependent development', within which all these contributions may have a place.

Development and change in history and in theory

Economic development and economic history

We have noted that until World War II, the subject of 'economic development' was widely regarded as forming part of the field of economic history. At an earlier period, however, a substantial part of economic and social theory was rooted in historical research, the most important contributor being Marx himself — outstandingly in his study of pre-capitalist economic formations, which was not published until long after his death (Marx 1939–41/1964T, with Hobsbawm). Max Weber's famous studies of the protestant ethic and the rise of capitalism, and Werner Sombart's work on capitalism, belong to the same basic methodological stream — different though their philosophy and conclusions might be. Clément Juglar was the first to recognize the phenomena of business cycles, by a pioneer study in quantitative economic history in 1860. The work of these early writers had little to do with development as it is now

[1] I have elsewhere (Brookfield 1973b) argued that the real meaning of the macro/micro distinction is not one of scale, but rather of aggregation or disaggregation. Thus a study of the economy of the Republic of Nauru, taken as a unit, is a rather extreme case of a macro-study; a study of the structure and operation of Rio Tinto Zinc, taken as a single organized unit, would be an extreme case of a micro-study. Most examples, however, would correspond more readily with the conventional meaning of the two terms.

understood, but it established a foundation for more disciplines than economics alone. The same is true of certain primary sources in the history of social classes under industrialization. Outstanding among these, not only by its penetrating observation but also by its theoretical structure, is F. Engels's *The condition of the working class in England*, first published in 1845; this work is the direct antecedent of the more numerous reports by observers and participant observers of the condition of the poor in the 'developing countries' of our own time.

By the early twentieth century, a growing understanding of the nature and concomitants of change in the industrialized countries was supplemented by a body of literature on the economic and social history of countries in the world 'periphery', and by informed accounts of contemporary conditions.[2] This body of writing was greatly enlarged in the inter-war period, but it is symptomatic of the prevailing anti-historicism of the development field that it has been virtually ignored. One reason is certainly that few of these writers attempted higher generalization approaching theory. A few that did have not been ignored, outstandingly Innis on Canada and Boeke and Furnivall on Indonesia, or Mariátegui on Peru at a different level. Little of what they said, however, has been taken up by the economists of development: the linkages from their work to the present run around the central core of development theory.[3]

My first proposition, then, is that the longest strands of continuity in development study run from distant nineteenth-century roots, through the pre-1945 economic historians of colonial areas and the industrial revolution, to the modern structuralists. There have been many branching strands. They have included the

[2] Certain of these latter had important results. One small example was the exposure of conditions of indentured Indian labourers in J. W. Burton, *The Fiji of today* (London, 1910), which did much to sharpen agitation against the disabilities of emigrant workers in India and contributed substantially to the termination of the system a few years later.

[3] In the countries of the 'periphery', less of the writing of this period has been superseded by modern research than in the richer countries, with their much higher density of scholars. Even in Australia, where there has been a lot of modern historical writing, the student of development differentials can still obtain much insight from E. O. G. Shann's pioneer *Economic history of Australia*, published in 1930.

entire debate about cultural, social and structural pluralism, the interpretative historical anthropology pioneered by Geertz, and even export-based growth theory, though this latter has meshed more closely with industrial analysis. Dependency economics originated with problems in the theory of international trade, but has become integrally a part of the structural school. The central characteristic that links this work together is the emphasis on social structure and its transformation, on the interrelation of social and economic systems, and on the search for the locus of power.

To write of this work as constituting a 'stream of thought' is not to endow it with unity. It is in the very nature of ideas derived from empirical generalization that they lack the coherence of deductive systems. But the relevance of the generalization to reality is of a high order, and the collective contribution is substantial. We can perhaps draw a broad distinction between those who have put primary weight on ascribed differences of class, race or culture, and those whose emphasis leans toward the common external force of the international capitalist system — which brings different initial structures into a common behavioural response — but the difference should not be over-emphasized. Boeke stressed culturally dependent behavioural differences between Indonesians and Europeans, and much of the hostility which his ideas have aroused seems to stem from his use of the concept of culture to explain the disadvantages of a marginalized population. But Boeke also explained these disadvantages by reference to the locus of power within the economic system. The evolution of plural society theory has departed from the 'developmental' stream by taking off from Furnivall's neutral insistence on the lack of a shared social will, so that continuity depends on government and on the balance achieved in the market place; an opposing group of writers criticized the absence of a common social will, and preferred an interpretation in terms of the theory of social stratification, or a combination of the two approaches.[4] But Furnivall also stressed, more specifically than

---

[4] Much of this large literature has a static rather than a dynamic quality, although a few writers, such as Leo Kuper, stressed the evolutionary potential of a class/caste situation. Particular landmarks in the discussion may be located in the more general chapters of M. G. Smith (1965), L. Kuper and M. G. Smith, *eds.* (1969) and L. Plotnicov and A. Tuden, *eds.* (1970), within which most of the views are clearly stated and surveyed.

Boeke, the role of an exploitative capitalism lacking in any social responsibility, in generating the conditions of dependency. This structural bias is prominent in Dutch work on Indonesia (e.g. W. F. Wertheim 1956; H. O. Schmitt 1962) and has also been taken up by some Indonesian scholars and foreign researchers. Clifford Geertz's (1963a; 1963b; 1965) work is illuminated by it more than most commentators — including myself — have recognized; his theory of 'agricultural involution' is also a theory of societal and ecological response to the pressures of marginalization under capitalist development, as W. R. Armstrong and T. G. McGee (1968/1971R) have correctly pointed out in the course of expanding Geertz's involution thesis in an urban context.

It is in the southeast Asian literature that the principal links between the older and the newer structural streams are to be found, but a few examples taken almost at random may be located elsewhere. The work of R. E. Baldwin and G. Arrighi in central Africa, to which I have referred above, is a particularly obvious illustration. However, so strong is the regional separation of the literature, and so massive the intrusion of development economics, that for the most part we are dealing with independent evolution of related ideas rather than with linkages, except of the most indirect sort. Sometimes connections can be traced through Marx himself, and even this much of a common root is often lacking. We should perhaps look to convergence rather than to continuity, and note not only parallel writing in and about the dependent countries and economies, but also the sort of structural reinterpretations that are appearing from time to time in the economic history of 'developed' regions.[5] In this latter area we might take particular note of E. J. Hobsbawm's (1968) treatment of Wales and Scotland,[6] and of the relative decline of Britain itself. In his reinterpretation of modern British economic history it is tempting to see not only the

[5] A marginal example here, but a particularly interesting one, is L. H. Fuchs's (1961) social history of Hawaii, an 'interpretation' which seems to have no connection whatever with the rest of the work discussed here, but which differs sharply in approach from the more traditional histories of the '50th State', and reaches conclusions which closely parallel those of students of Indonesia and Latin America.

[6] And also his scattered comments on the economic history of Ireland, which is otherwise excluded from his frame of reference.

continuity of his own long-established directions of inquiry but also perhaps some reflection of his more recent interest in Latin America.

Economy as 'instituted process'

Somewhat apart from the rest of this 'historical prose' — as some commentators disparagingly describe it — is the contribution of Karl Polanyi. A central theme runs through his work: the uniqueness, inhumanity and destructiveness of the free-market economy. His immensely stimulating study of the meaning of the industrial revolution (K. Polanyi 1944) has its core in a profound analysis of the Speenhamland poor law system of 1795 which guaranteed a minimum wage for rural workers and unemployed alike provided that they remained on the land.[7] The effect was to check the formation of a national labour market, and this continued until the abrupt reversal of policy in 1834, by which time, with growing underemployment, the rural masses were largely pauperized. The *laissez-faire* economy was then swiftly brought into being by deliberate state action, proletarianizing the workers, forcing other countries to drop trade barriers, and establishing the automatic gold standard. Polanyi sees Speenhamland as an attempt by the squirearchy to protect the old order, and retain cheap and tied labour. After its failure, the self-regulating economy was almost at once subjected to new forms of restriction, through acts regulating employment, the emergence of trade unions and the beginnings of public enterprise, and much later the return of international trade restrictions and the re-establishment of national control over currencies. This followed spontaneously but of necessity: '*laissez-faire* was planned; planning was not' (p. 141). The impact of a self-regulating market was so violent that society immediately, and without any change of opinion, had to begin the task of its own protection.

The more far-reaching consequence of establishing a market economy was the creation of world interdependence. Proletarianiz-ation of the industrial populations demanded an expansion of trade and markets that could only be achieved by exporting the system to new lands. Here, too, it was necessary to establish factor

[7] A briefer review of the Speenhamland controversy is to be found in Hobsbawm 1968: 82–6. This downgrades the effects of Speenhamland proposed by Polanyi, and puts them into a wider context of forces.

markets — to detach man from land, dissolving 'the body economic into its elements so that each element could fit that part of the system where it is most useful' (p. 179). The old mercantilist system had done this in some measure, but its motivation was the creation of a buyers' market in the metropoles. To this was now added the establishment of a sellers' market for industrial produce. But the need to sell in order to buy generated massive new supply of foodstuffs and raw materials, leading industrial countries later to return to protectionism in order to avoid total dislocation of their own societies. Free trade was soon a thing of the past.

Though Polanyi saw sectional interests as the vehicle of change, he saw classes as mobile in response to the changing needs of society as a whole. Standing and rank, status and security, seemed to him more important than economic motives in explaining class behaviour, and he also stressed the need of classes to obtain the support of other classes — in contrast to the doctrine of class war. In the same line of reasoning, cultural degeneration and the destruction of social systems are of greater consequence than economic exploitation alone. The destruction of English rural society was the unintended consequence of the Speenhamland system, and its effect was to pave the way for subsequent proletarianization. By the same token, we find in the expansion of the system abroad the same 'smashing up of social structures in order to extract the labour from them' (p. 164). But the politically unorganized colonial states could not protect themselves from the self-regulating market economy in the same way as the organized states of Europe: Polanyi therefore sees the revolt against imperialism as mainly an attempt to acquire the political status necessary to obtain shelter.[8]

[8] Polanyi's treatment of the international aspects of the market system is nowhere integrated, but is scattered through the book. He makes no reference to the mass of colonial legislation and practice, some of it as early as the 1870s, designed to offer some measure of protection to the colonial societies from these very disruptions. He leaves us with the contradiction between economic progress, but greater destruction of society, in India after the removal of the monopolistic East India Company, and the break-up of native lands elsewhere, but makes no reference to regulations designed to limit both land and labour markets that were already coming into being. Yet the argument runs parallel: regulation in the colonies began seriously to arise just as the self-regulating market economy was achieving its maximum impact: again, there was no real change of opinion, but the impact was so violent that

This analysis focused Polanyi's attention on forms of organization alternative to the market system, and the germs of thought already evident in the 1940s were then developed into a joint inquiry which he led, the results of which constitute his major contribution to theory (K. Polanyi, C. M. Arensberg and H. W. Pearson, *eds*. 1957; K. Polanyi 1968). In an essay central to the 1957 volume — with the title used for this subsection — Polanyi argued that economic theory should not be restricted to the price-fixing market system. Economy is simply 'an instituted process of interaction between man and his environment, which results in a continuous supply of want satisfying material means' (1957: 248). Three forms of transaction are envisaged: reciprocity, or movement through 'gift' between symmetrical individuals or groups; 'redistribution', or movement into a centre and out again; 'exchange', dependent on the atomistic price-fixing mechanisms of the market economy. Each requires its own system of social institutions. In the absence of a system of price-fixing markets, the whole calculus of modern economics is inapplicable.

This system of thought, and its corollaries, have been taken up and argued far more extensively in anthropology than in any other discipline. But its relative neglect in the study of complex societies and their development may be drawing to an end. Several of us have found it useful in discussions of the interrelationships of a so-called 'dual economy'.[9] Polanyi himself called attention to the fact that different systems may be found side by side in the same area and among the same population. This has been interestingly taken up by David Harvey (1973) in a manner relevant to this discussion. Seeking a theory of modern urbanism, Harvey finds inadequate explanation in market exchange, and identifies elements of reciprocity and redistribution so that the basic lineaments of residential structure in a modern metropolis 'can be interpreted only as the result of

---

some protection became necessary almost at once. It should also be noted that, writing in the 1940s, he did not foresee the weak power of political independence in offering shelter against a restructured world capitalism that later became evident. His treatment of the system internationally is suggestive, but incomplete.

[9] I made particular use of Polanyi's analysis of transaction modes in my study of Melanesia (Brookfield with Hart 1971).

individuals turning to the criteria of a rank society to differentiate themselves in the face of a homogenizing market process' (p. 281). In a pioneer attempt to comprehend a modern revolution as significant as the earlier one with which Polanyi was concerned, Harvey also concludes that cities are founded on the 'exploitation of the many by the few'. We see here possibilities of a convergence between interpretative economic history, development study and the comprehension of modern urbanism that is just beginning to emerge to light, but which has immense possibilities for the future. The key is 'operational structuralism', a method that has only begun to be clarified adequately for general use. I return to it below.

Economists as revisionists

In discussing the 'new economics' of the Latin American and Caribbean structuralists, Norman Girvan (1973: 24) asked a pointed question:

> Why then, did the new economics begin with a reaction against metropolitan economics, rather than take it as a starting point? It seems that the reason for this, basically, was not because metropolitan economics was irrelevant to the underdeveloped countries, but rather because it was irrelevant *to the developed countries themselves*. . Thus the search for a 'relevant' economics for the underdeveloped countries becomes a search for a relevant and valid economics for the metropolitan economies as well. (Italics in original)

This is to say that if a comprehension of structures, transformations and interrelationships is essential in the dependent economies, it must also be important for an understanding of the metropolitan economies. This is not a new idea: some elements of it can be found in Schumpeter's writings; Perroux's work implied it; the export-base group followed such a method without discussing its implications. Polanyi's insistence on the narrow historical relevance of the 'self-regulating market economy', and on the fact that it *never* in fact operated as in theory because of the reaction of society to its destructive effects, underlines this argument. But no one has yet stated the almost obvious facts more clearly than J. K. Galbraith, in a series of publications of which *The new industrial state* (J. K. Galbraith 1967) has been the most influential.

To Galbraith, the need for new thinking is obvious because the assumptions of economic theory are irrelevant to the structure of modern business. Whereas in 1900 the small, competitive firm still dominated capitalist business except in mining, transportation and heavy industry, by 1970 a very great range of primary production, manufacture and even services has been reorganized into a dominant, corporate, sector and a small-business sector that has become peripheral. The new industrial system rests primarily on the new technology, which makes necessary the more and more intricate subdivision of tasks, and demands more and more complex organization. Industrial planning requires that the 'self-regulating market' be superseded — by contract and the internal transaction made possible through vertical and horizontal integration, by internal financing, and by the establishment of control over the consumer by product-standardization and advertising.[10] The labour market is partly superseded by syndicalization. In all this, large size is the most obvious requirement for effective planning.

Hence arises Galbraith's central argument: the appropriation of power by what he calls the 'technostructure' — the collective of executives and specialists in whom decision-making comes to rest. This collective has replaced both the Schumpeterian entrepreneur and the Marshallian risk-bearing capitalist. He argues that (p. 67):

> Power goes to the factor which is hardest to obtain or hardest to replace. In precise language it adheres to the one that has the greatest inelasticity of supply at the margin. This inelasticity may be the result of a natural shortage, or an effective control over supply by some human agency, or both.

When land, labour and capital were the factors of production, power belonged to whichever of these best fitted this qualification. Once free markets had been established in land and labour, it was control over capital that first became centralized. But capital is no longer the constraint that it was, especially within the large corporation with its self-financing ability. Power now resides with an association of men

[10] The new role of the individual is characterized thus (Galbraith 1967: 49):

> The individual serves the industrial system not by supplying it with savings and the resulting capital; he serves it by consuming its products. On no other matter, religious, political or moral, is he so elaborately and skilfully and expensively instructed.

whose interest lies not in maximum profit, but in growth and diversification which will ensure their own continuity, status, expansion and promotion. In effect, leadership within organization has become the new and most critical factor of production.[11]

Galbraith is concerned with understanding the system itself, almost exclusively within the American context. He does not deal either with the continuing role of small business in the system, or with the international aspect. And in the immense literature on the new structure of the American economy that has now accumulated,[12] the role of small business, and the relationship of the poor to the new economic system, seem to be lesser matters of concern than the interrelationship of the corporation with the state, both at home and abroad. In all this literature, it is not generally in dispute that the growth goals of the corporation are a major contributor to aggregate national growth goals, or that the system ensures affluence, security and opportunity for its participants. There is also general agreement on the need for autonomy from public regulation if the corporation goals are to be secured. Herein, as many see it, lies the principal source of conflict: the alternative — the subordination of government itself to the corporate interests — was for long presented principally by journalists and certain science-fiction writers, but is becoming an issue for more serious analysis in the 1970s.

To summarize up to this point, a considerable continuity in ideas with those of the modern structuralists can be found in the writings of some economic historians of an earlier generation. But these writings have a wider span than those of the structuralists. In particular, Polanyi traced out the establishment against opposition, and the later regulation under 'collectivism', of the free-enterprise market economy. He argued that the effects of this economy were so destructive for society that protection was immediately necessary once it was established. This led him into a search for alternative means of regulating, or instituting, the interaction between man and

[11] This thesis, with its downgrading of the boardroom, has been disputed by some critics, who consider that top management has not become so relatively subordinate to the technocracy as Galbraith suggests. But the presence of a 'new class' is widely agreed.

[12] Among significant items in this literature are A. D. Chandler's (1962) historical survey, and R. T. Averitt's (1968; 1969) presentation of the 'centre-periphery' structure of the American economy.

his environment and between man and man, in which he postulated that redistribution and reciprocity were historically of equal importance with market exchange. More recently, Galbraith has shown that the 'free-market economy' no longer obtains in a system dominated by the 'centre economy' of the large corporation or conglomerate, and shows how the locus of power has shifted through time from the holders of land in the pre-capitalist era, through the holders of capital, to what he defines as a new 'technocracy' which guides not only production but also consumption in the new industrial state. The emphasis on organization and structure has in fact been sustained throughout, and led to some very major theoretical contributions, only a few of which are yet integrated with other approaches, even in 'dependency economics' itself.

Transnational capitalism and national disintegration
Transnational corporate enterprise is in no sense new: the largest corporations of the last century before the industrial revolution were the great colonial monopolies, and the interlocking and integrated structure of production, trade and finance that they evolved has its parallels in the international commercial system of modern dependent economies. Though monopoly has been replaced by oligopoly almost everywhere in these economies, the degree of interconnection far exceeds that of metropolitan economies,[13] and the traditional areas of transnational corporate operation remain well integrated.

control of a mkt by a few producers

However, the expansion of transnational capitalism since World War II has presented a situation of a different order. In a parallel and related manner to the metropolitan developments, TRANCOs have entered a far wider range of economic activity, and many small businesses marginal to the metropolitan 'centre economy' have followed them.[14] At the same time, the control over consumer

---

[13] This is well demonstrated by two inquiries of rather unfortunate history: R. Gendarme (1960) on Madagascar, and J. J. Puthucheary (1960) on Malaya. Both authors suffered for their efforts. Much more skeletal discussions can be found in Brookfield with Hart (1971) on Melanesia, Beckford (1972) on the West Indies, and J. Panglaykim (1968) on Indonesia.

[14] The transnational operations of small businesses have been almost totally neglected in the literature, but they are by no means insignificant, nor are they new. The operation may even run from periphery to periphery. For example, business in the Gaspé peninsula of Québec was for very many years dominated

demand, which Galbraith emphasized as a major element in the planning of metropolitan corporate enterprise, has also been extended to the peripheral economies not only by formal advertising — which is extensive[15] — but also through almost every possible indirect means of influencing consumer tastes. The obvious benefit in terms of access to new, standardized, and often cheaper products would doubtless be cited by the advocates of 'modernization' as wholly beneficial,[16] but there is a price to be paid.

The title of this subsection is drawn from a report, by the Chilean economist Osvaldo Sunkel (1973) on work in Santiago, designed to establish a fuller theoretical framework for 'dependency economics'. We drew on some elements of it in chapter 5. Sunkel examines the origin of high incomes in poor economies, which may arise in several ways: by achieving control of high productivity activities; by securing transfers of income from high productivity sectors to social groups not directly involved; by monopolistic exploitation of goods and/or factor markets in low-productivity activities; or by transfers from abroad. The recipients of high incomes tend to have internationalized consumption patterns, to maintain which they need to establish or retain social structures which will permit sharp income

---

by small companies from the Channel Islands; in the New Hebrides, most urban small businesses are branches of small companies resident in Nouméa, New Caledonia; companies based in Trinidad and Barbados, as well as in the metropoles, have been active in recent years in takeovers of small businesses in the Windward Islands.

[15] There can scarcely be a street in the business area of any Mexican small town — to cite only one example — which does not carry a density of 'Coca-Cola' advertisements significantly below one per hundred metres.

[16] An excellent illustration is the widespread popularity in the American tropics of 'Kentucky Fried Chicken'. This business, founded by a single man and seemingly a denial of the assertion that the age of Ford, Morris and Rockefeller is over, evolved as a piece of true Schumpeterian entrepreneurship in exploiting a new market opportunity. Galbraith would class it as an 'immature' corporation. By providing a standardized good, at reasonable prices, it has had an enormously successful impact among lower-income groups in America and abroad alike. It is not surprising that it should be so successful among middle-income groups in the poorer countries. In the Bahamas, for example, it is reputed that *per capita* consumption of this good is higher than anywhere in the United States.

differentials. The growth of this class is therefore associated with the expansion of a marginalized sector; furthermore, it is also correlated with widening of the external links of the economy.

The rise of this high-income class in poor countries is, in Sunkel's view, directly related to the shift of linkages with the metropoles from their older basis in trade to a newer basis in local production. Just as in the metropolitan economies, the new 'technocracy' here is taking over from whatever national entrepreneurial class may have existed. But the dependent-country technocracy is also dependent, for research and decision-making are concentrated in the metropole; so the new class, and the civil servants who share its consumption pattern, become integrated with the TRANCOs. This is perhaps what one American student of transnational business means when he says, of the possibility of achieving accommodation between TRANCO and national interests (Fayerweather 1969: 96):

> There would seem . . . to be at least some hope that localized third-culture groups or an intermediate subculture composed of international businessmen and the government officials who work with them around the globe may achieve such a sense of unity and dissociation from internal nationalism. . . . A key question . . . will be the extent to which a true community of interests exists, drawing managers of the multinational firm and officials of the host nation together.

Sunkel concludes that the world economy is in fact being reorganized into a new international industrial system structured around the TRANCOs, strongly supported both by rich-country governments and by their allies in poor-country governments. Not only the best managerial personnel but also a new 'labour aristocracy' is detached from national interests. Each social class is thus disintegrated, and those who do not succeed in becoming incorporated in the new system are marginalized.

In contrast to views of this order, we find contrary arguments concerning the benefits brought to poor countries by the operations of the TRANCOs. The contribution to aggregate growth, and hence to national revenue, is the first and most obvious of these. Capital inflow improves the balance of payments — at least in the short term; there may be significant gains from new employment generated, often a factor of considerable political weight. The economy may be usefully diversified through new activity and its multiplier effect. In this connection it is urged that the new wave of international direct investment, in manufacturing and services rather than in raw-material production or extraction, has a very different basis from the old. Whereas in the old transnational economy of plantations and mines (the role of the trading and agency houses, and banks, is usually ignored in this part of the discussion) the principal benefit to the host economy lay in employment, plus whatever share of returns they were able to extract, benefits with the new type of investment are far greater. Transnational investment supplies capital, technology and skills, and guaranteed marketing — all scarce commodities in poor countries; there is a major spin-off through technology transfer, both direct and through the training of skilled workers.

It is becoming increasingly clear, not least from the extensive studies made by the Harvard Business School,[17] that technology, management and marketing are crucial to an understanding of TRANCO operation. These are the areas of activity provided by the TRANCOs, but within an international framework. Opponents of the system agree that technology and management, and marketing skills are made available cheaply, but at the inevitable cost of a loss of local decision-making capability. Quite crucial here is the role of 'research and development' (R & D), an activity quite fundamental to the operation and growth of the new industrial system in view of its high and rising technology component. Singer (1970) has pointed out that 70 per cent of R & D expenditure is in the USA, 25 per cent in Europe and only 2 per cent in the 'less developed countries'. A. Herrera (1972) has additionally demonstrated that the growth of a modern research sector in the Latin American countries is stifled

[17] A large inquiry into the problems of multinational business, under the direction of Raymond Vernon, has for some years been in progress at Harvard University. A large number of articles in the *Harvard Business Review* now constitute a principal source on this topic. A good summary of the approach, which seems to assume the benefit and examine its operation and its problems, is given by R. Vernon (1960; 1966; 1968; 1970), the most prolific of writers on this question. One of his most recent statements, *in* C. A. Girault, *ed.* 1973, adheres to the basic view that TRANCO enterprise is conducive to both growth and development, however defined, and that the conflicts are essentially the result of conflicting interests within host countries, and even among the élites within the host countries.

because of the incongruity of this potentially revolutionary activity with the dependent *status quo* supported, in the interests of their own possession of control over land and labour, by the national oligarchies. It is therefore not only cheaper and more 'efficient' to import the skills of the technocracy; it is also in the short-term interests of the ruling groups to depend on foreign sources, rather than develop an indigenous technocracy. One consequence is the progressive stifling of local industry, administrative capability and research by importation of the more 'efficient' alternative.

There is thus a total and truly Marxian contradiction here. On the one hand, transnational business and the technical and financial aid that accompanies it have very positive effects on growth; they can also be seen as a major agency for the diffusion of modernization through the establishment of 'modern' sectors which will have trickle-down effects and, in time, transform the rest of the economy. On the other hand, we have the argument that they starve the less-developed countries of the opportunity for independent techno- logical development and structural transformation, by creating dependent, high-technology sectors, supporting existing oligarchies in power by means of their attachment to the benefits of corporate growth, and linking 'development' yet more firmly to centres of innovation located abroad. There is, in addition, the already remarked cost of imports of machinery, intermediate products, and services, which reinforces the dependence of such economies on primary exports. The social effect is seen by some as integration into a prosperous international economy, by others as the loss of a nation's soul.

Structuralism and development in richer lands

Views such as those of Sunkel have found abundant echoing noises in recent years from areas much closer — whether physically or psychologically — to the heartlands of the new industrial system. Polarized especially around the writings of J. J. Servan-Schreiber, French opposition to American economic penetration has been especially vocal, and a policy of national defence against foreign enterprise has been followed very consistently by different govern- ments of France. Similar concern at the loss of national indepen- dence through foreign ownership of a major share in the economy have been voiced in Britain, in New Zealand, and more recently but more effectively in terms of a change of public policy, in Australia. But the most profound controversy is unquestionably that which has arisen in Canada, where a massive literature has grown in the last decade, and the issue of foreign – meaning American – ownership has become a major political bone of contention. Kari Levitt's (1970) book on the subject is important not only for its effect on this debate, but also because it translates the 'dependency economics' thesis from her work in the Caribbean to the Canadian context, and in doing so with historical perspective, also offers perhaps the closest linkage between export-base theory, dependency economics and the concept of the new industrial system yet available in the literature.

The Canadian situation is complicated by internal pluralism, but the dominant fact is that massive direct investment by American-based companies had produced a situation by the mid-1960s in which more than half the capital in Canadian commodity production was controlled abroad, the proportion being much higher in manufacturing and the petroleum industry. National legislation has preserved the banking system, but Canadian dependency on American trade has become a critical weakness during the balance-of-payments crises of the 1970s when Canada, itself with a favourable trading balance, has been unable to protect its economy from the effect of American difficulties. A further aspect of the problem is that takeovers in Canada are now overwhelmingly financed from retained profits of foreign firms, with support where necessary from Canadian banks: there is no longer any chronic shortage of capital. The economic dependency is compounded by an overwhelming cultural impact,[18] by the 'international' trade unions formed mainly in the inter-war period, and by an admiring envy of higher American living standards which has, in recent years, been offset only by a sense of detachment from the rising problems of American city and political life.

Levitt sees Canada as forming part of the international 'peripheral economy', in which the dominant institution is the foreign affiliate or branch plant of the great corporation, and in which the con-

---

[18] While this impact is less effective among the French-Canadian population which retains a core of independent cultural life and productivity, the assimilation of French Canada to the 'North American way of life' is obvious to any observer, and a matter of great concern to Québec nationalists.

sequences include loss of independence at both national and firm levels, impoverishment of Canadian R & D and entrepreneurship, and most insidiously a weakening of the nation, as separate groups and separate provinces — not excluding Québec — find short-term advantages in making their own independent arrangements south of the border.[19]

She touches only lightly on the regional problem in Canada, but there may well be a connection. Unlike the situation in the United States, interprovincial differences in *per capita* income have shown no tendency to converge in Canada, even in periods of high 'growth' (Economic Council of Canada 1965). The principal problem concerns the whole area east of Montréal, where unemployment levels are seriously higher, and educational levels, rural and non-rural wages much lower, than almost anywhere else in the country (ARDA 1964). These inequalities, and some lesser inequalities in western Canada, have persisted notwithstanding a massive redistribution of population, substantial incentives and a redistributive policy of 'transfer payments' that has the effect of supporting the economy of large parts of eastern Canada from federal funds.[20] It has been implied that the persistence of Canada's regional problem is aggravated by the deep penetration of the national economy from abroad, with only a piecemeal protection offered to domestic industry or

[19] Levitt, herself an immigrant, sees this quite literally as the national disintegration of Canada, and her analysis — though not conducted on class lines — therefore parallels that of Sunkel. However, some Canadians would still argue that the multiple outlooks of Canada — to English Canada, Québec, America and the Commonwealth — constitute one of the few surviving instances of a nation not based on chauvinistic nationalism. Perhaps this might help explain the ready assumption of an international role by this small country in a recent — though past — time. However, Americanization has become so weighty in the past decade that this world view can now be sustained only by a minority, and with difficulty.

[20] In other terms, the 'transfer payments' policy offsets the balance-of-payments deficit of these areas. Precisely comparable policies are adopted in the development regions of Great Britain where, in some areas, as much as a third of the regional income is derived in this way. *The Economist* (248, 6788, 29 September 1973: 44) remarks that 'Scotland suffers from a balance of payments problem but as it is an integral part of Britain devaluation is ruled out'. It is interesting to note in Canada that the programme of the separatist Parti Québecois has included devaluation of the currency of an independent or quasi-independent Québec.

branchplant industry. The national economy as a whole is not protected, as is that of Japan for example, and the physical location of Canadian economic growth shows the closest association with that of American growth across the border. Such close linkage deprives the Canadian economy of a national framework and frustrates the pursuit — or even formation — of national policy goals. However, as all observers agree, the new industrial system has advantages for its participants and contributes to 'national' growth because growth is the central goal of the system. As Kindleberger (1969: 144) rather bluntly puts it:

> If the Canadian people understand the trade-offs between independence and growth or income, and choose independence, that is no-one's business but their own . . . The way to maximize independence is to close the economy and move to autarky . . . To talk of national independence as an absolute, and to work to maximize it, fails to put the issues in perspective . . . I suggest that companies and individuals should pursue their economic interests and leave to government the pursuit of the commonweal.

This is the ethos of the self-regulating economy combined with the benefits accruing to individuals who participate in the system: the marginalized are a residuum whose care belongs to government, and toward whom the 'centre economy' can assume benign neglect. The separation of public from private and corporative goals has seldom been more clearly expressed.

The Canadian case is, however, an extreme one. More generally in the world the centrally controlled transnational economy is having to give way to a structure exhibiting a greater degree of polycentrism under the impact of just the sort of conflict that Kindleberger outlines. This is true even in Latin America, at least in the larger countries (Furtado 1970T: 39–67). But this partial decentralization does not necessarily eliminate Sunkel's problem. A polycentric, but hierarchically organized structure of 'national' decision-making centres will still be a structure of closely linked 'centre economies' each surrounded by a 'periphery economy'. In some countries — Britain is the outstanding case — there is also the problem of a large economic sector composed of the 'stranded' industries of a former centre economy, organized in a way quite different from that of the modern growth industries, and constituting a different sort of enclave of 'persistent relative poverty'. The complexities of the situation are much greater than can be handled within the simple models we have outlined.

Towards a new approach to development study

The problems posed by what are interpreted as persistently 'lagging' regions and sectors in the richer countries are calling forth a growing tendency to introduce developing-country methods of analysis into the study of the advanced economies themselves. Structural analysis is penetrating ever more widely and deeply. We see this quite clearly in Britain, where the almost independent emergence of a 'structure and organization school' is having quite an important effect on British industrial geography,[21] and is reflected also in some recent surveys published in *The Economist*, at a different level of generality. In France, now one of the world's most dynamic economies, the persistence and even sharpening of inequalities — to say nothing of the problem of French agriculture as a whole — is demanding methods of inquiry some way beyond those adopted by the growth-pole-based French regional planning school.

Particular interest, however, attaches to work in an unlikely area — the new approaches to social urban geography that have been evolving for several years, and which have recently been catapulted into prominence as a leading area of controversy by David Harvey (1972; 1973). We introduced one aspect of his work a few pages above. Concern over persistent poverty, ghetto formation and the havoc being wrought by 'developers' has led workers away from 'neutral' ecological models and Pareto optimality toward a concern with social justice which not only parallels the concern inspiring development study, but also is leading toward some parallel interpretations. R. E. Pahl (*in* Chisholm and Manners, *eds.* 1971) focused attention on the concentration of the poor, and their worsening conditions, within the inner urban areas of cities in the advanced industrial countries. Harvey has made use of Marx's concepts of surplus value and appropriation, and with some reliance on A. G.

[21] For example, in the collection of papers in M. Chisholm and G. Manners, *eds.* (1971), and in a recent spate of articles in *Area*. The study of linkages in the West Midlands carried out by M. J. Taylor and P. A. Wood (1973) incorporates examination of plant size, capitalization and ownership category in a study of spatial agglomeration, in an instructive manner.

Frank has sought to demonstrate that the concentration of the 'transaction maximizing system' in the metropolitan areas reproduces there the differentiation through appropriative flows characteristic of dependent economies. He comments on the 'imperialism' of the Central Business District, achieved by the dominance of its oligopolistic organizations over the weaker structures elsewhere in the city, and also argues that the whole motive force of the system is represented by the rapidity of circulation of surplus value. The modern metropolis is likened to the great corporation whose control is exercised through its ability to maintain and increase this rate of flow, which in turn depends on its continued growth.

This, he maintains (1973: 267), is a qualitatively new phenomenon. Monopoly has always been a necessary feature of capitalism; towns have always maintained monopolistic (or oligopolistic) control over the transactions of their regions, and the stability of companies has required the acquisition of monopoly over some portion of the market. But the new system, in which survival has come to depend on the rate of current flow and hence on growth, puts corporation and metropolis alike on a Marxian treadmill. The implications of this interpretation – or hypothesis – for the structure of development are obvious: if he is right, the centre economy must grow and must 'appropriate surplus value' on an ever-increasing scale in order to survive. There is plenty of evidence that the interconnected system underlying development is becoming less stable – or alternatively that the rate of change is accelerating throughout the system. But national and international regulation of the system is also having to be enlarged in the manner and for the reasons postulated by Polanyi.

The point of this apparent digression is that the sort of analysis now being undertaken into the regional and metropolitan problems of the richer countries is creating a thickening web of methodological and theoretical links with the study of development. On yet another plane, Pahl notes the importance of the 'social capital' of kin links and supporting patterns in Western working-class communities; similar characteristics are called on in explaining resistance to the atomizing effects of 'modernization' in the wider world. And whatever the strength of these interpretations may be, it follows that where we are calling on similar processes we are also calling on structures of related organizational form. That is to say that development study is not a field concerned only with the poorer countries of the world, but is one aspect of a larger study of change in society and economy as a whole. Even more than that, since the 'developing' countries are orientated toward metropolitan economies and dependent on them,[22] what happens in the metropoles and their central cities has organic interrelation with the worldwide process of development. It is to say — as has already been obliquely remarked at several points in this book — that there is only one process of development in an interconnected world, a process which takes numerous forms, which can yield poverty and dependence as well as wealth and growth, and which is as operative as much in the American northeast as the Brazilian northeast. The material is different, the mode of operation varies greatly, and results differ widely, but we are dealing with parts of a single set of forces.

Some questions of method and theory

Interdependent development: some implications for inquiry

The central argument is thus stated: the interconnection of the world economy which has been progressively achieved over the last five centuries has brought into existence a set of processes which have operated, albeit in radically different ways, on all points and peoples touched by the interdependent system. The movement of slaves from Africa to America is one aspect of a set of processes which was also initiating the proletarianization of the English yeomanry; British support for Latin American independence movements, and the subsequent attachment of the Latin American economies to the British economic system, was part of the process which we narrowly call the British 'industrial revolution'; the conversion of many small islands in the south Pacific into coconut plantations was part of a general improvement in working-class living standards in Europe; the gross accentuation of polarization in the Venezuelan economy is part of the monumental growth of the American automobile industry; the chronic regional problems of Canada or France are produced by forces also operating on the marginalization of the Brazilian peasantry; the ills of Western democracy have some common causes, and even direct links, with the collapse of one democratic system after another in the 'developing' world.

[22] The assumption of one-way dependence is challenged in chapter 7, but is accepted at this stage of the argument.

The connections are sometimes obvious and direct, sometimes obscure and highly indirect; but they are there to be sought out. There are always both partial causes of general operation, and a complex of local partial causes. The problem of the 'backward' countries is not to adopt and adapt the technology already integrated into the 'advanced' economies, for this will not create a copy of the latter economies; a different structure will emerge, as it has in the past. Underdevelopment is not 'a discrete historical process'. It is true that no experience replicates that of any other, but the process is not discrete. The German industrial revolution did not replicate the English; it did not arise in the same way, nor did it reproduce the same structure; its new contributions may be said to have initiated, in one sense of the term, the 'underdevelopment' of Britain. Development can have negative as well as positive effects, and there may be both positive and negative feedback. It is likely for example that the forces which led the impact of change in Latin America and elsewhere into what we call 'underdevelopment', with consequent distortion of the economies to the short-term advantage of the 'advanced' economies, may have had long-run negative feedback in reducing the adaptability of the advanced economies themselves.

The principal implication of this argument for inquiry is that the range of questions we ask should be very greatly widened. In examining the development problems of any country or region, we should be searching not for answers specific to that economy, nor for clues drawn from the parallel experience of other countries and regions, but also for clues drawn from economies subjected to similar forces but whose paths did not run parallel. To take one example, I would suggest that some detailed comparison between the experiences of the southern countries of Latin America, and those of Australia and New Zealand, might prove very instructive. The economic relationship with the metropole was for a long period remarkably similar and some important parallels have remained, yet the paths have been very dissimilar.[23] Alternatively, we might ask

[23] No system of colonial development can rank much higher on the scale of exploitativeness than that with which Australia began, and early land policies might well have led the country into a Latin American pattern of land holding. Perhaps the gold rushes saved the country from this outcome. But by the later nineteenth century Australia, with a thoroughly dependent economy charac-

why Australia has never developed the strong regional differentials in income and opportunity which have characterized Canada. Or much might be gained from a comparative examination of 'dependency' in the economies of, say, Iceland, the Faeroes and Shetlands, just as well as in Latin America.

A second implication, which is also contained in the suggestions made in the previous paragraph, is that development problems need to be studied with awareness of the dimensions of both space and time if they are to be understood. The aggregate economy of most economic analysis has no spatial dimension and very little time dimension: it is a point economy in the one sense, and a very short line in the other. But it is vitally important both to establish what has happened, and how what has happened has been distributed over space. Not only geographical space is involved, for greater understanding may be achieved by first employing topological concepts such as economic space and social space before translating these into 'real' patterns on the ground. This also involves us in questions of the utility of aggregates, which is a major methodological issue in its own right.

Aggregation and disaggregation

Schumpeter was always hostile to the use of aggregates in economic analysis, maintaining that such totalities are essentially the creations of statisticians and that their use vitiates the search for actual causation. Many economic historians have urged that the proper unit for examination of change is the single firm. Yet we find it immensely convenient, indeed essential, to employ the spatial aggregates called countries and regions, the economic aggregates

---

terized by serious structural inflexibility, may well have led the world list of *per capita* incomes (J. D. Gould 1972: 34–5). There followed a long period of relatively slow growth and little transformation, then a period of import-substitution industry and major foreign investment especially in mining and manufacturing; among the growth sectors a high proportion of the economy is foreign owned. Yet Australia seems to have succeeded in achieving structural transformation, perhaps with some help from its own relatively important system of external economic enterprise. Substantial modern work on the Australian economy has now been done, but not in a comparative context: yet the most important lessons to be drawn from the Australian experience might lie in just such a context.

called sectors and industries — or centre and periphery economy — and the social aggregates called classes or ethnic groups.

The spatial aggregates called 'countries' have obvious relevance in certain respects, and this relevance has increased through time. They are fiscal and currency units; they have a single legal system and are the domain of single government policies; they are the units of national-level redistribution; they are also entities whose citizens have, or are expected to have, some common loyalty which shapes their external behaviour. Throughout the socialist countries, state monopoly of external trade is universal; elsewhere there are partial state monopolies such as statutory marketing boards and similar organizations whose importance varies widely; still more generally there is state control through import and export licensing and currency controls. State financial independence varies greatly; the degree to which there is a national economic policy varies not only between states, but also very greatly through time. The public sector is of major importance in some countries, and is hardly anywhere insignificant. But it is none the less superficial to generalize the system of economic relations at a state level, and to talk of a hierarchy of national economic independence, or the dependence of a national economy on a metropole or patron.

I have argued elsewhere that a 'country' should also be viewed 'as a frame within which individuals are aggregated, and into which multinational structures are disaggregated' (Brookfield 1975). A very different view of a national economy is thus obtained. For example, a small 'developing' country may seem to have overwhelming dependence on a single export staple. Yet the individual families and many small firms composing its economy may diversify their activities greatly, including subsistence production, production for or provision of services to the internal market, and employment in their total activity mix. By contrast, the units of the transnational organization domiciled within the country may be specialized, but the TRANCO as a whole is highly diversified, and able to support its weaker activities from the stronger if it so desires. Aggregating the whole into a point economy obscures all this, and most particularly obscures the considerable development of final demand linkage that can evolve without any weakening of the initial staple economy. Indeed, the one or two activities that may seem to dominate an economy at the aggregate level may be enclave industries in both an economic and geographical sense, having the most limited degree of linkage with the 'general' economy. In such a case, the principal points where the general economy is gathered together are likely to be the port towns, where we commonly find external transaction and even a large part of internal transaction very tightly controlled by a small number of trading and financial houses. The enclave sectors may be separate from this structure, which is what really matters in terms of the options available to individuals.

Proper analysis of the economy of a spatial aggregate thus demands examination of its production system and the whole structure and organization of its economy. It demands furthermore that this be done with historical perspective, and with attention to its spatial plan. The aggregate view still retains a role and is not irrelevant, but it will be obvious that two economies which look very similar when viewed as aggregates may look very different, and offer quite different possibilities, when examined in depth.

All this is still more true of the 'region' as a spatial aggregate, for in a great many instances the region has no corporate existence except as a collective of parts and a disaggregation of wholes. The utility of regional economic theory (e.g. Friedmann 1967/1972; Siebert 1969), and of regional economics which treat undefined regions as aggregates is limited to a very high order of generality. It is hardly surprising that it has been found to be of small help in the determination of practical policy. It is well known that the very definition of a 'region' has presented almost insoluble problems, as geographers discovered long ago, and as economists have now rediscovered in their turn. Siebert's attempt at a definition[24] is a masterpiece of imprecision in precise language — to say which is not

---

[24] Siebert (1969: 16) defines the concept of a region as:

an intermediate category between an aggregate economy with no spatial dimension and a highly disaggregated economic system defined as a set of spatial points. The region is not as disaggregated as a set of spatial points and therefore allows a simplification in the analysis of spatial structure and of economic processes in space. On the other hand it is not as aggregated as a national point economy without any spatial dimension. The new concept (*sic.*) is an in-between category similar to the sector, which makes possible some aggregation of the multitude of individual firms without requiring a complete aggregation into a national economic system.

But this supposes (a) that the economy can be resolved into a set of spatial points, (b) that firms engage in only one activity, and occupy only one point, and (c) that the partial aggregation does not rupture integrated units. The relevance of all these assumptions to reality is doubtful.

to denigrate Siebert's invaluable contribution to an economic regional development theory.

Yet the existence of regions, and of differentiation between regions, is part of common perception. It is also true, as with such statistics at the national level, that data on regional GDP or *per capita* income are a most valuable first approximation to understanding. Perhaps the last word lies with the 'new economic historian', J. D. Gould (1972: 431), who has a most thoughtful discussion of the value of aggregation, and of the utility of abstract economic models which can only be applied and tested with aggregated data. He remarks that these latter 'are *necessary* but not *sufficient* to explain the concrete detail of historical experience'.

Similar arguments hold concerning other forms of aggregation, though the problem of social classes is particularly thorny. Again, no one questions the existence of classes as perceived groupings, corresponding to a great many observable variables. But the role of classes changes, they grow and decline, individuals move in and out of them. 'Class behaviour' is a generalization on which a great deal of theory has been based, but which continues to be questioned. Once again, it is a valuable generalization when empirically based, but it cannot be projected as an assumption through history, nor can it be applied to the individual case. This may be reasonable in the realm of political argument, but it is a most unsound procedure in analysis or explanation.

I have long been identified with opposition to aggregation within geography, and have advocated for more than a decade the use of controlled comparison on micro-level data gathered in depth as an alternative path to generalization. I sustain my preference for this approach, but as a preference between alternatives rather than a choice between incompatibles. There are problems that can only be tackled at the aggregate level, using appropriate methodology on aggregate data. But there are others, and other parts of the same problems, that demand disaggregative approaches. Both may be necessary, neither sufficient alone, and each can and should feed the other with ideas and insights.

Do we need full Marx?

To conclude this chapter I turn to face directly an issue which has become insistent during the writing of the second half of this book:

this is a question of method and philosophy. Specifically, my preference for an 'historical-structural' approach has emerged very clearly, while at the same time my argument has at times come suspiciously close to dialectical materialism. Yet, equally obviously, I am not drawn toward Marxist conclusions. I seem, therefore, to be one of those of whom Mao Tse-tung (1968T; 57) complains, who:

> have their Marxism, but they have their liberalism as well – they talk Marxism but practise liberalism; they apply Marxism to others but liberalism to themselves. They keep both kinds of goods in stock and find a use for each.

It seems very likely. Most certainly, I do not find that I follow Harvey in leading either from my method or from my interest in 'social justice' toward a 'revolutionary theory' which will lead into revolutionary practice. There is a convergence, but also a divergence, yet I believe that the propositions which I have derived are firmly grounded in reality, can encompass conflict and contradiction within themselves, do have a contingent status and – despite the historical formulation which I have given them here – do hold out the prospect of creating truth as well as merely finding it (cf. Harvey 1973: 150–2).

Not being equipped by the necessary years of study to enter the field of Marxian exegesis, I confine myself here to Harvey's interpretation. It seems to me that the 'contradiction' delineated above might be resolvable on two levels. First is the level of methodology. The method into which I am drawn seems very close indeed to the 'operational structuralism' elucidated by Piaget (1970). I certainly view development as a totality that is a structure under transformation, in which it is the dynamic interrelationship among the elements that is of principal importance. Understanding the nature of the whole is subordinate to elucidation of the processes by which the parts become the whole; without continuous transformation structures become static, and the totality of development ceases to exist. I agree with Harvey that a methodology elaborated within this framework is the only way of reaching an understanding of development that is grounded in reality: no 'universal truth status' can attach to propositions based on the necessity for transformations, and real choices are clearly and constantly identified. Development, as I hinted in my introduction, is simply to be defined as the totality formed of constantly changing and interrelated structures.

But it seems to me that the *necessary* flexibility of this method of analysis is denied by the rigidities which Harvey, and a large number of Marxist writers,[25] seek to give to it. Marx identifies a hierarchy of structures, among which the economic basis is fundamental, so that where there is conflict between the evolution of this structure and that of other components of the totality, the latter have to 'give way, adapt or be eliminated' (Harvey 1973: 292). Polanyi's analysis, which we reviewed above, seems to provide a direct refutation of this assertion, and it would seem arguable that the structures of the economic base are not exempt from the laws of continuous, interactive transformation.

On a second matter, intersecting with the first, there would appear in Harvey's and Marxist writing to be strong elements of an *a priori* functionalism of the sort that attributes an active role to the structures within a totality. Thus, for example (Harvey 1973: 289):

> The totality seeks to shape the parts so that each part functions to preserve the existence and general structure of the whole. Capitalism, for example, seeks to shape the elements and relationships within itself in such a way that capitalism is reproduced as an ongoing system.

This seems to me almost indistinguishable from the structural functionalism of a generation of British social anthropologists who erected social systems into similar *gestalt* creatures. It troubles me not only because I was once a *de facto* functionalist myself, and because the earlier Harvey (1969: 433–46) was of help in my progressive escape from this heresy, but also because it surely denies the transformation of structures themselves into new structures of different form. Is Harvey calling on Adam Smith's famous 'hidden hand' here? It seems hardly likely. But the same difficulty is also encountered with the doctrine of the class struggle: classes are, again, things that act, and propositions about them acquire 'universal

[25] Harvey (1973: 17) merely admits the likelihood that he will be 'categorized as a "Marxist" of sorts': notwithstanding his use of Marx's analysis as a guide to inquiry, and his attachment to many Marxist propositions, he nowhere claims to be a Marxist himself, and indeed such an assertion of doctrinal affiliation would be hard to credit.

truth status'. It is this element of the Marxist doctrine which leads to the necessary place of revolution in the process of transformation.

It therefore seems to me possible to adopt the framework of operational structuralism from Marx without at the same time accepting certain of his basic assumptions and the historical laws derived, through operational structuralism, from these assumptions. Marx's assumptions are based on the reality of his time in Great Britain and some parts of Europe. The manner in which he reached these assumptions is still illuminating, but the assumptions themselves need to be recast and constantly re-examined. Structures can be recognized within the totality, formed of the processes and parts that make them, and make also their interaction and their contradictions. Comprehension of the processes and contradictions does facilitate the identification of choices, and also a certain degree of prediction. But, empirically, it seems to me that we must admit that the structures of the economic base are not dominant in all instances over all others, and also that if we find evidence with which to endow the structures with an independent life, the proper place to seek explanation is in the locus of power and its manipulation, not in unverifiable laws of disembodied behaviour.

It is for these reasons that I am able to work within a Marxist system of methodology, and to accept a large part of the conclusions reached by Marxist analysts as constituting partial truth, without being led to the necessity for revolutionary solutions. I do indeed 'keep both kinds of goods in stock and find a use for each'. If there is a fundamental contradiction in society, I would identify it in the endlessly reproduced, universally present, and continually reconciled yet ultimately irreconcilable conflict between private and collective goals. The recognition of this conflict, which is surely the stuff of liberalism, also does not prevent me seeing the formation of structures, their constant transformation and ever-changing contradictions. But the more fundamental contradiction intersects this totality throughout its domain in space and time. I am thus led to see a range of choices, and am permitted to prefer reformist solutions, that is, evolution, while not ruling out the necessity of revolution where the contradictions harden so much as to eliminate all other short-run possibilities of effecting an amelioration of injustice, or other forms of 'contradictions'.

I have one further difficulty with the Marxist approach which enters the discussion in my final chapter. At this point, however, I accept the inevitable conclusion that my own identification must be with those analysts whom I described as 'neo-Marxists' in chapter 5, and whom A. G. Frank (*in* Cockroft, Frank and Johnson 1972: 432) describes as 'sponsored by nationalist sectors of the bourgeoisie' and as revising 'the imperialist version' but diverting 'all attention from the class structure'.

7: A conclusion that is an introduction

Adoption of an holistic definition of development has important corollaries. Not only is development independent of growth, capable of both positive and negative dimensions, creative of 'persistent poverty' in the one area by processes related to those which have produced wealth in another, but also even development that raised the real income of the whole world might diminish social welfare, most specifically by causing deterioration of the environment. Moreover, the price of gain by present generations may be paid in scarcity for the yet-unborn, as resources of all kinds are squandered, not only to meet present needs, but even to generate new ones in the name of 'progress'.

This last chapter is concerned centrally with the ecological 'dimension' that we have so far neglected almost wholly, because the writers whom we have reviewed have neglected it. Not much can be said in one chapter, and I shall not try to say much. But I want to lead from the discussion of 'interdependency' into a little-considered aspect which is of truly basic importance, and which has, indeed, the effect of reversing some underlying notions about the relational aspects of development itself.

Who is dependent on whom?

There is a popular legend that the 'developed' condition of the advanced countries is due to internal causes. This legend, which is widespread, underlies the other legend of which I have complained, that 'underdevelopment' is a discrete process. It is well expressed, from the 'developed country' point of view, by R. T. Averitt (1969: 62-3):

> Any developed economy is characterized by a close structural interdependence. Although no national economy can hope to be self-sufficient in resources, advanced nations are usually able to supply the bulk of their domestic demand for manufactured goods. They tend toward economic self-sufficiency, while the underdeveloped nations tend toward dependence. Most of the world's wealth and income is generated by the highly diversified

economies of the United States, Western Europe, Japan and the U.S.S.R., and these areas have in common a relatively complete economic structure.

This is a convenient philosophy from several points of view. It permits advanced-country theorists to seek explanations in their own domestic virtues and to ignore the impact of advanced-country growth on the rest of the world. It invites dependent-country theorists to place emphasis on the disabilities under which they suffer, and to pinpoint causes in the machinations of the great transnational companies, or less specifically in 'capital'. Generally, it encourages compartmentalized thinking.

Yet we have seen that a major growth in world trade preceded and facilitated the transformations that brought about the first industrial revolution. The 'international specialization of labour' — and hence of resource use — is what made the great transformations possible. The 'energy crisis' of the early 1970s points up a weakness in the argument which Averitt exposes, but it does so on too restricted a plane. To take the example of agriculture, we can point to the achievements of such regions as the Netherlands or Denmark in attaining very high levels of productivity, and we might well attribute these to technological innovations and their skilful application. But this high productivity also depends on heavy inputs of fertilizer and animal feeding stuffs, and these are of very wide provenance. More specifically, since 1950 the formerly huge anchovy resources of the seas off Peru have been exploited, at a rate now demonstrated by experience to have been excessive, in order to supply fishmeal for feeding stuffs and fertilizer. The overwhelming bulk of this has supplied North American agriculture, and irrespective of who achieves the financial benefit this is an enormous resource transfer toward the already-wealthy countries. Like the use of space, soil and labour in poorer countries to enlarge the food supply of the wealthier,[1] the drawing-off of Caribbean labour to

---

[1] The most obvious instance, of course, is in the plantation system: this is why Adam Smith, who saw this point quite clearly, regarded the West Indian plantation colonies as simply an extension of the home economy — to link this view with mercantilism fogs the issue. Certain rather obvious modern uses include the American-owned vegetable farms established in Mexico entirely for the American and Canadian markets. Still more striking, perhaps, is the case cited in a forthcoming study of Haitian migration to the Bahamas by Dawn

meet seasonal peak demand in the vegetable farms of New Jersey and Ontario, and the whole massive modern search for minerals on land and now also under the 'international' sea, this has the effect of resource appropriation to enlarge the productive capacity of the industrialized countries. To ignore this selective use of production factors from abroad, and its scale, is to fail to understand the basis of the ability of the advanced countries 'to supply the bulk of their domestic demand for manufactured goods'. Our gains, in the advanced countries, have been based as much on widening resource exploitation as on our growing command of technology. The very real gains of our working classes, as well as our capitalists, rest on this worldwide *dependence*. In fact, in the larger sense of the interdependent economy, it is we in the advanced countries who tend most strongly toward dependence, while ability to provide for *basic domestic demand* remains more characteristic of the 'under-developed' nations than ourselves.

This inversion of a commonly held view follows logically from the abandonment of unreal compartmentalization in our thinking. From it also follows a different view of the institutions of development. These can be seen as the conversion of resource-dependence into the power of control, achieved through technology and institutional command over the means of redistribution. But this is not new. Similar principles apply in urban history. Chieftainship and feudal domain also entail command over allocation, but equally entail dependence on the resources thus controlled. Reduced to its essentials, our modern interconnected world system differs quantitatively, in scale and volume, from these earlier models: it does not differ qualitatively. An integrated view over space and time, over the material and non-material aspects of development, demands some substantial revision of many of our basic assumptions.

Marshall: certain American companies operating vegetable farms (with foreign labour) in Florida also maintain 'reserve' farms on the Bahamas, using mainly Haitian labour, the product of which is primarily an assurance against frost damage in Florida. When not required, or when its addition might oversupply the market and depress prices, this produce is sometimes destroyed. Meanwhile in Nassau, the Bahamian capital, the urban market is supplied from American sources.

Towards a relevant science of development

It seems likely that we are approaching a 'scientific revolution' in the development field in the sense proposed by T. S. Kuhn (1962). Reality cannot be resolved within the existing paradigm — or paradigms — and the contradictions are leading to an active search for new approaches; we have reviewed some elements of the search in this book. The sense of a new beginning applies not only in the economic theory of development, and the theory of modernization which has been its 'soft social science' dimension, but also in several applied areas, including family planning, technological transfer and agricultural extension — including, of course, the whole set of notions surrounding the 'green revolution'. Assumptions concerning the ready transferability of innovations, implying their automatic superiority, are being questioned, and a closer examination of existing family structures, existing technologies and their adaptive potential, and existing farming practices, are at last coming to be the vogue. Many of us who have criticized the 'development drive' from the edges might be tempted to crow, but we have weak grounds for such self-congratulation since we have offered no viable alternative and the rethinking is coming mainly from within.

Most fundamental of all, however, is a growing doubt concerning the basic goals of development. This is arising at two levels. Within the poorer countries there is some healthy questioning of the imitative nature of development, well expressed by the West Indian economist, Norman Girvan (1973: 26):

> One aspect of development study that is all too often overlooked is that related to the desired structure of consumption to which the society should aspire. If the goal is to 'catch up with the rich countries', and to 'close the widening gap', then the consumption patterns to which the society implicitly aspires are those of the developed countries. The ends of development, therefore, will be essentially imitative. But suppose it is precisely this imitative pattern which underlies the mechanisms of dependence?

Indeed, for to paraphrase an old saying, what greater form of dependence is there than imitation? But this is only partial, for dependence, as we have seen, is a two-edged sword. The desire of the wealthy to retain and increase their affluence constantly augments their own dependence — and hence also the aggressiveness with which they seek to retain command over the system. This desire for affluence is itself being questioned. The issue has been clouded by the recent upsurge of 'eco-doom' writing, much of it highly specific to limited megalopolitan areas; the more general truth of this writing has been greatly weakened by hyperbole and some thoroughly shoddy argument. The implications of shifting from material goals to goals of social welfare have been more seriously examined by a growing number of writers, among whom E. J. Mishan (1967/1969R) is one of the most penetrating. In such work it is argued that growth should be slowed, in order that resources can be diverted from 'production for production's sake' and applied to improving the habitability of the world that we have. Such views are gaining ground, but rather slowly, and meanwhile the 'development drive' is continuing. And so our land is despoiled, and the soul of our cities is torn out in the short-term interest of profit and some employment, and the long-term interest of 'progress'. The exploitation of natural resources certainly cannot be said to have been retarded. The heritage of future generations (if any) is being wantonly sacrificed for short-term gain in a manner that recalls to mind the old and almost-forgotten weight of criticism directed at farmers practising shifting cultivation. In denigrating the improvidence and lack of foresight of these supposedly primitive 'mangeurs de la forêt', it seems that we were in greater truth describing ourselves.[2]

---

[2] In the same context of forest resources, we might for emphasis note the opening up of what is described as the last really large-scale pulpwood area in North America, in eastern Québec. This development was initiated by a true Schumpeterian entrepreneur who was diverted over the area on a regular flight, and saw its possibilities which he then investigated further. He interested ITT Rayonier in the area, and ITT Rayonier were in turn greatly encouraged and helped by an obliging Québec government, one in a line which has consistently made 'growth' the overriding goal. The story is most candidly, even disarmingly, described in a reported interview with the Schumperterian entrepreneur ('How new pulp and paper projects are originated and executed', *Paper Trade Journal*, 1 November 1971) — a man 'who can see past the forests all the way to the market place': no considerations other than those of commerce are even breathed. Since no similar areas in North America still 'await' development, further expansion of the pulp and paper production — to meet anticipated growth in demand — must now, he says, turn to the tropical hardwoods: new technological breakthroughs are in sight which will facilitate the use of these resources. Most probably, the Amazon forests are in mind.

Among attempts to blaze a new trail in development study is one particularly interesting book by R. G. Wilkinson (1973), who offers what he calls an 'ecological model' of development. His thesis is essentially an expansion of that of Ester Boserup (1965), who makes agricultural intensification the dependent variable of population growth. Wilkinson argues persuasively that all the technical progress which structures development has arisen from the need to overcome resource scarcity, beginning in fact with the need to overcome shortages of wood in seventeenth- and eighteenth-century Britain. The argument is very simple:

> Although by far the most important increases in production have come from increasing factor productivity, there has obviously been some increase in the ratio of capital to labour . . . The ecological approach to development explains this trend quite simply: it is the result of having to use the less amenable raw materials and of other changes which increase the complexity and difficulty of the productive task. (p. 204)

To some extent, this interesting if rather simplistic argument converges with my own, in that it emphasizes the 'dependence' of the 'developed' countries. Such a material view, however, gives little weight to the redistributive aspects of the interconnected world system without which the enormous differentials of the modern world cannot plausibly be explained, and without which indeed the localization of the first industrial revolution in Britain becomes simply a matter of chance. Wilkinson, like W. C. Clarke (1973) in an elegant and effective appeal for the primacy of the goal of ecological equilibrium, does however emphasize the point that economics, and the allocative mechanisms on which it rests, arise from the presence of a condition of scarcity. However affluent the well-to-do have become, however much 'wealth' we have produced, there has never been enough to go around at any stage in the development process.

The 'development' of Amazonia is already shaping up into what may become the most classic of all examples of resource exploitation, carried out by a tiny wealthy majority of individuals, through international companies, for the benefit of the populations of already wealthy countries in maintaining and augmenting their high living standards, and with minimal gain for the Brazilian poor. It will be convenient to blame only the developers.

A disagreement about scarcity

Marxists agree that the market economy relies on scarcity for its successful operation, but claim that scarcity can be eliminated by adopting a system which does not require it. Scarcity, they say, is socially determined and does not arise naturally. It is true that, as Harvey (1973: 114, 139) argues, many social institutions are geared to the maintenance of scarcity, but to accept this is not to accept the absence of scarcity in nature. Resources, even though they are a creation of human perception and technology, exist also in a finite material base. The quantity of human labour power is limited. Space is limited. All these ultimately finite quantities must be allocated and all social systems exist fundamentally for their allocation. It is untrue to say that primitive social systems operate in the absence of scarcity, as Wilkinson seems to believe; even nature itself combines the resources available to life in such ways as to adapt to scarcity — what else, for example, is xerophytic vegetation but such an adaptation? For any particular location, or other segment of the whole, scarcity is also compounded by the absolute or relative immobility of resources. Social systems, whether based on reciprocity, redistribution or market exchange, or some combination of these modes, *all* exist to mediate this immobility and adapt to absolute scarcity. Market exchange, expanded into a worldwide system, has proved extraordinarily effective in this respect, but at the cost of accentuating scarcity for some while easing it for others. It is this relative, socially determined scarcity that *might* be eliminated under new forms of social organization, and which has been constrained by the regulation of the market system as Polanyi argues. But scarcity itself is an inherent condition, the effects of which are capable only of amelioration and not of removal.

It is worthwhile to dwell a little longer on this point, for it is fundamental. If scarcity did not exist there would be no limits to growth. If the constraints of absolute material scarcity and relative scarcity in the dimensions of space and time were absent, then Utopian solutions would be feasible. If the only evils in the world were the socially determined concentration of wealth, power and advantage, then the development problem would be simple. Revolution would solve everything. But conversely, if scarcity exists then the development problem becomes, at base, a problem of adaptation and allocation at all times and in all places. The goal becomes the most efficient *long-term* adaptation coupled with and consistent with the most equitable allocation. The problem is immensely deepened: let us develop it briefly in abstract terms.

The uneven distribution of scarce resources underlies the whole development problem. Systems of production create value from the resource base, and systems of allocation and redistribution complete the adaptation which we call economy and society. In ancient times, these systems were finely compartmented over the surface of the earth, and links between them were only supplementary to the local adaptive systems. The essential fact of development has been the creation of a worldwide interconnected system, which has facilitated much higher levels of adaptation and far more complex systems of allocation and redistribution. Any redistributive system must have nodes, which can be viewed in social, economic or geographical space. The holders of these nodes have become dependent on the network and its flows, but have compensated this dependence by acquiring control over the allocation of scarce resources and production — that is, power. Among the scarce goods have been innovations of many kinds, which have been integrated into the system by entrepreneurs with such a distribution as to increase control, wealth and power in certain nodes. These 'growth poles' have become the locus of an increasing measure of control, leading to the progressive marginalization of the rest of the network. Adaptation to scarcity has thus taken the form of alleviating scarcity for some at the cost of increasing its relative impact on others.

Changes in the weight of advantage through the system have taken place over time. Moreover, other changes have arisen as society has sought to constrain the forces leading to growing inequality, or at least to spread over a wider population the gains accruing to the holders of power. Such changes have, in the main, taken place within the framework of spatial aggregates called countries and, for a time, also through hierarchies of such aggregates, called empires. But internal conflicts and external pressures have led to the break-up of most of these hierarchies, and in the process the spatial aggregates have themselves, as collectives, come to play a much larger role in the management of their own resources, as well as in internal redistribution and in securing the gains of the larger redistributive system for their own clientèle. At all levels within the inter-dependent system conflicts have increasingly developed between the selective interest of gaining an unequal share within scarcity, and the forces seeking to regulate the system and overcome polarization.

The study of development has been concerned overwhelmingly with the problems of the latter group of forces; the operation of development, meanwhile, has on balance been mainly in favour of the former. But the study of development has remained partial, concerning itself almost exclusively with the instruments and mechanisms of allocation and redistribution. There has been very limited concern even with the technology of the adaptive systems of production, and the basic problems of resource scarcity have been pushed aside. Scarcity of capital and labour are recognized, but the underlying scarcity is not. Growth theory does not take account of it, either in its aggregative or dualistic forms. Regional development theory ignores it, except in certain detailed studies where the constraints become important.[3] Structuralism and dependency economics are almost predicated on the assumption that scarcity is not the fundamental constraint. Only when carried into the Caribbean environment does structuralism have to come to grips with the problems of absolute resource scarcity, yet even here the tendency in recent years has been to shrug them off, and look instead to marginalization as the fundamental cause of limited policy options.

But induced scarcity and real scarcity are not opposites; the former is merely the exploitation and intensification of the latter. While it is important to pay the closest attention to the one, it is equally important that we should not ignore the other, or wish it out of existence. It is only the fact of scarcity that makes it possible to exploit scarcity. Even if only because of their relative location, marginalized economies suffer from real scarcity of opportunity as well as induced scarcity. In order to obtain a closer approximation to reality in development study, therefore, it is necessary that adaptation to scarcity — or in other terms, rational ecosystem management under change — be incorporated within the agenda. Without this, we run the risk not only of continuing with very partial explanation, but also of encouraging policies which undermine the very foundation of what we are trying to achieve.

[3] An excellent illustration is D. Barkin and T. King (1970), where a theoretical introduction paying scant attention to resource scarcity is followed by a profound study of the real problems of regional development in a constrained environment, in Mexico.

An introduction to a future task

This book has been about theory, and I have had some hard things to say about geographers for failure to link their own theoretical systems adequately into the stream of development study. This is passing as I write, and at the empirical level the contribution of geographers is already substantial. In the 1973 edition of the *UK Development Register*, published by the Institute of Development Studies at Sussex, geography appears as the second-ranking discipline on the basis of a straight head-count of projects. This is illusory, for the link of many of these projects with development is tenuous, but the neglect of which I have complained is in process of being actively remedied, with consequences that will become apparent in the course of a few years.

But there is need for more, much more. It is not only the spatial dimension which, like the time dimension, needs to be introduced more strongly into development study. Development is also carried out in man's environment, utilizing resources which vary greatly in wealth and poverty both through space and through time. The variables of wealth distribution, employment and underemployment, apply to resources as well as to persons; they are expressed spatially and also ecologically. As society and economy are enlarged in the course of development, as communities trade autarky for access to a wider range of goods and services, new and coarser patterns of resource evaluation and selection replace the older, finer patterns. Specialization replaces diversity; economic risk is added to natural risk.

Development is change, and the understanding of change in man's use of environment opens up an enormous field. Habitually, geographers attuned to theorists from Darwin to Toynbee and Boserup have sought indicators of stress to explain change; they might equally pay attention to Schumpeter and Perroux and their emphasis on 'swarms' of innovators arising at points in the system where linkages exist to generate multiplier effects, and under social conditions favourable to their emergence and operation. The study of development, that is, joins directly with the study of all change in man's use of environment, and provides elements of positive theory for infusion with other theory in the task of generating a dynamic man-environment paradigm.

At the beginning of this book I carried the study of development back to the voyages of Columbus and da Gama; this is true in so far as 'development' is the process of linkage between widely spread parts of the world leading toward interdependence in a single world system. But in the last analysis this too is a parochial view. There have always been linkages, however tenuous. Clarke (1973: 282) points out that 'on spaceship earth, there and everywhere are here, and all costs are internal'. But then and whenever are also now, in the sense that common process underlie and arise from all change, from the neolithic revolution to the technocratic.

Narrowly, development study is a contemporary field concerned with the great inequalities of our age and their reduction. But its own enrichment, and the realization of its full contribution to the sum of knowledge, demand an immense expansion of its ideas in both space and time and its incorporation into a new understanding of man's changing use of environment and relation to environment. This is the domain of the 'higher-level paradigm' to which we should be aiming. The task is enormous. There is a large number of pointers in the literature which indicate how it might be approached, but the job itself is a field for argument that is still to come.

References

A preliminary note on conventions

A large proportion of the literature has been translated or reprinted. Since it is desirable to trace such work back to its original appearance, as well as to indicate its most recent or most available location, a complex system of referencing is employed. In the text, references are given thus:

J. Blow 1940/1960T/1971R

1940 is the date of original publication, in whatever language.

1960 is the date of translation into English (occasionally French).

1971 is the date of most readily available republication, thus corresponding with the referencing system normally found in modern texts.

In general, wherever a reprinted or republished version has been used, this is the final date shown; page references are always to this final citation. Reprinting in the same form is ignored (except in cases where the date of first publication is not shown), and the final date is that of first printing in the current format. Several papers have been reprinted in more than one place, but only a single location is shown here.

In the list of references, this order of referencing is reversed, and the most recent date of publication is shown first, with bibliographic detail, including details of translation. The date of translation (if applicable) follows, and the date of original publication comes last. These are keyed as follows:

(R) — Recent reprint

(T) — Translation

(O) — Original publication

An explanatory note accompanies the few titles where these conventions do not fit the case.

Where collections of essays or reprinted papers are cited more than once, they are shown with an asterisk in the left-hand margin: references to articles within such collections then show only the name of editor and date: further details can be found under the citation of the collection as a whole.

References to 1972a, 1972b in the text indicate the *order* of titles of the same year given in this list.

*AGARWALA, A. N. and SINGH, S. P., eds. *The economics of underdevelopment: a series of articles and papers*, (R) New York, 1963: (O) Bombay, 1958.

AMIN, S. *Le développement du capitalisme en Côte d'Ivoire*, Paris, 1967.

AMIN, S. *L'accumulation à l'echelle mondiale*, Paris, 1970.

ANON., ed. *Une politique dangéreuse: recueil* [qui] *contient les articles publiées dans la presse Soviétique qui dévoilent la caractère véritable de la politique des dirigeants Chinois hostile aux intérêts de socialisme, du mouvement révolutionaire, et de libération mondial*, Moscow, 1972 (T — no original cited).

ARDA (Agricultural and Rehabilitation and Development Administration) *Economic and social disadvantage in Canada: some graphic indicators of location and degree*, Ottawa, 1964.

ARMSTRONG, W. R. and McGEE, T. G. Revolutionary change and the Third World city: a theory of urban involution, (R) *in* McGEE 1971: 64-94; (O) *Civilizations* 18 (1968): 353-77.

ARRIGHI, G. *The political economy of Rhodesia*, The Hague, 1968.

ARRIGHI, G. Labour supplies in historical perspective: a study of the proletarianization of the African peasantry in Rhodesia, *Journal of Development Studies* 6 (1970): 197-234.

ARRIGHI, G. International corporations, labor aristocracies and economic development in tropical Africa, (R) *in* RHODES, *ed.* 1970: 220-67; (O) *in Italian*, 1967.

AVERITT, R. T. *The dual economy*, New York, 1968.

AVERITT, R. T. American business: achievement and challenge, *Daedalus* 98, 1 (1969): 60-77.

BAER, W. The economics of Prebisch and ECLA, *Economic Development and Cultural Change* 10 (1962): 169-82.

BALDWIN, R. E. Patterns of development in newly settled regions, (R) *in* FRIEDMANN and ALONSO, *eds.* 1964: 266-84; (O) *Manchester School of Economics and Social Studies* 24 (1956): 161-79.

BALDWIN, R. E. *Economic development and export growth: a study of Northern Rhodesia, 1920-1960*, Berkeley and Los Angeles, 1966.

BARKIN, D. and KING, T. *Regional economic development: the river basin approach in Mexico*, Cambridge, 1970.

BARRACLOUGH, S. L. and DOMIKE, A. L. Agrarian structure in seven Latin American countries, (R) *in* STAVENHAGEN, *ed.* 1970: 41-94; (O) *Land Economics* 42 (1966): 391-424.

BECKFORD, G. L. *Persistent poverty: underdevelopment in plantation economies of the Third World*, New York, 1972.

BÉJAR, H. *Peru 1965: notes on a guerrilla experience* (transl. by W. ROSE from *Perú 1965: apuntes sobre una experiencia guerrilla*), (T) New York, 1970; (O) Mexico, DF, 1969.

BENDIX, R. Tradition and modernity reconsidered, (R) *in* PLOTNICOV and TUDEN, *eds.* 1970: 273-336; (O) *Comparative Studies in Society and History* 6 (1967): 292-346.

BERNSTEIN, H. Modernization theory and the sociological study of development, *Journal of Development Studies* 7 (1971): 141-60.

BERRY, B. J. L. Hierarchical diffusion: the basis of developmental filtering and spread in a system of growth centers, *in* HANSEN, *ed.* 1972: 108-38.

BEST, L. A model of pure plantation economy, *Social and Economic Studies* 17 (1968): 283-326.

BEST, L. and LEVITT, K. *Export-propelled growth and industrialization in the Caribbean*, Montréal (multilith, 4 vols.), 1968.

BIANCHI, A. Notes on the theory of Latin American development, *Social and Economic Studies* 22 (1973): 96-121.

BLANCO, H. *Land or death: the peasant struggle in Peru* (transl. by N. ALLEN), (T) New York, 1972; (O) *in Spanish, details not given.*

BOARD, C., DAVIES, R. J. and FAIR, T. J. D. The structure of the South African space economy: an integrated approach, *Regional Studies* 4 (1970): 367-92.

BOEKE, J. H. *Economics and economic policy of dual societies*, New York, 1953.

BOSERUP, E. *The conditions of agricultural growth: the economics of agrarian change under population pressure*, London, 1965.

BOUDEVILLE, J.-R. *Problems of regional economic planning*, Edinburgh, 1966.

BROOKFIELD, H. C. *Colonialism, development and independence: the case of the Melanesian islands in the South Pacific*, Cambridge, 1972.

BROOKFIELD, H. C. On one geography and a Third World, *Institute of British Geographers, Transactions* 58 (1973): 1-20.

BROOKFIELD, H. C. Introduction: explaining or understanding, *in* BROOKFIELD, *ed.* 1973: 3-22.

BROOKFIELD, H. C. Full circle in Chimbu: a study of trends and cycles, *in* BROOKFIELD, *ed.* 1973: 127-60.

BROOKFIELD, H. C. Multum in parvo: some questions about diversification in small countries, *forthcoming in* P. SELWYN, *ed., Development policy in small countries*, London, 1975.

*BROOKFIELD, H. C., *ed. The Pacific in transition: geographical perspectives on adaptation and change*, London, 1973.

BROOKFIELD, H. C. with HART, D. *Melanesia: a geographical interpretation of an island world*, London, 1971.

BUKHARIN, N. and PREOBRAZHENSKY, E. *The ABC of Communism* (transl. anon. in 1922), (T) with an introduction by E. H. CARR, London, 1969; (O) *in Russian*, Moscow, 1920.

CASANOVA, P. G. Internal colonialism and national development, *in* HOROWITZ, de CASTRO and GERASSI, *eds.* 1969: 118-39.

CASANOVA, P. G. *Democracy in Mexico* (transl. by D. SALTI from *La Democracia en México*), (T) New York, 1970; (O) México, DF, 1965.

CHANDLER, A. D. *Strategy and structure: chapters in the history of industrial enterprise*, Cambridge, Mass., 1962.

CHAYANOV, A. V. *The theory of peasant economy* (transl. by R. E. F. SMITH, and edited by D. THORNER, B. KERBLAY and R. E. F. SMITH), (T) Homewood, Ill., 1966; (O) *in Russian*, Moscow, 1925.

CHEVALIER, F. Land and society in Colonial Mexico (transl. by E. EUSTIS from *La Formation des Grands Domaines au Mexique: terre et société aux XVIe-XVIIe siècles*), (T) Berkeley and Los Angeles, 1963; (O) Paris, 1952.

CHISHOLM, M. and MANNERS, G., *eds. Spatial policy problems of the British economy*, Cambridge, 1971.

CIDA (Comité Interamericano de Desarrollo Agricola) *Land tenure conditions and socio-economic development of the agricultural sector: Argentina*, Washington, 1965.

CIDA *Tenencia de la Tierra y Desarrollo Socio-Economico del Sector Agricola: Peru*, Washington, 1966.

CIDA *Tenencia de la Tierra y Reforma Agraria en América Latina: informe regional y resúmenes de los estudios por países*, Washington, 1971.

CIES (Consejo Interamericano economico y social) *Lineamentos para Alanzar el Mayor Empleo y Crecimento en América Latina*, Washington, 1973.

CLARK, C. *The conditions of economic progress*, second edition, London, 1957; (O) 1951.

CLARK, C., WILSON, F. and BRADLEY, J. Industrial location and economic potential in Western Europe, *Regional Studies* 3 (1969): 197-212.

CLARKE, W. C. The dilemma of development, *in* BROOKFIELD, *ed.* 1973: 275-98.

CMEA (Council for Mutual Economic Assistance) *Comprehensive programme for the further extension and improvement of co-operation and the development of socialist economic integration by the CMEA member countries*, Moscow, 1971 (T — no original cited).

COCKROFT, J. D., FRANK, A. G. and JOHNSON, D. L. *Dependence and underdevelopment: Latin America's political economy*, New York, 1971.

COMMISSION OF THE CC OF THE CPSU, *ed. History of the Communist Party of the Soviet Union (Bolsheviks): short course*, Moscow, 1943 (T — no original cited).

CRUISE O'BRIEN, D. Modernization, order and the erosion of a democratic ideal: American political science 1960-1970, *Journal of Development Studies* 8 (1972): 351-78.

DAHRENDORF, R. *Class conflict in industrial society*, Stanford, Calif., 1959.

DARWENT, R. F. Growth poles and growth centers in regional development — a review (*earlier as:* Growth pole and growth center concepts: a review, evaluation and bibliography), (R) *Environment and Planning* 1 (1969): 5-32; (O) *Center for Planning and Development Research, Institute of Urban and Regional Development, University of California, Working Paper* 89 (1968).

DEAN, G. A note on the sources of technological innovation in the People's Republic of China, *Journal of Development Studies* 9 (1972): 187-99.

DEBRAY, R. Latin America: some problems of revolutionary strategy (transl. by M. MARKS and R. NOVICK from an original in Spanish), (R) *in* HOROWITZ, de CASTRO and GERASSI, *eds.* 1969: 499–531; (O) *in Spanish* in *Casa de las Américas,* La Habana, 1965.

DE KADT, E., ed. *Patterns of foreign influence in the Caribbean,* London, 1972.

DEMAS, W. G. *The economics of development in small countries, with special reference to the Caribbean,* Montréal, 1965.

DEUTSCH, K. W. and FOLTZ, W. J., eds. *Nation-building,* New York, 1963.

DJILAS, M. *The new class: an analysis of the communist system,* New York, 1957.

DURKHEIM, E. *The division of labour in society* (transl. by G. SIMPSON from *De la division du travail social: étude sur l'organisation des sociétes supérieures*), (T) London, 1933; (O) Paris, 1893.

ECKAUS, R. S. The factor proportions problem in underdeveloped areas, (R) in AGARWALA and SINGH, *eds.* 1958/1963R: 348–78; (O) *American Economic Review* 45 (1955): 539–65.

ECLA (UN Economic Commission for Latin America) Theoretical and practical problems of economic growth (*E.CN 12/221*), (R) *in* ECLA with QUINTANA, 1970: 32–60; (O) New York, 1951.

ECLA A contribution to economic integration policy in Latin America (*E.CN 12/728*), (R) *in* ECLA with QUINTANA, 1970: 133–60; (O) New York, 1967.

ECLA *Income distribution in Latin America,* New York, 1971.

ECLA REPORT *Economic survey for Latin America for 1948 . . . 71,* New York, 1951.

*ECLA with QUINTANA, C. *Development problems in Latin America: an analysis by the United Nations Economic Commission for Latin America, with a foreword by C. Quintana,* Austin, Texas, 1970.

ECONOMIC COUNCIL OF CANADA *Second annual review: toward sustained and balanced economic growth,* Ottawa, 1965.

EISENSTADT, S. N. *Modernization: protest and change,* Englewood Cliffs, NJ, 1966.

ENGERMAN, S. L. The effects of slavery on the Southern economy: a review of the recent debate, (R) *in* TEMIN, *ed.* 1973: 398-428; (O) *Explorations in Entrepreneurial History* 4 (1967): 71-97.

EPSTEIN, T. S. *Capitalism, primitive and modern: some aspects of Tolai economic growth*, Canberra, 1970.

FAYERWEATHER, J. *International business management: a conceptual framework*, New York, 1969.

FEDER, E. *The rape of the peasantry: Latin America's landholding system*, New York, 1971.

FEI, J. C. H. and RANIS, G. A theory of economic development, *American Economic Review* 51 (1961): 533-64.

FEI, J. C. H. and RANIS, G. *Development of the labor surplus economy*, Homewood, Ill., 1964.

FINNEY, B. R. *Big men and business: entrepreneurship and economic growth in the New Guinea highlands*, Honolulu, 1973.

FISK, E. K. Planning in a primitive economy: special problems of Papua and New Guinea, *Economic Record* (Melbourne) 40 (1962): 462-78.

FISK, E. K. Response of non-monetary production units to contact with the exchange economy. Paper presented to a Conference on Agriculture in Development Theory, at Villa Serbilloni, Bellagio, Italy, 23-29 May 1973, MS, Canberra, 1973.

FISK, E. K. and SHAND, R. T. The early stages of development in a primitive economy: the evolution from subsistence to trade and specialization, *in* WHARTON, *ed.* 1969: 257-74.

FITZGERALD, C. P., *ed.* *Supplement to quotations from Chairman Mao Tse-tung*, Melbourne, 1969.

FLANDERS, M. J. The economics of Prebisch and ECLA: a comment, *Economic Development and Cultural Change* 12 (1964): 312-14.

FRANCO, J. *The modern culture of Latin America: society and the artist*, (R) revised edition, Harmondsworth, 1970; (O) London, 1967.

FRANK, A. G. *Capitalism and underdevelopment in Latin America: historical studies of Chile and Brazil*, (R) revised edition, New York, 1969; (O) 1967.

FRIEDMANN, J. *Regional development policy: a case study of Venezuela*, Cambridge, Mass., 1966.

FRIEDMANN, J. A general theory of polarized development, (R) *in* HANSEN, *ed.* 1972: 82–107; (Oii) *University of California School of Architecture and Urban Planning, Los Angeles, Paper,* 1969; (Oi) *The Ford Foundation Urban and Regional Advisory Program in Chile, Paper,* Santiago, 1967.

FRIEDMANN, J. The spatial organization of power in the development of urban systems, *Comparative Urban Research* 1 (1972): 5–42.

*FRIEDMANN, J. and ALONSO, W., *eds. Regional development and planning: a reader,* Cambridge, Mass., 1964.

FUCHS, L. H. *Hawaii Pono: a social history,* New York, 1961.

FURNIVALL, J. S. *Netherlands India: a study of plural economy,* Cambridge, 1939.

FURTADO, C. Capital formation and economic development (transl. by J. CAIRNCROSS from 'Formacão de capital e desinvolvimento economico'), (R) *in* AGARWALA and SINGH, *eds.* 1958/1963R: 309–37; (T) *International Economic Papers* 4 (1954): 124–44; (O) *Revista Brasileira de Economica* 6 (1952).

FURTADO, C. *The economic growth of Brazil: a survey from colonial to modern times* (transl. by R. W. de AGUIAR and E. C. DRYSDALE from *Formacão Económica do Brasil*), (T) Berkeley and Los Angeles, 1963; (O) Rio de Janeiro, 1959.

FURTADO, C. *Development and underdevelopment* (transl. by R. W. de AGUIAR and E. C. DRYSDALE from *Desinvolvimento e subdesinvolvimento*), (T) Berkeley and Los Angeles, 1964; (O) Rio de Janeiro, 1961.

FURTADO, C. *Diagnosis of the Brazilian crisis* (transl. by S. MACEDO from *Dialéctica do desinvolvimento*), (T) Berkeley and Los Angeles, 1965; (O) Rio de Janeiro, 1964.

FURTADO, C. *Economic development of Latin America: a survey from colonial times to the Cuban revolution* (transl. by S. MACEDO from *La Economía Latino-americana: una síntesa desde la conquista Ibérica hasta la revolución Cubana*), (T) Cambridge, 1970; (O) Santiago, 1969.

FURTADO, C. *Obstacles of development in Latin America* (transl. by C. EKKER from pieces published at various dates during the 1960s, but not detailed), (T) New York, 1970.

FURTADO, C. The Brazilian 'model', *Social and Economic Studies* 22 (1973): 122–31.

GALBRAITH, J. K. *The new industrial state*, Boston, 1967.

GALEANO, E. *Guatemala: occupied country* (transl. by C. BELFRAGE from *Guatemala: país occupado*), (T) New York, 1969; (O) Mexico, DF, 1967.

GEERTZ, C. *Agricultural involution: the process of ecological change in Indonesia*, Berkeley and Los Angeles, 1963.

GEERTZ, C. *Peddlers and princes: social change and economic modernization in two Indonesian towns*, Chicago, 1963.

GEERTZ, C. *The social history of an Indonesian town*, Cambridge, Mass., 1965.

GENDARME, R. *L'économie de Madagascar*, Paris, 1960.

GILMOUR, J. M. *Spatial evolution of manufacturing: southern Ontario 1851-1891*, Toronto, 1972.

GINSBURG, N. S. From colonialism to national development: geographical perspectives on patterns and policies, *Annals of the Association of American Geographers* 63 (1973): 1-21.

GIRAULT, C. A., ed. *Dépendance, marginalité, développement: essais sur les Amériques Latines*, Montréal, 1973.

GIRVAN, N. The development of dependency economics in the Caribbean and Latin America: review and comparison, *Social and Economic Studies* 22 (1973): 1-33.

GLACKEN, C. *Traces on the Rhodian shore*, Berkeley and Los Angeles, 1967.

GOULD, J. D. *Economic growth in history: survey and analysis*, London, 1972.

GOULD, P. R. A note on research into the diffusion of development, *Journal of Modern African Affairs* 2 (1964): 123-5.

GOULD, P. R. On the geographical interpretation of eigenvalues, *Institute of British Geographers, Transactions* 42 (1967): 53-86.

GOULD, P. R. Tanzania, 1920-63: the spatial impress of the modernization process, *World Politics* 22 (1970): 149-70.

GOULD, P. R. The open geographic curriculum, *in* R. J. CHORLEY, ed. *Directions in geography*, London, 1973: 253-84.

GREEN, L. P. and FAIR, T. J. D. *Development in Africa: a study in regional analysis with special reference to southern Africa*, Johannesburg, 1962.

GRIFFIN, K. *Underdevelopment in Spanish America: an interpretation*, London, 1969.

HÄGERSTRAND, T. Aspects of the spatial structure of social communication and the diffusion of information, *Papers of the Regional Science Association* 16 (1965): 28–42.

HÄGERSTRAND, T. A Monte Carlo approach to diffusion, *Archives Européennes de Sociologie* 6 (1965): 43–67.

HÄGERSTRAND, T. *Innovation diffusion as spatial process* (transl. by A. R. PRED from *Innovationsfölopet ur kurologisk synpunkt*), (T) Chicago, 1967; (O) *Medelanden från Lunds Universitets Geografiska Institution, Avhandlingar* 25 (1953).

HAGGETT, P. *Geography: a modern synthesis*, New York, 1972.

HAILEY, LORD *Britain and her dependencies*, London, 1943.

HANSEN, N. M. Development pole theory in a regional context, *Kyklos* 20 (1967): 709–27.

HANSEN, N. M. A note on urban hierarchy stability and spatial polarization, *Program on the Role of Growth Centers in Regional Economic Development, Paper 2*, Lexington, Ky., 1969.

HANSEN, N. M. Regional economics and the new regionalism, *Program on the Role of Growth Centers in Regional Economic Development, Paper 15*, Lexington, Ky., 1969.

HANSEN, N. M., ed. Growth centers in regional economic development, New York, 1972.

HARROD, R. F. An essay in dynamic theory, *Economic Journal* 49 (1939): 14–33.

HARVEY, D. *Explanation in geography*, London, 1969.

HARVEY, D. Society, the city and the space-economy of urbanism, *Association of American Geographers, Commission on College Geography Resource Paper* 18, 1972.

HARVEY, D. *Social justice and the city*, London, 1973.

HEILBRONER, R. L. *The worldly philosophers: the lives, times and ideas of the great economic thinkers*, fourth edition revised, New York, 1972.

HEIMANN, E. *History of economic doctrines: an introduction to economic theory*, New York, 1945.

HELLEINER, G. K. *International trade and economic development*, Harmondsworth, 1972.

HERMANSEN, T. Development poles and related theories: a synoptic review (*earlier as: Growth poles and growth centres in national and regional development – a synthetic approach*), (R) *in* HANSEN, *ed.* 1972: 160-203; (O) *United Nations Research Institute for Social Development, UNRISD/69/C.26*, Geneva, 1969.

HERRERA, A. Social determinants of science policy in Latin America: explicit science policy and implicit science policy, *Journal of Development Studies* 9 (1972): 19-38.

HIGGINS, B. *Economic development: problems, principles and policies*, (R) second edition revised, New York, 1968; (O) 1959.

HILHORST, J. La théorie du développement régional: un essai de synthèse, *in* OECD (Organisation de Coopération et de Développement Economiques), Centre de Développement, *Aspects Multidisciplinaires du Développement Régional*, Paris, 1969: 21-38.

HIRSCHMAN, A. O. *The strategy of economic development*, New Haven, Conn., 1958.

HIRSCHMAN, A. O. *A bias for hope: essays on development and Latin America* (originally published at various dates during the 1960s), New Haven, Conn., 1971.

HOBSBAWM, E. J. *Industry and empire: an economic history of Britain since 1750*, London, 1968.

HOBSON, J. A. *Imperialism: a study*, London, 1902.

*HOROWITZ, I. L., de CASTRO, J. and GERASSI, J., *eds. Latin American radicalism: a documentary report on left and nationalist movements*, New York, 1969.

HOWLETT, D. R. Terminal development: from tribalism to peasantry, *in* BROOKFIELD, *ed.* 1973: 249-73.

HUIZER, G. Emiliano Zapata and the peasant guerrillas in the Mexican revolution, *in* STAVENHAGEN, *ed.* 1970: 375-406.

INNIS, H. A. *The fur trade in Canada: an introduction to Canadian economic history*, Toronto, 1930.

INNIS, H. A. *The cod fisheries: the history of an international economy*, Toronto, 1940.

ISARD, W. *Location and the space economy: a general theory relating to industrial location, market areas, land use, trade, and urban structure*, New York, 1956.

ISARD, W. *Methods of regional analysis: an introduction to regional science*, Cambridge, Mass., 1960.

ISHIKAWA, S. A note on the choice of technology in China, *Journal of Development Studies* 9 (1972): 161-86.

JACOBY, E. H. with JACOBY, C. F. *Man and land: the fundamental issue in development*, London, 1971.

JAMES, C. L. R. *The Black Jacobins: Toussaint l'Ouverture and the San Domingo revolution*, (R) with an appendix, New York, 1963; (O) London, 1938.

JOHNSON, E. A. J. *Market towns and spatial development in India*, New Delhi, 1965.

JOHNSON, E. A. J. *The organization of space in developing countries*, Cambridge, Mass., 1970.

JORGENSON, D. W. The development of a dual economy, *Economic Journal* 71 (1961): 309-34.

JORGENSON, D. W. The role of agriculture in economic development: classical versus neoclassical models of growth, *in* WHARTON, *ed. Subsistence agriculture and economic development*, Chicago, 1969: 320-48.

JULIÃO, F. *Cambão – the Yoke; the hidden face of Brazil* (transl. by J. BUTT from an uncited work in Portuguese), (T) Harmondsworth, 1972.

KASER, M. C., *ed. Economic development for Eastern Europe: proceedings of a conference held by the International Economic Association*, London, 1968.

KERR, C. Changing social structure, *in* W. E. MOORE and A. S. FELDMAN, *eds. Labor commitment and social change in developing areas*, New York, 1960: 348-59.

KERR, C., DUNLOP, J. T., HARBISON, F. and MYERS, C. A., *eds. Industrialism and industrial man*, Cambridge, Mass., 1960.

KINDLEBERGER, C. P. *Economic development*, (R) second edition revised, New York, 1965; (O) 1958.

KINDLEBERGER, C. P. *American business abroad: six lectures on direct investment*, New Haven, Conn., 1969.

KUHN, T. S. *The structure of scientific revolutions*, Chicago, 1962.

KUPER, L. and SMITH, M. G., *eds. Pluralism in Africa*, Berkeley and Los Angeles, 1969.

LASAQA, I. Q. Melanesians' choice: Tadhimboko participation in the Solomon Islands cash economy, *New Guinea Research Bulletin* 46 (1972).

LASAQA, I. Q. Geography and geographers in the changing Pacific, *in* BROOKFIELD, *ed.* 1973: 299-311.

LAS CASAS, B. de *History of the Indies* (transl. and ed. by A. M. COLLARD from *Historia de las Indias*), (T) New York, 1971; (O) Mexico, DF, *ed.* by A. MILARES from MS c. 1555.

LASUÉN, J. R. On growth poles, (R) *in* HANSEN, *ed.* 1972: 20–49; (O) *Urban Studies* 6 (1969): 20–49.

LENIN, V. I. *Imperialism, the highest stage of capitalism: a popular outline*, (R) Moscow, 1970; (T) Moscow, 1926, translator not stated; (O) *in Russian*, Petrograd, 1917.

LEONTIEF, W. W. *The structure of the American economy, 1919–1939*, New York, 1951.

LE RIVEREND, J. *Economic history of Cuba* (transl. by M. J. CABAZON and H. LEON from *Historia Economica de Cuba*), (T) La Habana, 1967; (O) La Habana, 1965.

LERNER, D. *The passing of traditional society: modernizing the Middle East*, New York, 1958.

LEVITT, K. *Silent surrender: the multinational corporation in Canada*, Toronto, 1970.

LEWIS, G. K. *The growth of the modern West Indies*, London, 1968.

LEWIS, W. A. The industrialization of the British West Indies, *Caribbean Economic Review* (1950).

LEWIS, W. A. *The theory of economic growth*, London, 1955.

LEWIS, W. A. Economic development with unlimited supplies of labour, (R) *in* AGARWALA and SINGH, *eds.* 1958/1963R: 400–49; (O) *Manchester School of Economics and Social Sciences* 22 (1954): 139–91.

LIPSET, S. M. and SOLARI, A., *eds. Elites in Latin America*, New York, 1967.

LIPTON, M. Interdisciplinary studies in less developed countries. *Journal of Development Studies* 7 (1970): 5–18.

LOGAN, M. I. The spatial systems and planning strategies in developing countries, *Geographical Review* 62 (1972): 229–44.

LOGAN, M. I. The development process in the less developed countries, *Australian Geographer* 12 (1972): 146–53.

LUXEMBURG, R. *The accumulation of capital* (transl. by A. SCHWARZCHILD from *Die Akkumulation der Kapitals: ein betrag zur oekonomischen erklärung der imperialismus*), (T) London, 1951; (O) Berlin, 1912.

McGEE, T. G. *The southeast Asian city*, London, 1967.

*McGEE, T. G. *The urbanization process in the Third World: explorations in search of a theory*, London, 1971.

MACMILLAN, W. M. *Africa emergent*, (R) second edition revised, Harmondsworth, 1964; (O) 1938.

MAINE, H. S. *Ancient law*, London, 1861.

MAO TSE-TUNG. *Five articles by Chairman Mao Tse-tung*, Peking, 1968 (T) translator not stated.

MARIÁTEGUI, J. C. *Seven interpretative essays on Peruvian reality* (transl. by M. URQUIDI with a foreword by J. BASADRE, from *Siete Ensayos de Interpretacion de la Realidid Peruana*), (T) Austin, Texas, 1971; (O) Lima, 1928.

MARX, K. Pre-capitalist economic formations (transl. from German by J. COHEN with an introduction by E. J. HOBSBAWM), (T) New York, 1964; (O) *in German*, Moscow, 1939–41.

MAUDE, A. M. Land shortage and population pressure in Tonga, *in* BROOKFIELD, *ed.* 1973: 163–85.

MIRACLE, M. P. African markets and trade in the Copperbelt, *in* P. BOHANNAN and G. DALTON, *eds. Markets in Africa* Evanston, Ill., 1962: 698–738.

MISHAN, E. J. *The costs of economic growth*, (R) Harmondsworth, 1969; (O) London, 1967.

MOSELEY, M. J. Growth centres — a shibboleth?, *Area* 5 (1973): 143–50.

MYINT, H. *The economics of developing countries*, London, 1964.

MYRDAL, G. *The American dilemma: the negro problem and modern democracy*, New York, 1944.

MYRDAL, G. *Economic theory and underdeveloped regions*, London, 1957.

NAKAJIMA, C. Subsistence and commercial family farms: some theoretical models of subjective equilibrium, *in* WHARTON, *ed.* 1969: 165–85.

NASH, M. *Primitive and peasant economic systems*, San Francisco, 1966.

NKRUMAH, K. *Neo-colonialism: the last stage of imperialism*, New York, 1965.

NORTH, D. C. Location theory and regional economic growth, (R) *in* FRIEDMANN and ALONSO, *eds.* 1964: 240–55; (O) *Journal of Political Economy* 63 (1955): 243–58.

NURKSE, R. *Problems of capital formation in underdeveloped countries*, (R) with *Patterns of trade and development* (New York, 1961), New York, 1967; (O) New York, 1953, originally delivered as lectures in Brazil in 1951, and published in Portuguese.

OAS (Organization of American States) *El Desarollo de América Latina y la Alianza para el Progreso*, Washington, 1973.

PANGLAYKIM, A. Marketing organization in transition, *Bulletin of Indonesian Economic Studies* (Canberra) 9 (1968): 35–59.

PARSONS, T. and SHILS, E. A. *Toward a general theory of action*, Cambridge, Mass., 1951.

PERHAM, M. *Colonial sequence 1930 to 1949: a chronological commentary upon British colonial policy especially in Africa*, London, 1967.

PERROUX, F. Economic space: theory and applications, (R) in FRIEDMANN and ALONSO, eds. 1964: 21–36; (O) *Quarterly Journal of Economics* 64 (1950): 89–104.

PERROUX, F. Note on the concept of growth poles (transl. by I. LIVINGSTONE from 'Note sur la notion de pôle de croissance'), (R) *in* I. LIVINGSTONE, *ed. Economic policy for development: selected readings*, Harmondsworth, 1971: 278–89; (O) *Economie Apliquée* 8 (1955): 307–20.

PETRAS, J. F. and LaPORTE, R. Modernization from above versus reform from below: US policy toward Latin American agricultural development, *Journal of Development Studies* 6 (1970): 248–66.

PIAGET, J. *Structuralism*, New York, 1970.

PINTO, A. and KÑAKAL, J. The centre-periphery system twenty years later (transl. by C. GIRVAN from 'El sistema centroperifera viente anos despues'), (T) *Social and Economic Studies* 22 (1973): 34–89; (O) *ECLA/IDE/DRAFT/41*, Santiago, 1971.

*PLOTNICOV, L. and TUDEN, A., eds. *Essays in comparative social stratification*, Pittsburgh, 1970.

POLANYI, K. *The great transformation*, Boston, 1944.

POLANYI, K. *Primitive, archaic and modern economies: essays of Karl Polanyi*, ed. by G. DALTON, Boston, 1968.

POLANYI, K., ARENSBERG, C. M. and PEARSON, H. W., eds. *Trade and market in the early empires: economies in history and theory*, Glencoe, Ill., 1957.

POPOV, Y. *Marxist political economy as applied to the African scene*, Moscow, 1973.

PORTER, P. W. and de SOUZA, A. The underdevelopment and modernization of the third world, *Association of American Geographers, Commission on College Geography Resource Paper* (1974), forthcoming.

PREBISCH, R. The economic development of Latin America and its principal problems, (R) *Economic Review of Latin America* 7 (1962), Part I; (T) New York, 1950; (O) *in Spanish*, 1949.

PRESTON, D. A. The revolutionary landscape of highland Bolivia, *Geographical Journal* 135 (1969): 1-16.

PUTHUCHEARY, J. J. *Ownership and control in the Malayan economy*, Singapore, 1960.

REDFIELD, R. The folk society, *American Journal of Sociology* 52 (1947): 293-308.

REDFIELD, R. *The primitive world and its transformations*, Ithaca, NY, 1953.

*RHODES, R. I., ed. *Imperialism and underdevelopment: a reader*, New York, 1970.

RICHARDSON, H. W. *Regional economics: location theory, urban structure and regional change*, London, 1969.

RIDDELL, J. B. *The spatial dynamics of modernization in Sierra Leone: structure, diffusion and response*, Evanston, Ill., 1970.

RITTER, A. R. M. Growth strategy and economic performance in revolutionary Cuba: past, present and prospective, *Social and Economic Studies* 21 (1972): 313-37.

ROBINSON, R., ed. *Developing the Third World: the experience of the nineteen-sixties*, Cambridge, 1971.

ROBINSON, R., GALLAGHER, J. with DENNY, A. *Africa and the Victorians: the climax of imperialism*, London, 1961.

ROSENSTEIN-RODAN, P. N. Problems of industrialization of eastern and south-eastern Europe, (R) *in* AGARWALA and SINGH, *eds.* 1958/1963R: 245-55; (O) *Economic Journal* 53 (1943): 202-11.

ROSTOW, W. W. *The stages of economic growth: a non-communist manifesto*, Cambridge, 1960.

SANTOS, M. *Les villes du tiers monde*, Paris, 1971.

SCHMITT, H. O. Foreign capital and social conflict in Indonesia, 1950-58, *Economic Development and Cultural Change* 10

(1962): 284–93; Economic policy making in Indonesia: a reply (to B. Glassburner, ibid.: 113–33), ibid.: 432–3; Economic interest and Indonesian politics once again, *Economic Development and Cultural Change* 12 (1963): 87–8.

SCHUMPETER, J. A. *The theory of economic development: an inquiry* (transl. by R. OPIE with additions by J. A. SCHUMPETER, from *Die Theorie des Wirtschaftlichen Entwicklung*), (T) Cambridge, Mass., 1934; (O) Leipzig, 1911.

SCHUMPETER, J. A. *Imperialism* (transl. by H. NORDEN from original in *Archiv für Sozialwissenschaft und Sozialpolitik*, Tübingen, 1919), (T) New York, 1934.

SCITOVSKY, T. Two concepts of external economies, (R) *in* AGARWALA and SINGH, *eds.* 1958/1963R: 295–308; (O) *Journal of Political Economy* 62 (1954): 143–51.

SEERS, D. Big companies and small countries: a practical proposal, *Kyklos* 16 (1963): 599–608.

SEERS, D. The mechanism of the open petroleum economy, *Social and Economic Studies* 13 (1964).

SEERS, D. A step toward a political economy of development: the case of Trinidad/Tobago, *Social and Economic Studies* 19 (1969): 218–53.

SELWYN, P. The dual economy transgressing national frontiers: the case of industrial development in Lesotho, *Institute of Development Studies Communication* 105, 1973.

SEMPLE, R. K., GAUTHIER, H. L. and YOUNGMAN, C. E. Growth poles in São Paulo, Brazil, *Annals of the Association of American Geographers* 62 (1972): 591–8.

SEN, A. *Growth economics: selected readings*, Harmondsworth, 1970.

SHIH CHUN *On studying some world history*, Peking, 1973.

SIEBERT, H. *Regional economic growth: theory and policy*, Scranton, Pa., 1969.

SINGER, H. W. Dualism revisited: a new approach to the problems of the dual society in developing countries, *Journal of Development Studies* 7 (1970): 60–75.

SMITH, M. G. *The plural society in the British West Indies*, Berkeley and Los Angeles, 1965.

SOJA, E. W. *The geography of modernization in Kenya: a spatial analysis of social, economic and political change*, Syracuse, NY, 1968.

SOJA, E. W. The geography of modernization: some comments on the relevance to Latin America of recent research in Africa, *in* A. D. BUSHONG, *ed. National Conference of Latin American Geographers, Muncie, Ind., 30 April-3 May 1970*, 1970: 413-27.

SOJA, E. W. African geographical studies and comparative regional development, *in* M. W. MIKESELL, *ed. Geographers abroad: essays on the problems and prospects of research in foreign areas*, Chicago, 1973: 165-84.

SOJA, E. W. and TOBIN, R. J. The geography of modernization: paths, patterns and processes of spatial change in developing countries, *in* R. BRUNNER and G. BREWER, *eds. Ordered complexity: empirical theories of political development*, New York, 1972.

STAVENHAGEN, R. Seven erroneous theses about Latin America, (R) *in* HOROWITZ, de CASTRO and GERASSI, *eds.* 1969: 102-17; (O) *New University Thought* (Detroit) 4, 4 (1966): 25-37.

STAVENHAGEN, R. Social aspects of agrarian structure in Mexico, *in* STAVENHAGEN, *ed.* 1970: 225-70.

STAVENHAGEN, R. *Agrarian structure and underdevelopment in Africa and Latin America*, Paper presented to an IDEP-IDS-IEDES Conference on Strategies for Economic Development: Africa versus Latin America, Dakar, 4-17 September 1972, MS.

STAVENHAGEN, R. L'Amérique Latine demain: entre le sous-développement et la révolution, (R) *in* STAVENHAGEN, 1973: 33-82; (O) Séries Rencontres Intérnationales de Genève, *Où va la civilisation humaine?*, Neuchâtel, 1972: 43-85.

*STAVENHAGEN, R. *Sept thèses erronées dur l'Amérique Latine, ou comment décoloniser les sciences humaines*, Paris, 1973.

*STAVENHAGEN, R., *ed. Agrarian problems and peasant movements in Latin America*, New York, 1970.

STEWARD, J. *The theory of culture change*, Urbana, Ill., 1955.

SUNKEL, O. National development policy and external dependence in Latin America, *Journal of Development Studies* 6 (1969): 23-48.

SUNKEL, O. Transnational capitalism and national disintegration in Latin America, *Social and Economic Studies* 22 (1973): 132-76.

TAAFE, E. J., MORRILL, R. L. and GOULD, P. R. Transport expansion in underdeveloped countries: a comparative analysis, *Geographical Review* 53 (1963): 503-29.

TAYLOR, M. J. and WOOD, P. A. Industrial linkage and local agglomeration in the West Midlands metal industries, *Institute of British Geographers, Transactions* 59 (1973): 127-54.

*TEMIN, P., *ed. New economic history: selected readings*, Harmondsworth, 1973.

THOMAS, M. D. Growth pole theory: an examination of some of its basic concepts, *in* HANSEN, *ed.* 1972: 50-81.

TIEBOUT, C. M. Exports and regional economic growth (with reply by D. C. NORTH, and rejoinder), (R) *in* FRIEDMANN and ALONSO, *eds.* 1964: 256-65; (O) *Journal of Political Economy* 64 (1956): 160-9.

TÖNNIES, F. *Gemeinschaft und Gesellschaft*, Leipzig, 1935.

VANCE, J. E. *The merchant's world: the geography of wholesaling*, Englewood Cliffs, NJ, 1970.

VEILLEUX, L. Rapport dur une visite en Chine, été 1973, Montréal, MS.

VERNON, R. Foreign-owned enterprise in the developing countries, *Public Policy* 15 (1960): 361-80.

VERNON, R. International investment and international trade in the product cycle, *Quarterly Journal of Economics* 80 (1966): 190-207.

VERNON, R. *Report of the research project on the multinational corporation* (Harvard Business School), Cambridge, Mass., 1970.

VERNON, R., *ed. Multinational enterprise in the 1960s*, London, 1968.

VINER, J. Studies in the theory of international trade, London, 1937.

WATKINS, M. H. A staple theory of economic growth, *Canadian Journal of Economics and Political Science* 29 (1963): 141-58.

WERTHEIM, W. F. *Indonesian society in transition: a study of social change*, Bandung and The Hague, 1956.

*WHARTON, C. R., *ed. Subsistence agriculture and economic development*, Chicago, 1969.

WILKIE, J. W. *The Mexican revolution: federal expenditure and social change since 1910*, Berkeley and Los Angeles, 1970.

WILKINSON, R. G. *Poverty and progress: an ecological model for economic development*, London, 1973.

WILLIAMS, E. *Capitalism and slavery*, London, 1964.

WILSON, E. *To the Finland Station: a study in the writing and acting of history*, (R) London, 1960; (O) London, 1940.

WOLPERT, J. The decision process in a spatial context, *Annals of the Association of American Geographers* 54 (1964): 537–58.

WOMACK, J. *Zapata and the Mexican revolution*, New York, 1968.

ZAMMIT, J. A., ed. *The Chilean road to socialism: proceedings of an ODEPLAN-IDS round table, March 1972*, Brighton, 1973.

ZIMMERMAN, L. J. *Poor lands, rich lands: the widening gap*, New York, 1964.

Index of persons